MYSTIC BIBLE

DR. RANDOLPH STONE

"In the beginning was the Word,
and the Word was with God, and the Word was God."
(John 1:1)

RADHA SOAMI SATSANG BEAS
PUNJAB (INDIA)

Printed in the United States of America

ISBN 978-1-941489-61-1

www.AudioEnlightenmentPress.com

Dedicated to My Beloved Master Whose Grace and Inspiration Made This Book Possible.

BIBLES USED

When 'The Mystic Bible' was composed during the summer of 1955 in America, all Biblical quotations were taken from the Holy Bible containing the Old and New Testaments translated out of the original tongues, being the version set forth A.D. 1611; compared with most ancient authorities and revised A.D. 1881-1885; edited by the American Revision Committee A.D. 1901; Standard Edition; copyright 1901, and published by Thomas Nelson & Sons. The reason for using this particular edition was because many original terms were carried over into the English translation. This distinction of terminology was very helpful in clarifying degrees and meanings in explaining the Mystic Science of Soul.

But while traveling in other parts of the world, this edition was not available; so, taking into consideration this same difficulty for others who may wish to use the Holy Bible for confirmation and comparison, the quotations have been checked with and made to conform with the more popular and more easily obtainable edition of the Holy Bible, published by the Oxford University press. However, wherever the original terms are helpful, they are retained in parenthetical form within the actual Biblical quotations from the more recent edition. For example, 'Jehovah', 'Jehovah God' and the 'Spirit of Jehovah' are all translated as "Lord" in most modern Bibles. The original term, 'Spirit of Jehovah', in the Old Testament, is so typical of the Holy Ghost or the Holy Spirit in the New Testament, and of the Holy Sound Current or Word, that it did not seem advisable to omit it from 'The Mystic Bible'.

CONTENTS

PREFACE

Dr. Stone kindly gave me an opportunity to look through the manuscript of 'The Mystic Bible' and I must say that I was deeply impressed by his interesting comparisons.

The author is evidently well versed in Biblical and other types of Western Mysticism and has also drunk deep at the fount of Oriental Mysticism. He has disclosed much learning and ingenuity in solving several knotty problems and in clarifying a number of obscure points; in particular, the mystery of THE WORD which was with God and which was God.

Mystics and lovers of Biblical lore will appreciate the feast he has spread before them.

There is a proverb in the East: We should enjoy the mangoes and not bother about counting the trees. He has made it possible to enjoy the mangoes as well as to count the trees.

JAGMOHAN LAL

Dera Baba Jaimal Singh
Via BEAS, Disst. Amritsar
Punjab, India
January, 1956

FOREWORD

There comes a time when the honest seeker after Truth admits to himself that the Holy Bible, in its present form, does not make sense. The true teachings of the ancient Hebrews and the WORD of God as preached by Jesus are now obscured by the mists of time. We need a fresh Revelation from God. Or else some means must be found by which we can penetrate these mists and make those precious Truths our very own. The Pearl of Great Price is just as valuable and just as essential now as it was when Jesus Christ first offered it to the mankind. How are we to get it?

It is therefore a pleasant surprise to find that the Mystic Truths of the Bible and the WORD can still be attained. The key to all this still exists if one would take the trouble to look for it. This book does not claim to explain fully either the Old Testament or the New — no mortal hand can ever turn the key unaided! However, the earnest pilgrim, whether he be a learned theologian or just an humble layman, cannot fail to get some inkling of the astounding Truth, on reading this book.

What the author of this book seems to have acquired with patient study and honest endeavor, we readers can also acquire with far less difficulty. But we must seek!

Poona (Bombay State)   **(COL.) P. K. KURIYAN**
India   [later retired as Brigadier]
January, 1956

INTRODUCTION

Truth, as taught by the Saviors and by Saints, Mystics, Prophets and Sages of all ages and races is the Universal Solvent, and at the same time it is the catalyst which blends the basis of all creeds and shows the seeker the way back to his real Home of everlasting peace and happiness. Truth is the Word and the Light of God, reflected in the facets of devoted souls, minds and hearts. It is for such seekers that this book Was written.

Many versions and interpretations of the Holy Bible have been published from intellectual, philosophical, historical and other view-points. The purpose of 'The Mystic Bible' is to bring to light the meaning of the Holy Word and how to find it as an actual, living Reality within ourselves. The Word is the Truth and Essence of God Who created all things by this vital current of spiritual energy of Sound and Light. He Himself is Light. From Him proceeded the Sound, and from that Sound again proceeded Light and so on down through many regions, into this world.

The 'Word' of God or the Logos is the key to all Sacred Scriptures and the alpha and omega of all creation. It is the One River of Life which flows out of the Throne of God. The 'Word' is often referred to as 'The Pearl of Great Price', 'The Philosopher's Stone', 'The Father of All', 'The Great Mother', 'The Beloved', 'The Redeemer', etc. It is That for which all souls are searching, either consciously or unconsciously, within and without. The Holy Melody is Its highest secret. Only the human soul can know and experience the bliss of this 'Song of Songs' through the grace of a living Saint. Blessed are those who find it. It is the 'Wedding Feast' of the Lord of souls, to which all are invited, but few endeavor to attain this inner grace.

(MAT. 22; LUKE 12: 31-40)

Only the central beam of Truth itself can shed light on the way by which the soul came into this world and can find the pathway which leads back to the Father's House of eternal bliss. The Saviors, Saints, Mystics, Prophets and Sages have revealed some portion of this Light to mankind in each age, according to the measure of human capacity to benefit thereby at that time. Sacred Scriptures are the recordings of the Truth revealed in that particular period; but only to the extent that mortal language can convey, for it is up to each individual to have the actual experience within himself or herself. 'The Mystic Bible' is intended to point out to the reader how he can find and follow the path which will lead him to THAT IMMORTAL TRUTH.

The records are left for us to read, ponder and decipher. But man has lost sight of the 'Living Word' because the has wandered away from it through greater attraction and attention every human being, as 'The Lost Word', and must be found by each individual before the Homeward Journey can actually started. When the soul is linked to the current of The Holy Word by a living Saint, then it is literally lifter inward and upward to its Eternal Source.

Man should therefore strive to know himself as he really is, and be vitally interested I "that Light within, which lighteth everyman who cometh into this world" (JOHN 1:9). Only a living Saint can link the soul to the Word which leads to God-Realization. This latent Holy Sound Current is referred to by Job as the Redeemer which liveth and transcendeth the mortal form.

"For I know that my Redeemer liveth"   (JOB 19:25)
"Yet in my flesh shall I see God"   (JOB 19:26)

Therefore, first we should seek a living Saint who can link us with the Holy Word, and then follow His instructions so that we may realize God within ourselves while in the flesh.

When the Holy Bible is read in that light of understanding and search, then the Old Testament enriches the New, the latter explains the former and vice versa. And the Truth, the Word, as taught by the Saints, sheds much light on both as the One Mystic Thread which links the Old and the New, the first and the last, the cause and the effect. They Mystic Thread of the Holy Word is the key, the One Truth woven throughout all Sacred Writings. It is the central theme in this book and it is the One living Reality within each and every human being.

The material in this book is an inspirational gift from the Great Teacher Himself, the writing of which is really a privilege and a *blessing beyond human comprehension. I am overwhelmed at the very thought of being permitted to place these pages at the feet of the Beloved living Teacher, Maharaj Sardar Charan Singh Ji.*

My Niece, Louise Hilger, edited, typed and rearranged the material into its present form. She also added many references and much valuable authentic material which she gathered during the four years she has been going to the Radha Swami Satsang at Beas, which is located near Amritsar in the Punjab, India. During this time she has made five trips to India to gather Spiritual Gems of great prize. This most valuable information has been freely used to explain the Holy Bible in the Mystic Light, especially for the western world.

While in India, Miss Hilger has the great advantage of personal contact with the Living Teacher, which brings her in close touch with the working knowledge of the profound Truth as taught by Him and his illustrious Predecessors. Except for His Grace and Inspiration, this book could never have been written.

This opportunity is being utilized to express my gratitude to my dear friend and brother, Professor Jagmohan Lal of the Dera for going over the manuscript with me and suggesting slight changes and certain deletions wherever the additional information might seem confusing to a seeker. These have been gratefully complied with and approved by the present Living Teacher. The writer also wishes to acknowledge the suggestions of additional points of interest in the Bible which many Christian readers would like to have explained from a Mystic view-point; such as 'The Lord's Prayer', 'The Miracle of the Loaves and Fishes', etc. These have also been explained and incorporated in 'The Mystic Bible' prior to going over same with the Professor.

CHAPTER I
TRUE MYSTICISM

Nearly every seeker after Truth stands baffled at its gates and asks the question: "What is the Truth and where can I find it?"

Most races and nations have their own Sacred Scriptures, and the interpretations of them are many, as also are the religions which teach the creeds founded on those Sacred Texts. Intuitive souls sense the existence of a living Reality within the sealed, Sacred Scriptures; that is, not within the books themselves, but that the writings pertain to a "Living Reality" which cannot be perceived by the physical senses. It is actually within every human being, yearning to be brought into Conscious Realization. This is proven by the lives of true Saints in different countries in the Past, and by living Saints in the present age, who are hard to find. He who has found and come under the guidance and protection of such a True Mystic during his lifetime on this earth is most fortunate indeed.

An Ariadrian thread of devotion and faith seems to run through all religions, like a single pathway to the Truth in life, cleaving asunder many theories and external observations and rules. Love and Devotion transcend all forms, because these are living energy currents and qualities of the soul. They are not to be confused with mere physical emotions and attachments. Truth itself is the common denominator which is the reward in understanding. It is a life of devotion, love and service to the Supreme Being and His creation, under the guidance of a true Mystic in human form.

Mysticism is the pathway of the soul to God-Realization. A true Mystic, Master or Saint is one who has attained this goal during his lifetime on this earth, and those who are his devoted followers and aspire to attain this same goal are also called mystics, disciples, *satsangis*, etc., depending upon the language that is being used, but all have the same meaning. Truth is the mystic thread which links the pearls of every creed into a rosary of Life. But it must be **lived** in order to be realized. Mere lip service is useless.

Jesus lived this Ideal so completely that He merged His being into that pattern of thinking and feeling where He became identified with this Truth. Out of this consciousness came His wonderful declaration:

"I am the Way, and the Truth and the Life: no man cometh unto the Father, but by me."   (JOHN 14:6)

Similar is Laotzu's declaration of the Great Tao-The (virtue or power) and Wu Wei (effortless way of the gentleness of non-resistance).

The effortless effort **of true devotion** does all things naturally, from within, outward, as all fountains flow. It is the Life of the Spirit, uncensored by mind and personal preferences or considerations. There is not a trace of ego where God's Will direct and supreme. Jesus explained this simple way of life in a few words:

"For my yoke is easy and my burden is light."

(MAT. 11:30)

"If any man will come after me, let him deny himself, and take up his cross, and follow me."

(MAT. 16:24, *also* MARK 8:34)

This is the crossing over of the self-interests and currents into the selfless way of God and Love. It is the true way of gentleness and devotion by effort which is not born of self or selfish interest but of Love. This can be achieved by surrendering the self and all the cunning of the mind and ego to the Will of God.

Further, Jesus said:

"If a man love me, he will keep my Words: and my Father will love him, and we will come unto him, and make Our abode with him."   (JOHN 14:23)

"A new commandment I give unto you, that ye love one another; as I have loved you, that ye also love one another. By this shall all men know that ye are my disciples, if ye have love one to another."   (JOHN 13:34, 35)

"Inasmuch as ye have done it unto one of these my brethren, **even** these least, ye have done it unto me."

(MAT. 25:40)

"And I have declared unto them **Thy Name**, and will declare it; that the love wherewith Thou lovedst me may be in them, and I in them." (JOHN 17:26)

These simple statements solve all the problems of service and who is our neighbor. "**Thy Name**" is the secret Word of Power within every human being. It is the Holy Shabd or Sound Essence.

Such a true and simple religion is a WAY OF LIFE rather than a fixed creed of rules and observations. This is always noticeable at the fountainhead of that religion where there is a living Mystic or Master, and a few sincere followers. Truth reveals itself as a **Life** rather than a mere belief to cling to. A living faith is a definite Way of energy flow in an inward and upward direction, through the mind and emotions of the individual. It is a Reality, and is always rewarded by the Supreme Being. Faith is accredited only to him who **lives** it; and, as was said in the case of Abraham, that is counted as Righteousness (ROM 4:3). It then becomes the right pathway of Life and Understanding.

Living the life by doing the deeds of Love, expresses the Inner Life of the soul. It flowers and grows on the still lagoon of life's emotions, when riding on the Holy Shabd Current. This serenity is a gift of God, attained only by means of overcoming the self through His Love and Mercy. Success in this pursuit is as definite as any enterprise or business venture or scientific experiment. Yet it is the simple way of Life, spoken of by Jesus, Laotzu, and other Great Mystics.

Devotion and attention the Great Work are the first requisites to success in a mystic life. God, the Ideal, is the North Star to every devotee on this sea of Life. This constant awareness of God as the Giver, the Gift and the Receiver, solves many puzzling problems, leads to the sublimation of the separate self, and ends in the Bliss of Conscious Union with God, the Supreme Being. This is the meaning of True Mysticism and is the goal of all real Mystics or Saints in any land or at any time, regardless of race, creed or nationality. **It is life's supreme purpose and goal**.

The reason for writing this book is to follow the rosary thread of Mysticism in the Bible, through some of its hidden meanings in obscure passages and a few well-known ones, and to show how it is identical with other Sacred Scriptures such as the teachings of Radha Swami, and of the Saints and Mystic of other lands and ages.

Finding the hidden Light within ourselves (LUKE 11:34, 35, 36; MAT. 6:22 JOHN 1:9), and listening to the "still small Voice" within (I KINGS 19:12, 13), also called the Holy Shabd, the Sound Current, and Holy Sound; and actually **practicing** what is taught in the Bible and other Sacred Scriptures—as a new life and revelation—under the guidance of a true living Mystic or Master, ultimately leads to genuine Love and God-Realization.

As Truth is One, Mysticism is One. It is the Way, the Truth and the Life of the devotee. God is One and the Way to Him is One. The avenues of the starting points may be far apart; but, like brooks and rivers, they all lead to the Ocean.

CHAPTER II
INDIVIDUAL AWAKENING

There comes a time in the life of an individual when he begins to question set forms and values of religious beliefs and tries to find a reason for their observance, which is based upon understanding and inner need rather than mere outward routine. His intuitive longing for an inner understanding of the essential Essence of Life and a closer tuning into those vibratory waves of a deeper significance of the Soul Principles in Life is the start of the search for the hidden values within his very being, and not in mere external rituals. And that is when the living Master or Mystic comes to the rescue and shows him the way.

All religions exist because they fill a need which is best suited for the guidance of a race, a nation or a tribe, at the particular time or era. Religions, like the Sabbath, are made for men — not mankind for religion. When the consciousness evolves or changes, then all old values are questioned and a search for new ones is in progress. All set forms have a way of changing in the economy of Nature. The mind of man is no exception to this adaptation of growth, or expansion from within outward.

Everything in Nature sprouts, develops and fully expresses itself as mature sentient beings or vegetation. From the unconscious to the Conscious, is the way of life. If this is true of the growth of the body, the emotions and the mind, then why not the Soul Life and Consciousness also? **The latter is the real actor and the Essence** of the entire being. It is the very reason and cause of living. It is slow to mature and comes to the surface in the daily consciousness among the pressure of the body's material needs and the grosser frictions and attractions in life. But when once awakened, such individuals are heard of in history and act as a leaven for awakening many other souls, as one lamp can light another. They become the first fruits of that season or age.

Spiritual growth and fruition is an individual progress. It depends upon purification and development of the consciousness of each soul as a unit. That soul's awareness and attraction is toward the core and Inner Essence of all Being, whence it originally came. It is the cry of the soul to go back home to the Father's House, no matter where it is located or how it is conditioned on earth; that very conditioning being the fruit of its own previous actions and desires. Kings and beggars alike have received that call and set their faces toward the "East" the Inner Sensory Origin of their very being, the rising Sun of Reality.

The awakening of souls is a process of the ages, and the purpose of creation. All creation furnishes the material, condition and friction for further conscious development, through pleasure and through pain. Some have labored in this Vineyard of the Lord of Soul Growth for many ages; others begin, while a few enter at the tenth hour of the day, and they receive the same wages at the end of their day of labor. Soul growth, soul awakening, God-Realization is the reward.

Each age has its message of the Creator to mankind. This Truth is proclaimed by great Mystics, Saints, Sages, Seers, Sadhus, Yogishwars, Prophets, Lawgivers, and followers of great Teachers. Through the mercy and grace of the Supreme Father, none are forgotten or left out. To each race and nation, an interpretation of the Great Truth is given, which is best suited to the needs and the characteristics of the mental and emotional background.

Only that can be given which the conscious mind is ready to receive and to which it can respond. This is necessary for each era and clime, and need not be the whole Truth at any one time, as progress or evolution is not a sudden ultimate either. Hence, the great variance in religions and teachers at every epoch of time. Instructions to the many must necessarily be adaptable to them and accepted as a step forward in a better understanding of the Soul Life and its higher values standard, in a gross material world of experience.

All creation is but for man's benefit, as a Kindergarten of Life. The Eternal Father furnishes all the material and the environment, plus the instruments or vehicles with which to enjoy this experience of His Grace. The physical body, the emotional nature and the mind of man are all tools for the expression of the Soul, the Real Self or Being, as the One Essence in every form and substance.

Gradually, this realization dawns on the consciousness of the Soul in this journey of life in the Vineyard of the Lord, the Kindergarten of Souls. Little by little the gross is worn away and the Essence begins to be revealed within and shines forth consciously as a Diamond Soul, a real jewel in its own nature. All that had previously been sought for on the outside — and much more — is revealed and given within, a thousand-fold greater and richer than the earth could give or hold. This is the literal explanation of the experience of Job who surrendered all, endured all in this pilgrimage of life, in order to find God-Realization. In the end, his faith was rewarded, and he received thousand-fold rewards of Realities, of which the most precious earthly things were but mere shadows.

Spiritual values and gifts cannot be compared with physical things, even though they are recorded as such for the sake of those who know nothing of the Inner Jewels of Life. How else could the Saints tell the multitude of those Inner Values and describe them to those who know only material things? Spiritual things must be spiritually discerned:

"And I, brethren, could not speak unto you as unto spiritual, but as unto carnal, even as unto babes in Christ. I have fed you with milk, and not with meat: for hitherto ye were not able to bear it, neither yet now are ye able. For ye are yet carnal: for whereas there is among you envying, and strife, and divisions, are ye not carnal, and walk as men?"

(I COR. 3:1, 2, 3)

Religious renaissance or awakenings come periodically, as cycles of time in the life of souls on earth. Then a Great

Teacher is sent, who calls the souls, who are ready for one great stride forward. Such are the seasons of the soul. Their cycles are slower than material things because they are deeper and more lasting, the soul being an eternal verity.

The Soul is the Mystery of Life and the Darling of God, for which all creation was formed. All other things grow and perish. Even planets and solar systems grow cold. **Only the Soul endures** as the spark of the One Eternal Essence of the Supreme Father Himself.

Within every mortal is concealed the mystery of the Word of Life and Creation. It is the Lost Word found and is also symbolized by the Lost Chord. The parable of the Prodigal Son is symbolic of the experiences of the soul. It returns to its Father's House from its wanderings on earth and material existence, after having worn its garments or vehicles to shreds, or so thin, that it can find and see the way Home by the Inner Light of Love and Grace bestowed on it through the Living Master. Then the Heavenly Father bestows a new set of robes for the wedding feast of the soul. This wedding feast is not the celebration of a physical union, but that of the soul with its Divine Source, and that is termed 'God-Realization' (MAT. 22:1-15)

All ceremonial robes, and the wedding garment spoken of by Jesus in the parable of the call to the feast, as well as the multicolored coat of Joseph, are all symbols of the finer vehicles of man, beside his physical form or body. These are actual inner experiences of souls on the Homeward journey, back to their own conscious being in the Father's House, the Eternal Essence of the One substance.

Most great Teachers had and still have a secret doctrine for the few, and creeds and customs for the masses. Jesus said to His apostles:

"And the disciples came, and said unto him, Why speakest thou unto them in parables? He answered and said unto them, Because it is given unto you to know the mysteries of the kingdom of heaven, but to them it is not given. For whosoever hath, to him shall be given, and he shall have more abundance: but whosoever hath not, from him shall be taken away even that he hath. Therefore speak I to them in parables: because they seeing see not; and hearing they hear not, neither do they understand. And in them is fulfilled the prophecy of Isaiah, which saith,

By hearing ye shall hear, and shall not understand; and seeing ye shall see. And shall not perceive: For this people's heart is waxed gross, and their ears are dull of hearing, and their eyes they have closed; lest at an time they should see with their eyes, and hear with their ears, and should understand with their heart, and should be converted, and I should heal them.

But blessed are your eyes, for they see: and your ears, for they hear. For verily I say unto you, That many prophets and righteous men have desired to see those things which ye see, and have not seen them; and to hear those things which ye hear, and have not heard them." (MAT. 13:10-17)

"All these things spake Jesus unto the multitude in parables; and without a parable spake he not unto them." (MAT. 13:34)

Even the temples had an inner court where only the priests entered, and an outer court for the multitude.

In most of the Sacred Texts there is a promise of Saviors or *Avatars*, who are to come from time to time in the progression of cycles, to reveal a new aspect of the Great Truth to a particular nation or race at that time. The Hindus had the nine *Avatars of Vishnu*. The tenth is yet to come as Maitraya Acharya, also called Kalki. The Christians are looking for the second coming of Christ. The Jews are also still looking forward to a Messiah. While they acknowledge Jesus as a Prophet, His message did not blend with their particular type of consciousness and therefore they could not benefit by it. In the teachings of Jesus the Mosaic Laws and rituals were not emphasized enough to be a fulfillment to them. Jesus brought to earth a new aspect of the same Truth, and those who were not ready to evolve with and by it, persecuted Him. And so the cyclic expectation and prayers for further revelation by the multitudes on earth goes on, while they themselves may persecute or ridicule the very answer to their prayers during His lifetime among them!

However, in every uplift of the general consciousness, there were many who were the first fruits of that vintage of spiritual effort and Soul Growth, who gave their entire attention to this Reality in preference to earthly pursuits. Religious order perpetuated the forms which were established by their prominent leaders in the effort of Spiritual Growth.

As there are first fruits in Nature, which ripen before the rest of the fruits on the tree, so it is in humanity with the souls and their inner fruition on the Tree of Life in this material existence. There are awakenings of souls and longings and midnight tears of many whose consciousness does not fit any more to the forms they find themselves in, or to the trend of thoughts and values they were accustomed to before this awakening. These souls struggle and seek, either within or without the folds of formal creeds. The spirit is not bound by form but seeks to reveal itself to the consciousness daily, through experience, by practicing and living according to soul qualities.

Truth is the Essence of all existence. It is omnipresent, like the air on earth. Where can these souls present, like the air on earth. Where can these souls find the answer? Some type of air is more suitable to some individuals than the others. For these seekers after Truth, the Supreme Father has provided an answer in this age in order to show the shortest way Home to these first fruits of His Vineyard. In this Iron Age, the Supreme Father sends Saints out from the highest region of Spirituality to gather and bring in these souls by Their teachings and guidance.

These Saints do not start new creeds of religions, nor do They attempt to convert the multitude into formal observances, and they do not seek numbers. They merely attract and instruct those souls who come to them in all sincerity and want to find the Way to God-Realization.

The Goal is achieved by His Grace and Love, and the individual's own attitude of mine plus effort of attention to the development of soul consciousness. The direction for inner devotion and concentration is given by the Master at the time of Initiation. Otherwise, the disciple works and toils like others, in whatever station of life he may be, to earn his own living and fulfill his *karmic* obligations. He does not have to leave his church or creed; rather, by a process of better understanding and deeper devotion, he fulfills all these requirements until he does not need this outer help any longer to steady him in his inner progress. Naturally, he curtails his animal nature and lessens his *karmic* burden by following the strict instructions not to ear anything that must be killed or stopped in its progress of development, like eggs, meat, fish and fowl, or anything containing them. Alcoholic beverages of any kind are also to be definitely avoided because they dull the mind and senses and stimulate the nervous system and the earthy *pranas* which have a downward material tendency and result in deterioration.

The aspirant aims to ascend the Tree of Life from which he had originally descended, and to again reach Kether, the Crown of Consciousness. He is literally going back Home by the One Road of Life itself. And this is the straight and narrow way of Inner Devotion and Understanding, under the guidance of a living Master who has Himself traversed the Way. Just as His time, Jesus said:

> "I am the Way, and the Truth and the Life: no man cometh unto the Father, but by me."   (JOHN 14:6)
> "He that hath seen me hath seen the Father; and how sayest thou then, Shew us the Father? Believest thou not that I am in the Father, and the Father in me? The words that I say unto you, I speak not of myself: but the Father that dwelleth in me, He doeth the works. Believe me that I **am** in the Father, and the Father in me: or else

believe me for the very works' sake. Verily, verily, I say unto you, He that believeth on me, the works that I do shall he do also; and **greater works** than these shall he do; because I go unto my Father."   (JOHN 14:9-12)

"And he that seeth me seeth Him that sent me."

(JOHN 12:45)

This great Truth was a Reality when Jesus was on earth and could be seen by men. How many have actually seen Jesus since His departure from this earth, and yet they think that His work continues for ever on this earth. However, His Love and Truth remain for the guidance of the people, with the personal help of a living Mystic.

Every man's earthly work ceases when he leaves the earth. All obligations and promises made by Jesus were fulfilled when He was on earth. His earth life and obligations ceased when He entered the higher Spiritual Regions.

"In my Father's house are many mansions."

(JOHN 14:2)

He can descend within and show Himself to His devotees, who contacted Him during His lifetime on this earth, but after ascension, cannot assume the Physical body without re-incarnating. He can work through a successor, duly appointed by Him, or through any duly appointed successor of the previous successor, until that line runs out; providing the successor is sufficiently developed spiritually to go within consciously, by the process of Inner Transport, and meet the Savior on the inner planes of consciousness. Such is the teaching of the real Saints and Mystics of all times.

The Truth of the Saints is the consciousness of the Mystic life of the spirit, lived daily. It is a living of the soul for its conscious reunion with God. It is the process of the spiritual child, growing up to meet the Father in a distant country, from whence it originally wandered, so long ago that it has forgotten its origin. This is told in many myths and stories by the Greeks, like the story of the hero, Theseus, who was recognized by the Father when he brought back with him the sword of spiritual Truth, left by the Father when He had visited that region, and with which the son had girded his loins after finding it where it had been hidden from other eyes under the Rock of the Word.

The initiate, hero, or the son of the Father does the work of the Father by the strength of the Spirit of Truth, the Sword of Truth, which conquers all things and obstacles. The son's love and longing, coupled with patient and courageous effort, lead him on the Way to his Father's House in a distant land, which is really the spiritual world within. Such are the literal meanings of these marvelous myths of old, when truly understood for the message which they hold.

It is not for all, but for the children of the Household of Spirituality, who live the life and walk on the Way to the Kingdom of God within man. None other can use this great spiritual Sword of Truth or benefit by the mere possession of its form. Only he who **lives** the life can know the doctrine of the One Truth.

Truth is the Inner Life, while the conscious existence in a form is called the outer life and is actually **unconsciousness**, away from the bliss of consciousness and kingship of the realms within. Jesus stated this clearly when He said:

"My kingdom is not of this world: if my kingdom were of this world, then would my servants fight."

(JOHN 18:36)

"Thinkest thou that I cannot now pray to my Father, and he shall presently give me more than twelve legions of angels?" (MAT. 26:53)

Pilate found no fault in Jesus and washed his hands of the matter, in order to show his innocence. (MAT. 27:22-27).

Forms and customs which were originally meant for the security of life, become hard and lifeless as they grow old and crystallize, and are replaced in Nature by young and new forms as time goes on. The spirit or soul always remains solvent as the active pole of life itself.

Laws become forms which bind the Life eventually, because the within moves swiftly while the without crystallizes and cannot keep up the pace of the need of the spirit. New bottles are required for the new wine of life, or both are lost. (MAT. 9:17)

"For to be carnally minded is death; but to be spiritually minded is life and peace." (ROM. 8:16)

St. Paul admonished the Christians to be one in Spirit, as it was in Christ Jesus. (ROM. 8:9-12)

When the children grow up, it is both a joy and a sorrow to the mother of life, because the love of the babe must be replaced by the love of the adult, which is different. All growth is painful to physical forms, bodies and customs of established ways. One moves constantly like the hands of the clock, while the other stands still like the face of the clock to measure time itself and gathers the dust of the ages, which buries the life of any civilization.

Where the consciousness is, there is the life. A dead thing has neither. Life and consciousness are One in Essence. Therefore, the Saints advise their students to raise the consciousness to the center of the forehead and hold it there, consciously. The head is Kether, the Crown of Creation, and the center of the highest consciousness possible. The lesser centers and *chakras* — situated below the eyes — belong to the unconscious realm, and the true Mystics do not go in at these lower centers.

That part of the body which is situated below eyes is in the field of Nature and is automatic in function, to supply the needs of the body by attraction or repulsion to the great outer realm of Nature's energy fields. The psychic realm is in this subconscious field. The Spiritual Realms are situated above the eyes, the actual center of consciousness in the body. That is the abode of the soul in the body and is referred to as the *heart center* by the Saints.

The physical heart center is ruled by the emotions, while the spiritual heart center is governed by soul qualities, and that is where the Mystic Union takes place. When in deep thought, man's consciousness is normally in the head, so the Saints teach us how to utilize that faculty to enable us to go in and up from there, instead of wasting a lot of time and energy and perhaps becoming confused besides, in concentrating on the lower *chakras*.

In the first place, man is not so constructed as to be able to properly go in and govern these lower *chakras*, as he was in the ages past; and secondly, the life span is not long enough in this age to accomplish such a long and arduous task. And, even after all that has been done, it is still necessary to go in and up from the topmost conscious *chakra* in the body. Then why delay and take all the detours, when the straight and narrow has to be taken eventually if we wish to reach the Goal, and **can** be taken RIGHT NOW! **Now** is the time of the Lord. The degrees of life are measured in sentient sensitiveness and conscious awareness at each center or region.

The good Lord has many shepherds for His sheep, and not even a sparrow falleth off the roof without His knowledge:

> "Are not two sparrows sold for a farthing? And one of them shall not fall on the ground without your Father: But the very hairs of your head are all numbered. Fear ye not therefore, ye are of more value than many sparrows." (MAT. 10:29-31)

There have been a number of Mystics and Saints in the East. Since the advent of Saint Kabir in the fifteenth century, there have been quite a few Saints who brought the Great Truth to mankind, in a very simple manner. The Radha Swami teaching, known also as *Sant Mat*, is a direct revelation of the Path of the Soul and its Inward Ascension, without attention to the lower five *chakras* or centers in the body, as was previously practiced in all the earlier teachings in every land.

The Mysticism of all ancient Sacred Lore began at the bottom of the Tree of Life; namely, at the rectal center—Called the Muladhara Chakra—to evolve the consciousness through it and upward. In the Vedas, these six centers in the body, with the seventh at the center above the eyes — the thousand-petalled Lotus — was the height of attainment revealed.

In the Old Testament of the Christian Bible, which is based upon the Talmud and the Zohar, there are many hints and references to a secret process of concentration practiced by the Patriarchs of old, and their success was announced in terms of positive results in the spiritual life, symbolized as male off-spring; or negative results, symbolized by female off-spring, in their message to other mystics. These terms are similes and do not refer to the begetting of physical off-spring.

The Esoteric Kabbala, with its Tree of Life as the symbolic form of the finer essences of the human body, the Temple of God, was based upon the teachings of the Talmud and the Zohar. It has a system of centers or whirling energy virtues called Sephiroth, similar to the *Chakras*, built or designed as a replica of the temple seen by Moses on Mount Sinai. The hidden mystery of the Life Energy in the human body is clearly shown to be the objective of the entire system. Definite centers are given as stations for concentration, for devotion, for the showbreads, for incense and for sacrifice of thoughts and animal emotions at the abdominal center of digestion and absorption. Ceremonial magic was the method of concentration in this system.

In the Vedas, it was the control of the *Prana* to still the emotions and the mind. Other methods of control by the will were also used.

In all these systems, the methods differed somewhat, but the goal and the objective were the same; namely, to purify and still the mind by concentration, so that the Light of the Soul can shine forth. Thus, the consciousness may meet God in the stillness of the Garden of Life, the Paradise within.

The seat of the center of consciousness in the human body is the central axis of the brain. Here the Sound Current, called the Holy Shabd or the Word is consciously contacted. This is the first station and step on the ladder of human ascent above the eyes. Elijah's experience on Mount Horeb (I KINGS 19:8-15) tells of such an even.

Jesus also referred to it:

"The wind bloweth where it listeth, and thou hearest the sound thereof, but canst not tell whence it cometh, and whither it goeth: so is every one that is born of the Spirit." (JOHN 3:8)

In fact, all of the verses from 3 to 14 in John, Chapter 3, pertain to this subject, as well as many other passages in the Bible which can easily be recognized and understood when one has found the key.

Elijah also used the squatting posture of Yoga when he produced the rain for King Ahab at the time of great drought (I KINGS 18:42). Again, this shows that these secret methods for soul development and for power (which a true Mystic never squanders for material gain) were known to the ancient Prophets, Sages, Yogis, Rishis and Law Givers. In fact, this type of knowledge was the science of that age and much sought after by scholars. Even Alexander the Great was instructed by Diogenes. Most rulers revered the sages and those learned in the secrets of the finer forces in Nature and in man.

Our present-day material science does not satisfy the soul, no matter how much comfort and ease it may provide for the body. The emphasis is too much on the material side, and the soul feels the pressure, like the bondage in Egypt of Biblical times. Of course, these very bonds are the individual's own mind and senses, in their attachment to outer things. A living, vital understanding is necessary at this time, to strike at the core and the essence rather than the form and the belief alone. Can it be proven? Can it be done? Or has God forsaken His creation in this age of materialism?

The answer is that the Saints have done it and do it daily. They actually **live** this Mystic Inner Life and can show the true seeker the simple Path of God-Realization, which is to be trodden, not as an ascetic, but while living a normal life, performing our worldly duties and earning our own livelihood. But how many will give it time, thought and effort, when material things pay odd in cash? Man, in his purely material pursuits, is turning his mind away from God. God never leaves His creation. Without His eternal support, it would pass away into non-existence.

The consciousness of the Supreme Being is not limited, but man's awareness has been limited by his own acts of indulgence and desires, until the veil between himself and God has reached the proportion of a veritable mountain. The Saints show us how to wear away this mountainous obstruction, without at the same time is increasing its height or its depth at some other point while doing so. Thus, They help us to again reach the blissful state of conscious union with God — *God-Realization*. This human life has been given to us for that very purpose, and it is up to us to make the best use of it. That is the talent which we all have to account for when we leave this earth.

And mere physical death is not the answer; in fact, suicide or despair is one of the sins against the Holy Ghost and is definitely an unforgivable sin. We are here to learn to control the energies through a body of resistance, in conscious actions and reactions. What is really meant is the overcoming of the deadly vices of lust, anger, greed, attachment and egotism. These are tools of the lower mind and desire body. They can be sublimated only by the practice of CHASTITY, FORGIVENESS, CHARITY, DETACHMENT AND HUMILITY, under the guidance of a living, True Mystic or Master.

The Holy Word is the One Power which can overcome human weakness, by linking the consciousness to the Inner Life Stream of the Holy Spirit of Shabd. By lifting up the attention to this "living Redeemer" of the Holy Sound Current, all lower obstacles are automatically left behind and forgotten; much the same as children grow up and automatically give up their babyhood toys.

The tendencies of the lower self or animal nature in man can only be slain or overcome by **diverting** our **attention from** them **to** the higher, spiritual tendencies and developing them according to the teachings of the Holy Scriptures, under the guidance of a living Mystic, Saint or Master. It is not a matter of suppression, but of exchanging the lesser for the greater. If a child is playing with a dangerous weapon which it does not understand, a wise parent does not frighten the child by quickly snatching the weapon away, but rather diverts the child's attention from the weapon to a more attractive but harmless object. So, with the Great Mystics and Saints; They never compel, but through love and mercy point out the higher potentialities in such a way that we automatically abandon the lower and make an effort to reach the Highest. First, man must convince himself that he wants to let go of the lesser values, like a seed which dies unto itself to bring forth new fruit. So is the soul reborn in the Nectar of Inner Life, out of the shell of matter.

Every parent knows that it takes many years and tears to develop a human body to the age of maturity; but only God can make a soul, which is the inhabitant and the very life of that body, as it is a particle of the Supreme Being Himself. The human body is a great gift and opportunity for the soul to work out its deep-seated desires and cravings, through the protection of form as a media and as a measure for sensory indications of action and reaction.

Only in a realm where all planes and forces are fully represented can man work out his own ideas, emotions, desires and impulses, and reap the fruits of his previous acts. The earth is specially fitted for this purpose, like a Kindergarten or preparatory school. Only by sublimating the lower energies and using them wisely, as a skilled master craftsman uses tools, can man ever hope to become a Master Builder like the Grand Architect of the Universe.

A child must learn in order to grow up to the stature of his father. Jesus said:

"Be ye therefore perfect, even as your Father which is in heaven is perfect." (MAT. 5:48)

"The Lord is of Great Eminence, exalted is His Name. He who would know His height, must in stature be the same." (JAPJI — Verse 24)

Human emotions are young and immature and love to wallow in the indulgences of infancy. Even when they try to overcome on single item of weakness or pleasure, instead of realizing that they are being relieved of an impediment, they feel that they are making a great sacrifice, and expect immediate reward and praise. Wise parents know this trait of childhood. Mere years of body age do not spell growth or maturity of the mind or the emotions. Many a big man is but a child to the wife who loves him, and many a grownup lady is but a child to the man who loves her. Through love and opposites in qualities they learn forbearance, wisdom, patience and service in Love.

It is not always strength that is the best teacher. Weakness in one, usually brings out the strength of character in the other, if they make a success of their marriage. "A hard and a soft stone grind best" is an old proverb. That is why the earth itself is in such a muddle all the time, like loose and broken toys in a nursery. Mere perfection in external things has a way of deteriorating that is surprising. It takes constant care, time and thought to keep fit and in balance with the surroundings. Love and Patience are the real teachers in life. Earth is a nursery for mankind. It was never intended as a heaven nor even as a permanent dwelling. The Saints refer to this earth as a *wilderness*. The record of the Children of Israel passing through such a wilderness, is the key to the Books of Moses.

It is by this same process of obstacles and resistance, difficulties and problems in life on earth, that souls grow gradually mature by seeking **depth** and **purpose** in life;

and not mere physical indulgences as a pastime, and the material success which makes this waste of time possible. Jesus said:

"But seek ye first the kingdom of God and His righteousness; and all these things shall be added unto you."

(MAT. 6:33)

"And Jesus looked round about, and saith unto his disciples,

How hardly shall they that have riches enter the kingdom of God!

And the disciples were astonished at his words. But Jesus answereth again, and saith unto them, Children, how hard is it for them that trust in riches to enter into the kingdom of God! It is easier for a camel to go through the eye of a needle, than for a rich man to enter into the kingdom of God.

And they were astonished out of measure, saying among themselves, Who then can be saved?

And Jesus looking upon them saith, With men it is impossible, but not with God: for with God all things are possible.

Then Peter began to say unto him, Lo, we have left all, and have followed thee.

And Jesus answered and said, Verily I say unto you,

There is no man that hath left house, or brethren, or sisters, or father, or mother or wife, or children, or lands, for my sake, and the gospel's,

But he shall receive an hundredfold now in this time, in houses, and brethren, and sisters, and mothers, and children, and lands, with persecutions; and in the world to come, eternal life.

But many that are first shall be last; and the last first."

(MARK 10:23-31)

Souls, like children, must learn from life and grow up or remain in the background among other struggling souls until they can apply the talents given them by the Father. How can we expect to enter the kingdom of God while we are attached to and long for worldly possessions and relationships. It is such attachments which prevent us from attaining God-Realization.

Severe physical handicaps in life have many a time been turned into a stimulus for a greater effort in achievement and for a deeper understanding and appreciation of all the gifts which have been given to man to work out his Salvation. One who is endowed with the qualities of Love and Creativeness, searched for and finds a Teacher of Spiritual Wisdom, much the same as one would search for a teacher in the realms of art and science if one desired to become proficient in a given field.

CHAPTER III
A MYSTIC VIEWPOINT ON CREATION

The Bible and most other Sacred Scriptures begin with a vivid account of the Creation. Details and descriptions differ somewhat, but in essence the accounts are much alike. The unity of accord on the central ideas is amazing in such an endless scope and field, when in daily life few persons can agree even on small matters and undertakings. In the Bible, St. John, like a true mystic, also starts his gospel with a very brief statement of the Creation and mentions the Word or the Logos as the Primal Energy out of which it proceeded. In some writings it is referred to as the Spermatic Word. According to Sant Mat or Radha Swami teachings, it is called the Holy Shabd or the Sound Current, the Primal Essence or the Word.

The aim is to start with beginnings in the field of Primal Energy, before there was matter of any sort or kind. From a standpoint of reason, this is good logic. But the Mystics have something better and finer in mind for their followers, by constantly keeping before the mind the principle of the First Cause as the beginning and origin to which all things must return.

God created all — gives all! That is the Essence and the Keynote of all Sacred Texts. He is the Giver and the Gift, which Mystics never forget for one moment, and so they keep the mind humble and appreciative; hence, they have a greater sense of awareness of the deeper values and essence in life. Their mind — Soul and heart — is always open to God the Giver of all. In this manner they fulfill the law and the Prophets. They never forget the Lord God, the Supreme Father, and they do not create false images and gods (including their own ego) before their mind. The clever mind and intellect are great artificers in spinning webs of illusions created by material evidence, with the individual ego as the doer. This is the real idolatry and binds the soul and mind to the things craved and produced, or with which the mind identifies itself.

So, each person becomes a keeper of his own creation, and not only forgets the Real, but wanders into further mental bondage of what appears to be real to the senses at the time. Things which the mind grasps in order to own and possess, in turn possess the mind and soul, like the fowler's glue does the bird which has become stuck in it. The Saints also compare this illusion to a net, because the more we struggle to free ourselves, the more we become entangled. Until we have come under the guidance and protection of a true, living Master, the soul struggles and tries to free itself from this trap of illusion, but the mind and the senses are so totally ensnared and caught in the sensation and the pleasure of this illusion, that they cannot let go. And to indulge in grief or self-pity is just as great a sin, if not greater than indulging in pleasures. The reason is quite obvious.

The senses cry like babes when they are pried loose from one of their ruinous indulgences. And the mind has more affinity downward, toward the senses, than upward toward the soul, because the mind itself is the finest essence of matter as an Energy Ray. It is the neutron or neuter pole of all material in Creation. That is why it is so powerful in producing illusion and in determining the patterns and events in matter. The will is the positive pole, and the senses and their particles of dancing Tan Mantras are the electrons of this atom of mind substance, as the negative pole. All miracles and phenomena in matter are possible by the proper control of this mental atom as the energy unit in this field of Creation, because it controls the patterns and designs which give shape and limits to all individual units.

It took years of research and planning by many thousands of the best brains in this world to find ways and means to crack the material atom and use its latent energy. Billions upon billions of dollars were expended on this one venture in America alone, before it could be utilized as a mere destructive agent in explosives. If that much effort, thought and research were expended upon the research of this mental unit and its **constructive** possibility, much could be accomplished.

But as this is a problem for each individual to solve to conquer and understand his **own** mind and sense activity as energy distributions for health and disease, it lags behind all external achievement because it involves the control of personal desires, as well as the sublimation of indulgences of the mind and senses. Hence, this entire process of life, who really wish to understand the reason for Creation, and its mystery in their own life and being.

Only by the Supreme Father's Grace can this Light be bestowed on sincere seekers who have exhausted or surmounted some of their ties to pleasure, by bitter experience in the life in matter. A wise man soon finds the limitations in matter and seeks to ascend to control this energy field by understanding of its process, and by devotion to the Almighty Source.

The Mystic is a true alchemist who turns the lower values in life, symbolized by lead and iron, into the pure gold of understanding the energy potential within them and the motive power behind these crystallized essences. This is the permanent method, whereas mere suppression is only like placing ashes on the fire, for it continues to smoulder underneath only to flare up again at the slightest breeze of temptation or forgetfulness. Therefore, the Mystic and His devoted followers always keep in mind their Source, whence they came and whither they go, and follow that path of energy travel to learn of the Ways and Mystery of the Essence Itself.

Atomic research has definitely proven that all matter is but a mass of energy particles and fields in motion, which become fixed in a definite rate of vibratory balance. The pattern design of each object is in the mind field of the cosmos and of the unit. The substance is the attractive power of a sensory or desire action which holds energy particles which it attracts out of the cosmic reservoir. Desire and motive precede all expression of motor activity, mentally and physically—whether conscious or sub-conscious. Even in criminology there is a slogan, "There is no crime without a motive".

Energy itself has intelligence which must have a direction of flow or a way to go, or it defeats itself in useless expenditure and destruction. Every energy block in mind, emotion and in matter is an obstacle which often necessitates eruptions of a volcanic type in Nature, and as disease in man and beast or in vegetation. In such conditions the norm of the mental pattern of energy flow in form and use has been interrupted and must right itself. The wise man and physician looks for the **cause** and assists Nature in balancing this directional energy circuit back to its norm—physically, mentally and emotionally.

The Mystic goes deeper than that and seeks out the causes and blocks or obstacles of his soul currents, and uses all his strength of will and soul qualities to right this central axis of his very being in relationship to the design and purpose of the Supreme Father. The mind of the Mystic is ever in devotion and contemplation of the Source and Origin of all energy and beings. He does his work with his hands and feet, but his soul, heart and mind are in devotion to the Beloved God who is his All. He thus follows the 'North Star' of all currents of directional energy, flowing inward and upward, back to the Source whence they came as centrifugal energy of creativeness.

The Mystic longs to go Home and directs all his energy to that alchemical task of the great work of OVERCOMING AND SUBLIMATING THE EGO and all its outward-bound currents which create further bondage in matter. Externally it is a cleansing and reforming of the direction of the person's mind, emotions and energies in action. Internally it is a hidden process, called alchemy in the Middle Ages, which raises the baser tendencies up to the standard of Gold in their Vibration and values. This is His work, which was referred to by Jesus as *the Father's business* when He said to those who found Him in the temple, on being told that they had feared Him to be lost:

"Wist ye not that I must be about my Father's business?"
(LUKE 2:49)

The Father calls His humble and devoted souls Home because He loves them as the first fruits of His creative process. These have overcome the ego and proved their true love and longing by crossing over the outward currents leading into matter, and choosing the inward Path of Love and Devotion by which to ride Home on the return Current, the Holy Spirit or Holy Shabd. Such have either worn out or sublimated their fervor of material life and its excitement and attachments, and in all humility, they can be absorbed into the Essence of LOVE, BLISS and REALITY. The soul is itself made of this same material and is a particle of this WHOLE. In other words, it is as a drop returning to the Ocean of the Spiritual Essence.

The Mystic or true seeker is the lonely and weary wanderer on earth. Jesus stated this plainly when He said:

"The foxes have holes and the birds of the air have nests; but the Son of man hath not where to lay His head." (MAT. 8:20)

Laotzu, the great Chinese Mystic and Philosopher, said practically the same thing when he expressed his dire loneliness in the valedictory part of the 20th sonnet:

"Common people are joyful; they celebrate a feast day; they flock to a pavilion in spring time. I alone am calm, as one who has as yet received no omen; I am as a babe who has not learned to smile. I am forlorn, like a homeless wanderer! Common people have plenty; I alone am in want. I am a foolish man at heart! I am ignorant. Common people are vivacious and smart, I alone am dull and confused."

"Knowledge of the Tao, how vast I am like a sailor far beyond a place of anchorage, adrift on a boundless ocean. Common people are useful; I am awkward. I stand in contrast to them—but oh, the prize I seek is food from our Mother Tao!"

(from translation by Dwight Goddard, published by Brentano's Publishers, N.Y. 1919)

The Great Tao which is everywhere, eludes the soul when it seeks to embrace it in its entirety. After having lived It and taught Its way of non-resistance and the simple life, It seems to forsake the consciousness of the devotee in the lonely hour of need. This is also illustrated by the words of Jesus on the Cross, at the final moment of crossing over into the Father's Bosom:

"And about the ninth hour Jesus cried with a loud voice, saying: Eli, Eli, lama sabachthani? that is (to say) My God, My God, why hast Thou forsaken me?"

(MAT. 27:46)

The Great Spiritual Teachers from the Highest Inner Regions also have an answer to this mystery of consciousness. *Sant Sat Gurus* or Saints of the Highest order and True Spiritual Teachers always instruct their disciples to stand still in the Inner Essence by means of conscious devotion, and thus blend with the One Essence. The student is cautioned not to go outside of this Inner Core of Being during the process of concentration. This is *conscious devotion*.

It is the mind which rules in the world of phenomena time and space. When we become anxious, or attached to objects of sound or light, we are leaving the Inner Center of the Essence where the Reality exists and are allowing the mind to go out after created things. The mind becomes self-conscious rather than absorbed in the Inner Essence of Oneness. The All seems as nothing to the outer consciousness in this world. Is it any wonder then, when the Mystic writers state that the universe was created out of nothing? For the Essence is not a thing. It is a nothing or a

Reality which is a Oneness of substance and being, and no foreign particles can exist in that which endures for ever. When the Mystic's consciousness is still on earth, he feels and senses this vast inward whirl of Purity to which his soul is attracted, as a Nothingness, an inverted vortex. He does not fit on earth nor in the heavens, for he is a conscious part of that Reality even while he walks the earth. This nostalgia of the Mystic is his real home sickness and causes him to shed midnight tears of longing for the Beloved God.

To such souls, physical things are of no consequence, for these are not in their consciousness. Both Laotzu and Jesus had all their physical needs, supplied, Laotzu was welcomed and longed for in many of His disciples' homes. His disciples kept a purse for their common needs. Laotzu was a librarian for many years and lived a frugal life and had more than he needed physically. The cry of the Mystic is ever for the Beloved, but never for the things of the mortal mind and consciousness. The true mystic seeker is a chrysalis in the process of becoming a beautiful butterfly in soul stature. He is in the process of becoming a Diamond Soul by the pressure of the earthy mind elements upon it, and these are its symptoms of growth, of transcendence and ascension toward its Source.

The process and pressure, plus the heat which is necessary in order to form diamonds, emeralds and other jewels in the depths of mother earth is similar to the process which souls go through in time and space of creation, to consciously bring forth the inner brilliance of the soul's radiance as the Diamond Soul. This very process is the theme of all dramas.

Jewels and souls are all gems of creation. The process which is necessary to create a living consciousness in form is similar to the cutting of facets on the diamonds and to polishing them so they can radiate the inner light. The mounting of the diamond or jewel is symbolic of the creation of a body, a form, a garden of Paradise, a place to set the jewel into the lotus flower or the lily, of life. Truly,

"even Solomon in all his glory was not arrayed like one of these." (MAT. 6:29; LUKE 12:27)

The Buddhist mystic has this in mind when he repeats his *mantram*:

"Om Mani Padmi Hum."

(Oh, the Jewel in the Lotus.)

Love is the soft and yielding principle in Nature. It is the neuter essence of all things. It is the Word Essence. It supports all things, endures all things and is above all law because it is the Oneness which is unconditioned. It is in all creation, because all proceed from this Essence as a spark of the One Reality. Therefore, it is the brilliance in the diamond, the light in the sun and moon, the roar of the lion and the life in all there is, was or will be. All creation and manifestation is but Love's revealing itself in form, as geometric proportions of Love.

In mathematics it is the zero which mysteriously multiplies by ten. It either adds or takes away tenfold, depending on whether it is placed in front of or after the figure. So, it also illustrates the parable of Jesus "To them that have, shall be given, and those who have not, from them shall be taken away what they have." A purely mathematical formula, by the placing of the jewel of attention and the consciousness of the soul on either the physical or the spiritual journey. Where is the heart's desire? There will the attention operate as the carpenter or builder of the temple of the soul or in the region of the mind in matter and physical things.

"If any man defile the temple of God, him shall God destroy; for the temple of God is holy, which temple ye are.

Let no man deceive himself. If any man among you seemeth to be wise in this world, let him become a fool, that he may be wise.

For the wisdom of this world is foolishness with God.
For it is written, He taketh the wise in their own craftiness.
And again, The Lord knoweth the thoughts of the wise,
   that they are vain.
Therefore let no man glory in men."

(I COR. 3:17-21)

Love is the gentle and preserving principle in Nature. Without love we become hard shells, void of the inner spark of life and its radiance and die for want of this very substance. It is the Eternal Essence which brings forth life, beauty, art and the true proportions of things created. This is the effort and the struggle of all true art and artists everywhere.

When one sees the magnificent structures of old, such as the art of ancient Greece, and the remains of some of them, as well as the smaller objects of art and sculpture, then one can truly see where their heart and attention was. That is why these nations were great, when the inner life radiated through their efforts, their works and in their daily lives. Life flowed freely. Petty ideas were swept aside and surmounted. Were it not for the motor energy of the centrifugal force which resulted in war and destruction, more of their early glory of thought and vision would still remain for us to admire.

But only love can survive as the immutable solvent of all true art and proportions. Love is the soft center, as the heart of all. Form and force are but empty shells which sometimes hold the life. Love is the cup of life, as the heart of things material and spiritual. The Cup of the Holy Grail in the drama of Wagner's *Parsifal* is a mystic symbol of that life within, in its upward struggle.

Life must flow, or it leaves the form or body and the shell is dead when the life is not in it. Love is the gateway of life. "Be ye lifted up ye everlasting gates" cries out the writer of the Psalms. Where there is love, there is life. Love is not a duty; it is life itself. When the personal emotions crowd out the true Love energy and essence of Life, then there are created blocks of interference which cause great suffering—physically, mentally and emotionally. Such a one punishes himself by mental and emotional fixation and selfish determination. The soul starves for lack of the water of Love, of Forgiveness, of the real vision and purpose of life. Many physical pains, rheumatic and arthritic fixations in joints are due to a stoppage of this Life Energy flow because of mental or emotional dams in the conscious or subconscious field of mind energy. That is why hatred, jealousy, pride and even entertaining grief are considered sins against the Holy Ghost, the Spirit of Life within us. All these blocks, self-created and maintained as fixations, "are not forgiven", said Jesus briefly.

Only the floodgates of a greater Love can be the answer to these personal grievances and fixations. Forgiveness is a natural process in a life full of Love. It is natural to the Saints, to the Sages, the Mystics and little children. No wonder Jesus said that we must become as little children in order to enter into the kingdom of heaven. Heaven is where love flows freely and impersonally. It is the Oneness of life and it is the One Real Essence.

Creation has an outward purpose for the body and an inward purpose for the soul. Whichever road the consciousness travels on, is the way. The centrifugal path outward, toward the mind and senses, is the path of involution. The centripetal path inward, beyond mind and sense attraction, into the pure realm of Soul and Spirit itself is the way Homeward. We all come to this crossing of the way sometime in the soul's journey. It is like the question of Peter, when he left Rome and saw the vision of Jesus walking toward Rome: "Quo vadis Domine? Whither goest Thou, oh Lord?"

Life's paths are many and confusing. But in Nature and in life there is only an in-breathing and an out-breathing. Life is that simple; like the hand which only opens and shuts, and yet is capable of all skill. The mind creates multiplicity everywhere to cover the simplicity in Nature. All natural things are simple and pure, when not mis-used or abused. All Nature's patterns are fixed according to definite lines of a simple direction and directness.

"For naught so vile that on the earth doth live
But to the earth some special good doth give;
Nor aught so good but, straine'd from that fair use,
Revolts from true birth, stumbling on abuse:
Virtue itself turns vice, being misapplied;
And vice sometime by action dignified."
(words spoke by Friar Lawrence in Shakespeare's
ROMEO AND JULIET)

Man, as a soul, is a child of the Supreme Father, and is of His Essence. He imitates his Father in creativeness and learns the hard way by many mistakes in mind and matter, and through suffering in his outward efforts. When he has satisfied all his external cravings, like the Prodigal Son, then he is ready to go Home to the Father's House of Reality. Such is the life of the mystic soul as a wanderer on earth; who finds no resting place, no security, no satisfaction in things of pleasure and possession. His soul cries out in homesickness. He is aware of the snare of the mind and senses, and these can no longer hold him bound. He is ever asking, seeking and knocking on the door of Life and of Knowledge and of Truth, to show him the way out.

It is by such a sincere seeker that a Master is found, to show him the Way. Then his inward journey begins in Reality, and by definite, regular effort at concentration, to raise the consciousness and currents of awareness into the higher Realms of Soul and Spirit. Finally, the mystic devotee will be able to gather all his sensory energy currents at the center of consciousness between the eyes. This center is called the Tisra Til by Saints, and was referred to by Jesus as the *narrow-gate*.

"Because strait is the gate, and narrow is the way, which leadeth unto life, and few there be that find it."
(MAT. 7:14)

Here, at the entrance to the conscious Spiritual Life, renunciation must take place. All desires and cravings are to be sublimated because no such coarseness can enter this gate. The mind itself must become small and humble before it can find this door. This is also illustrated by the narrow passage up to the Queen's Chamber in the Great Pyramid of Gizeh. The body itself must bend low before it can ascent the narrow passage leading to this chamber. From there to the King's Chamber it is a steep climb, but spacious. In the King's Chamber we find the most perfect acoustics, a symbol of the Spiritual Sound Current which lies latent in this space and faculty in our brain.

The Great Pyramid was made a symbol of the body, the most perfect structure known to man. Truth is the same everywhere, whether it is symbolized by a temple or a pyramid or is given in the desert by a great Teacher. The messages symbolized by all the temples and structures were hidden in the secret process and concealed passage or way to go within and meet the Deity within the temple of the human body and to consciously commune with Him in silence.

Thus, man can leave this physical body **consciously** in a state of inner awareness called Transport. So, he can, during his lifetime, enter those regions spoken of in the Holy Scriptures, and return at will, under the guidance and protection of his Master or Teacher or Guru. This is the state referred to by St. Paul when he said:

"I die daily" (I COR. 15:31)

Then the consciousness of the devotee will have the satisfaction of Inner Knowledge and Union, and he will be lonesome no more. St. Paul wrote of such mystic transport in the following words:

"I knew a man in Christ above fourteen years ago, (whether in the body, I cannot tell; or whether out of the body, I cannot tell: God knoweth;) such an one caught up to the third heaven. And I knew such a man (whether in the body, or out of the body, I cannot tell: God knoweth;) How that he was caught up into paradise, and heard unspeakable words, which it is not lawful for a man to utter. Of such an one will I glory; yet of myself I will not glory, but in mine infirmities. For though I would desire to glory, I shall not be a fool; for I will say the Truth; but now I forbear, lest any man should think of me above that which he seeth me to be, or that he heareth of me."

(II COR. 12:2-7)

All true mystic effort culminates in this Inner Path of Reality and Transport. This is known to the few who are the real seekers. It is too straight and narrow a road for the multitudes. Only he who seeks shall find, and to him who knocks shall the door of spiritual life open and lead to Eternity while yet in this body. It is literally living in the world but not of it. The Truth is one; so is the Way and the Life in all true Mysticism.

CHAPTER IV
MYSTERIES IN CREATION

*(The object of this chapter is to start with
the One Primal Essence of all Energy and carry it
through to its practical daily application.)*

All Creation is a mystery because its real origin is in
the higher realms of energy fields, which are beyond the
sense comprehension and the intellect of man. The Saints
says that man neglects to use even the full faculties of
his intellect. He is under the impression that he is acting according to the promptings of his mind, but in reality, he is actually being ruled by his own emotions; and
only in rare instances does he act according to and make
use of his reasoning power. But as soon as the mind is
purified to the extent that it allows the soul to rule and
govern the body and its actions, then it joyfully accompanies the soul until it reached its own Home, from whence
the soul travels on to its Source. The mind is no more at
home in this world than is the soul, but it has become so
enslaved by the senses that it is our own worst enemy
until it turns about face and accompanies the soul to the
higher regions.

As the white light contains all the chromatic gradations of colors, which are not apparent to the eye until separated by a prism, even so does the One Primal Essence
of Nothingness contains all varieties of elements and substances, all ideals, ideas and creeds which proceed from it
as energy waves and circuits, and precipitate into matter
as we see it and know it.

Primordial Sound is the Voice of Command of the Supreme Creator in the first Essence of Emanation out of the
Unknown Cause. There is a beautiful quotation from the
sixteenth stanza of the JAPJI—the morning prayer—from
the Granth Sahib, the Sacred Scripture of the Sikhs:
"How speak of Him who with one Word
Did the whole universe create,

And made a thousand rivers flow therein?
What might have I to praise Thy might?
I have not power to give it praise."

(GURU NANAK)

The Thousand rivers referred to above are the thousand energy currents which flow out of the heart center of the Essence of material creation. This center is referred to as Sahasra Dal Kamal or The Thousand Petalled Lotus. It is the region of the inner sky in the plane of Akash, the ether of the universe, and is the powerhouse of the material creation. The thousand petalled Lotus of Jehovah God is referred to here as the multiple of the mysterious *Yod-He-Vau-He*.

In the human body this center is located in the center of the forehead, about three-eighths of an inch above the Tisra Til region between the eyes. It is the heart or pivot of consciousness and life incarnated. The physical heart is controlled from this life center in the brain, which is the center of light and fiery energy in the optic thalamus in the cerebrum. When the energy current of life and warmth and light leaves this center, the eyes grow dim, the heart ceases beating, respiration stops, and the life is drawn up into the next higher center, from whence it came. When death takes place, the silver thread is broken and the pitcher goeth to the well no more:

"Or ever the silver cord be loosed, or the golden bowl be broken, or the pitcher be broken, or the pitcher be broken at the fountain, or the wheel broken at the cistern. Then shall the dust return to the earth as it was; and the spirit shall return unto God who gave it."

(ECC. 12:6, 7)

The Golden bowl, the pitcher, and the wheel broken at the cistern or well, symbolize the circulation of the blood stream in the heart, which dips up the Life or Pranic energy from the respiratory tract and pumps it in rhythmic quantities, through the heart, like a wheel with buckets on it, still in use in the old time wells in the Orient.

The silver thread symbolizes the energy link which binds the conscious being to this life center in the finer etheric world, just as the umbilical cord connects the fetus from that sphere into the physical world. As physical birth is an involution (we originally came from the heights, no matter how low we may have descended in the meantime), so the conscious death while living in the body—known as Spiritual Transport—is a Spiritual New-birth. It is an evolution or ascension back into the realm of Perfect Bliss eventually; but first through the immediate energy realms until it reaches the Source. In spiritual Transport, the consciousness leaves the low stages and dwells consciously in higher Inner Realms of Being and Spiritual Vibrations of great Happiness, until the Region of Perfect Bliss is reached.

According to Gen. 1:3, "God said". This action is the first attribute of the Infinite One who is beyond all qualities, *gunas* and attributes. He is Akal Purush, the Timeless One, according to the Sacred Scriptures of the modern Saints; and is similarly referred to in the Bible. When "He" spoke, time began to run its course as energy currents of Sound and Light, in the process of Creation. Thus, He brought the Inner Consciousness to the outer layer of energy, enlivening the shapes and forms of Creation on all Regions, until the physical realm was born out of the higher ones by means of energy crystallization.

The Trinity of Consciousness or Bliss, plus Sound as Life Essence and Light as Love Essence, are the nearest approach to describing the Indescribable. The modern Saints, like Kabir Sahib, Guru Nanak, Swami Ji of Agra, the late Gurus Baba Jaimal Singh Ji, Baba Sawan Singh Ji Maharaj and Sardar Bahadur Maharaj Ji of Beas, who have traversed these exalted Regions in their inner reach of Transport, have described these High Planes in their Sacred Discourses which formed a message for the souls of true seekers and devotees.

In such Sacred Writings are described, as nearly as our language can convey, four gradations of Creation on Spiritual Planes in the Eternal Realm. The Infinite One emerged from the consciousness of Inner Bliss to radiate that Energy, Love and Bliss to all lower realms of vibratory essences, and to the myriads of beings who were in a state of blissful inactivity, of semi-consciousness. Each one was given an opportunity to step up its vibratory frequency by one step in the scale of his present consciousness, by this impetus from the center outward.

In the beginning, the One Essence and center of consciousness became myriads of centers of Being. Each is a spark from the Eternal Fire of Life, as a soul or citizen in the realm of Spirit, which can wander either up or down in this infinite realm of experience, as a Paradise or a Kindergarten of Life.

Each soul is like a drop of water from this Infinite Ocean of Eternal Energy, Whose Sound and mighty roar of Power pervade and sustain all Creation. This is also referred to as the Word of Power or the Logos is the ancient Greek writings, as well as by St. John in the New Testament of the Bible. It is also called the Holy Spirit or Holy Ghost in the New Testament:

"And suddenly there came a sound from heaven as of the rushing mighty wind and it filled all the house where they were sitting." (ACTS 2:2)

We also find references to this Holy Sound in the Old Testament:

"And it shall be upon Aaron to minister: and his sound shall be heard when he **goeth in** unto the Holy Place before the Lord (Jehovah), and when he cometh out, that he died not." (EXO. 28:35)

"and the sound of a shaken leaf shall chase them (the enemy); and they shall flee, as fleeing from a sword; and they shall fall when none pursueth." (LEV. 26:36)

"Blessed is the people that know the joyful sound:" (PSM. 89:15)

Many times in the Bible this Holy Sound is also referred to as a Voice, "And a Voice was heard saying". According to I Kings 19:12, 13, a still small Voice was heard by Elijah, etc. Translators of the Bible used the term 'Tao' as a satisfactory interpretation of the Holy Word, the Logos, the Holy Shabd, The Voice, The Sound, etc.

Who can describe Essences and Powers to the finite intellect which craves particulars and limitations only to judge and to discuss them, because it is accustomed to deal with these toys of Maya (illusion) in this material world. Only a brief survey of the over-all picture of various Sacred Scriptures is attempted in this book, in order to show how each one substantiates and clarifies the other, and to give us a better understanding of the mysteries otherwise sealed.

However, no matter how much is revealed in any Sacred Text, the mere reading and attempting to practice what is written therein, without the guidance and protection of a true, living Mystic or Master, leads only to confusion. But, once one has been shown the Path by a living Master, and sincerely follows it to the best of his ability, then one can understand and follow what is written in all the Sacred Scriptures of ancient and modern times. The WORD is the key.

"By hearing the word
Is acquired the Wisdom of all Scriptures."
by Guru Nanak, from 'Japji', the Morning
Prayer in the Granth Sahib.

In the world of economics, it was found that competition by various firms or individuals acted as a tremendous stimuli toward creativeness in each line, and as a great push to the general progress and welfare of the people of nations who used it. The mind has an immense scope in which to express itself and find the strong points, as well as the weak points, and the better values and uses of any item or article manufactured.

Could not this principle of research, free thinking, comparing and searching for the Jewels of the Spiritual Life (which have been revealed on this planet and written down in Sacred Texts in many lands) apply to all humanity as a new impetus to a better understanding of the Spiritual Life? The joy and happiness is in the hunt, in the unexpected. The Unknown is intriguing and leads on to concentration, by forgetting the self in the chase and in the search, which can become creative instead of destructive. The ego or self only leads to destruction of all its environment, because it wants to heap everything on its own pile as either live or dead accumulations.

Early settler in America, or in any new country, found it quite essential to be physically helpful to each other in order to survive. However, this scope of helpfulness did not extend to the mental or spiritual realms, only because they were not conscious of any pressing need of survival in that sphere. Each group sought the supremacy of their own religious interpretation, which was a remnant of the old countries from which they had fled for opportunities of better living, because of persecution or limitation of mind and body.

The question now arises whether our spiritual vision is keen enough to embrace real spiritual values as a Life, by finding its direct simplicity and application through comparison and search of all revealed values in that line. Have we done any spiritual searching, thinking and selecting of real values to live by, and then for a true, living Master or Mystic to protect us and show us how? On the contrary, we seem to have lost the zeal and interest even in that which we have followed for so long, without discovering the Jewel in that Lotus of Sacred Text or Belief. Are we satisfied with only languidly imitating our predecessors, or are we looking for a life more abundant and richer, as promised in our own Sacred Scriptures?

All thing—whether spiritual, mental, emotional or physical—take thought, time and constant effort of application before we can become efficient in a branch of any one of them. Physically, we know that success depends on clear thinking and effort in any line. When we chosen a vocation in life, we spend many years in studying under teachers in schools, colleges, universities, and then take post-graduate courses along with the actual and practical work and experience gained thereby. But spiritually, we assume to become proficient by the mere reading of a book or listening to sermons. The exercise of spiritual faculties, like muscles of action in that field, has been utterly neglected and forgotten.

A belief held but not used, is like the "light under a bushel" (Mat. 5:15), (Mark 4:21) and (Luke 11:33), for then it does not light the way for the possessor of it. The value lies not only in keeping the lamp in repair and full of fuel, but in **lighting** the lamp of understanding and discrimination, like the five wise virgins in the Bible. We ourselves must **live** the life and find the way to union with that Essence within us and beyond us, which is the Supreme Being, and results in Conscious exultation of Inner Bliss, Love and Truth. "Only those who live the life shall know the Truth" is an old Hermetic saying. Jesus said:

"Not everyone that saith unto me, Lord, Lord, shall enter into the kingdom of heaven; but he that **doeth** the will of my Father which is in heaven."

(MAT. 7:21)

"Therefore, whosoever **heareth** these sayings of mine, and **doeth** them, I will liken him unto a wise man, which built his house upon a rock:
And the rain descended, and the floods came, and the winds blew, and beat upon that house; and it fell not; for it was founded upon a rock."

(MAT. 7:24, 25)

"**that** observe and do."　　　　　　　　(MAT. 23:3)
"Blessed are they that **hear** the Word of God **and keep it.**"　　　　　　　　(LUKE 11:28)

In essence, Jesus inferred many times: "if you love me, you will keep my commandments and follow me."

The real values and riches lie at the core of all Sacred Scripture, and not in the mere circumference of ceremony or belief. True spirituality is a Life within this outer, material life, expressed to some extent by a good artist in any profession. It is a constant striving and effort to become more proficient in this art. The reward of such effort is greater capacity to understand, to love and to serve, due to the Inner Happiness and exaltation of the soul.

As the Supreme Deity serves all creation from the very core of things, so does the true Mystic accomplish much from within outward, in an effortless way, by a greater understanding of **how** to serve the needs of each of His disciples, and a greater Love **with which to serve** and endure all things. Saints do not use external force or compulsion of any kind; neither do They seek to reform anyone.

When a fruit is ripe, it drops from the tree all by itself. No external effort is needed. So, it is with souls when they have ripened on this Tree of Life, planted in the Kindergarten of emotions, which is the Paradise of young souls in their descent from the astral region to this physical one of resistance and pain. And let us not forget that the reason we have descended to the physical plane of opposites is to fulfill our own desires and reap the fruits of our own previous actions. Therefore, it behoves us to entertain only such desires as will ultimately lift us out of this vale of tears for all time. That can be done only under the guidance of a true, living Mystic or Master Who will show us how to fulfill our present destiny without further entangling ourselves in the net of illusion, which we are bound to do if we try to extricate ourselves without proper guidance.

Personal experience is the greatest teacher in the physical life. So, also spiritually we need the guidance of a true Master who has Himself travelled this Path, in order to save us from the many pitfalls, detours, and even from travelling faster in the opposite direction by thinking we are facing up whereas we are heading downward without being conscious of it. The Master consciously links us to the Voice of God, the Holy Shabd or Sound which directs us to the Goal of Eternal Bliss. Only a real Master can do this for us, as He alone is familiar with all the mirages and dangers on the way, because He has gone all the Way Himself, under the guidance of His Master. Even physically, we would not think of attempting to traverse an unknown jungle without the aid of a competent guide. Only a proficient artist can teach a great art, and the same applies to any profession, trade or science. Skilled teachers are a definite necessity in all educational institutions. How much more so is a competent Teacher necessary for Spiritual Progress!

In this physical life, mankind works hard and strains every nerve in order to earn a living and become successful. And when we stop to think about it, what is it all for? Only for the sustenance of the human body, which really needs so very little in order to function at its best. All this time in life is spent for mere physical comfort and satisfaction of the vehicle with which the mind and soul are to work. But even if we spend the whole of life in such endeavors, we can never find peace of mind, without which nothing can be enjoyed for any length of time. That peace of mind comes only when we allow the soul to lead the way, instead of permitting our senses to lead us by the nose. The soul, imprisoned as it is by the mind and senses, cannot lead the way until it is **consciously** put in touch with the Voice of God, the Holy Ghost or Shabd, by a living Mystic or Master Who is Himself merged in it. Then the soul, after having been cleansed, is attracted upward by that Holy Grace, like an iron filing to a magnet.

So, what about the soul life, our real spiritual redevelopment, which is our real object in coming here? When will there be a propitious day to do the Great Work for the Liberation of our own soul from this bondage in which we ourselves have carelessly placed it, and enter the Vineyard of our Lord and Creator in Reality?

These problems face each soul and must be solved by each one. None on the outside can aid the soul until it lights its own light of interest in its liberation from bondage, for the search of the soul jewels in this body and in this life. Then will he seek the guidance of a true Mystic or Master, and will himself become a master builder who works intelligently and erects the temple of God "not build by hands" in his own being, as a mystic architect. Until such a time he cannot claim the reward or wages of a master builder who journeys in many lands. The Bible states clearly, that only faith **lived**, and work done by faith is accounted as righteousness. In the process of building this temple within, man fulfills God's commandment and grows to the maturity of imitating the Great Architect of the Universe. The temple first seen by Moses on Mount Sinai is symbolic of the human body, the temple made by God Himself.

CHAPTER V
STAGES IN CREATION AND THEIR APPLICATION IN THE MICROCOSM OF MAN

The creation which we see with our material eyes and only part of which we can comprehend, is but a very, very small part of the total Creation. Even though science has gone a long way in calculating and describing the extent of the whole universe that is known to man, and our view of the heavens through a telescope seems vast and almost limitless, it is nevertheless but a speck of the Real Grand Total of the entire expanse of finer and still finer Substance and Vastness beyond the comprehension of the mind.

Our material creation is called Pind in the writings of the Saints. They do not include it in their description of Regions, because it has not an audible Life Stream or Sound Current in its keynote, which can be listened to and which leads the mind, and soul upward. It is the region of gross matter and corresponds to the entire portion of the human body which situates below the eyes. In the material creation, it extends up to the Astral Region.

Matter is energy stepped down to a fixed point in its vibratory activity, where it appears as a solid, liquid, gaseous or fiery substance. The shell of things is matter, which becomes either a shrine or a grave for the expanding Life Spirit or Energy Essence within the form. Matter is substance and form, and is perceptible by the senses. It is the opposite of mind and spirit.

Spirit is soul, the Essence of Life, and is the Center and Core or every being. In Creation, shells and forms are necessary for the soul to function in and through, to limit its expansion, and protect the soft and tender organs, like the brain is protected by the hard shell of the skull. The same is true of the egg shell and its substance, the earth's crust and its liquid and hot interior, etc.

Real Saints deal only with the Sound Essence or Current which is the One Word of God, which proceeds from the supreme Father in the very Highest Region down as far as the top of Pind, and returns to Him. It permeates all the higher Regions in various grades of intensity. When It reaches the Causal Plane, called Trikurti, It is still of a high Spiritual nature, but has taken on part matter. The next station below, known as the Astral Plane and called Sahasra Dal Kamal, consists of some Spirituality, but the greater part is matter. Then below that, in this material world, it is all matter. Hence in order to make contact with the Divine Sound, it is necessary for the attention to be concentrated at the top of Pind, from whence the soul may experience Transport to the higher regions. This is the Royal Road of all Saints. It is the Alpha and Omega of all true Mystics.

The Astral or Etheric Region is the realm called Eden in the Bible. Saints call it Anda, and Sahasra Dal Kamal is the main station, so to speak, in that realm. This is the Region immediately above the physical region. It is the one in which most of the creation took place, as recorded in Genesis, because the Lord God Jehovah is the Ruler and Creator in Anda. And the Bible speaks mostly of Jehovah as the Creator.

Other names are also mentioned in the Zohar, but these are principalities **under** Jehovah, and assist in the creation. Such are the Elohim, the Archangels and other powers and agencies which do the will of the Lord of Hosts. Creation was no simple affair. It required active and willing cooperation, as all real business does.

The Spirit of Jehovah is mentioned in many places in the Old Testament, in addition to Genesis. No explanation has been given as to why distinction is made between 'Lord God Jehovah' and the 'Spirit of Jehovah'. The Spirit of Jehovah, mentioned in the Old Testament, is really the Audible Life Stream or the Holy Shabd Current in the realm of Eden or Akash. It flows out of Eden and supports all visible creation.

In the realm of Eden or Akash there are ten different Sounds and Currents. The Kabbalists have called them the ten Sephiroth or virtues and powers.

The Astral Region is the last step of the Eternal Sound Essence downward into creation, where it can be heard before the material grossness covers it up in the physical creation. The soul and the mind must ascend into this region, after passing through the starry sky, the inner sun and the moon realm, before it can come to this Central Current in the Sahasra Dal Kamal Center. There the first True Sound is heard in its beauty and Reality.

As the involution or descent **into** matter took place at the time of creation, so must also be the evolution and ascend of our daily consciousness **out** of matter. If the consciousness of the man Adam fell into a deep sleep in this descent, then that consciousness must have a great awakening or rebirth in order to again ascend into the higher regions on its upward journey. Truly, the soul must be reborn in the Energy of this Living Water of space, the Eternal Shabd or Sound Current, before it can ascend into the kingdom of heaven. Baptism by immersion or application of water symbolizes this very ideal.

"But as many as received Him, to them gave He power to become the sons of God, **even** to them that believe on His Name: which were born, not of blood, nor of the will of the flesh, nor of the will of man, but of God. And the WORD was made flesh," (JOHN 1:12-14)

"Jesus answered and said unto him, Verily, verily, I say unto thee, Except one be born again, he cannot see the kingdom of God. Nicodemus saith unto him, How can a man be born when he is old? Can he enter the second time into his mother's womb, and be born? Jesus answered, Verily, verily, I say unto thee, Except a man be born of water and of the Spirit, he cannot enter into the kingdom of God. That which is born of the flesh is flesh; and that which is born of the Spirit is spirit. Marvel not that I said unto thee, Ye must be born again.

The wind bloweth where it listeth and thou hearest the sound thereof, but canst not tell whence it cometh, and whither it goeth: so is every one that is born of Spirit."
(JOHN 3:3-9)

"As newborn babes, desire the sincere milk of the Word, that ye may grow thereby: If so be ye have tasted that the Lord is gracious." (I PETER 2:2-3)

The 'sincere milk' mentioned by Peter is the Nectar of this Holy Shabd Current which flows freely in that 'Promised Land of Milk and Honey', within ourselves. This is the taste of the graciousness of the Lord, referred to in the last line of the above quotation.

As all life travels in circuits and cycles, so does the soul in its experience of involution into matter and evolution out of matter as a new birth into a higher region and consciousness. Here, the understanding is supported by reason and facts, as the soul travels onward and upward in the Mystic Way to Everlasting Life.

The soul falls into a deep sleep, dies in the higher realm, and comes to the earth. Now, if it wished to return to the higher, it has to renounce the earth and earthly things which keep it in bondage. The True Master teaches us how to do this by withdrawing the conscious energy currents of sensation and awareness from things outside of the body and from the body itself, into the single eye center, **located between the two eyes**. Once collected there and purified, the mind and the soul can rise into higher regions, stage by stage; and can come and go at will. This is the literal and logical path of re-birth or being born again and becoming a walker or traveler in and beyond the regions of the starry sky.

Cause and effect complete a circuit which is easy to understand but slow to prove, because of the resistance of the lower mind-habits and sensory current directions. The soul must go in backwards into Noah's tent, to find the new wine, after the flood of involution. (This is explained under the sub title 'Noah's Ark' in the chapter entitle, 'Breezing Through the Hexateuch')

In the Kabbala, Eden, the Astral is referred to as the region of Briah. The energy currents which flow out of it and form the four elements or the four rivers of life out of Paradise, out of the One Current, are called the world of Yetzirah or the formative stage. And the result of this action is referred to as the world of Assiah or the physical world.

The region above Briah, the Astral world, is referred to as Yesod or the Atziluth. This is the archetypal world of the ancient Kabbalists. It is where mind patterns were formed and designs of things to be were made, like architects make all blueprints. They are all necessary in the creative process and its stages, and many powers and hosts carried out orders of the blueprint patterns.

These are the steps and stages of creation in different regions. And it certainly would be most inadequate to measure these periods of time according to our earthly nights and days, when the action took place in a different world each time. II Peter 3:8 states clearly that one day with the Lord is as a thousand years and a thousand years as one day. That gives an idea of the Bliss of that region, which transcends our material concept of time on earth.

The Vedas call this mind region of Atziluth, the Causal World or Plane. The Saints call it Trikuti or the World of Three Prominences, the three mountains being called Meru, Sumeru and Kailash. These fields express themselves in action as the three gunas or **modes of motion** in mind, emotions, sensations and actions in all matter. Sat is the neuter pole of the gunas. It is the mind principle, which is sustained by a ray from the Creator. Raj is the positive pole, the motor power and the restless drive of the emotions, the desires for action and fulfillment. And Tamas is the precipitate of these two. It is inertia, darkness, resistance and reaction to all action.

The mountain of Meru, in the cosmos, is the center of the earth, according to Buddhist Mythology, and is called Maru. The same is referred to as Mount Olympus in Greek Mythology. In the Microcosm, it becomes the crown or the head. In the physical body, it designated the superior pole as the crown of creation, in the top area of the brain, where all regions are represented, and through which the higher regions my function in the physical consciousness of man. It is also represented as Mount Sinai or Mount Horeb in the Bible. All pyramids and man-made structures like the Tower of Babel, were results of efforts to illustrate this idea. Going up into this mountain, means ascending in consciousness to that Inner Height of Vibration **in the Sound Current**, where the soul becomes lifted up and literally sees and talks with God. Such experiences were recorded by Moses on Mount Sinai and by Elijah on Mount Horeb.

These references do not pertain to mountains as we know them in this world. They are located in the Inner Regions and are known to the Mystics. Inspiration and direction for soul life are given here to Mystics and to Messengers of the Lord for His people. This has happened throughout the ages, continues to happen today and will be so in the future. Ascending the mountain means going up in concentration.

Rajoguna the positive guna of action flows through the brain for direction and light on the Way within, and to the feet and hands without in daily work. The Sound Current and the higher inner consciousness can transcend this region and the three gunas. The Creator views His creation as a witness and sees that all things are good:

"and God saw that it was good"   (GEN. 1:10, 21, 25)
"And God saw everything that he had made, and, behold, it was very good."   (GEN. 1:31)

Mount Sumeru expresses the opposite pole in the body as the Brahm Chakra in the etheric place, through which the negative psychic prana flows for generation and procreation of the species. This energy must be controlled and sublimated or lifted up into the positive region, by ascension of consciousness, often called Redemption or Regeneration.

Mount Kailash becomes the middle, neuter pole or axis as the Sukshma Sharira—of sustaining the body as the neuter, heart region for emotional expression. Physically, it is the power of digestion to sustain and nourish the body.

These three regions and functions have been symbolized by the Three Wise Men of the East in the Bible. They come from the East, the rising Sun, down to earth, the West, to find the Savior of mankind and Salvation of the soul which inhabits these three major regions, the head, the heart and the generative system.

According to the Kabbalistic theory of Creation, the descent from Spirit into creation was described as:

AIN, the vacuum of Pure Spirit

AINSOPH, the Limitless and Bondless

AINSOPH AUR, the Limitless Light

The Macroprosophus is the first emanation of the Ainsoph. This is the Universal Man, the Adam Kadmon of the Kabbala, or the Prototypal Man, the One Adam or the whole material creation. The Grand Man of the Zohar is the same universal presentation as the Great Universal Tree of Life, the Yggdrasil Tree planted in the great cleft in space called the Ginnungagap in Norse Mythology. It is the Sephirothic Tree of Life in the Kabbala. The Great Pyramid is also such a macrocosmic symbol.

The region of Trikuti is the region of the Universal Mind. This is the true home of the individual mind, the height of which it can only reach by accompanying the soul up to this point. This region is also called a fort because of the firm stability. The Saints declare those who have reached this height to be true soldiers, for they have indeed fought and won a great battle. Here the color is a reddish hue, and the Sound of thunder is heard.

Trikuti is the Causal or Pattern Word, where Brahm the Creator or Universal Patterns performs his artifices as the designer of individual forms, shapes and things to be, with the souls entrusted to him by the Supreme Being. This is all done in mind substances, by mental energy currents. Viewing from the top, down to this stage, no physical substance is yet precipitates as gross matter.

The realm has a virile beauty, and mystics who reach this stage in their upward journey are called Yogishwars and Mahatmas or Great Souls. It is the ideal stage of attainment of the Master Masons who wish to be master builders like the Great Architect of the Universe. While in its downward trend, mind energy whirls its substance and precipitates it into a lower vibratory rate, forming the plane of the Astral Region, or the sky below Trikuti.

The region below Trikurti is the Psychic World of sensitive action and reaction, and is also called the Astral Light and the Etheric World. In the Astral World or the Realm of the Etheric is engraved the pattern of the mind world from above as well as the report of the sensory reactions from below in the physical world. In this manner does the consciousness keep aware of sensations from without inward, and from above downward. It is cross road of energy currents and has much to do with the health and disease of the body, mind and the emotions; because the energy currents are the active factors which precipitate the form according to their design, direction and speed of vibratory activity.

Out of the realm of the mind substance, called Chit, is precipitated the Akash or Ether in five pattern fields, as substance for the five senses and the five fingers and the five toes to work through. This is the negative field of the body, precipitated in the five ovals of the body, with the arms and legs as extension levers for motion and action. Its polarity, like the five regions, is from above downward in potential.

Also out of this Chit Akash is precipitated the Life Essence called Prana, which is the positive pole of energy as a step-down from the neuter pole of mind energy itself. It is the activating, life-giving and moving energy in the body. It also has five keys of vibratory action to match the five Tattwas or fields, and by flowing through five sensory and five motor actions which animate this house called the human body, the actual temple of God on earth.

The energy at work is unseen; but the fields and the senses are quite evident in their action. The sensory energy is of the finer type, of the astral light or psychic prana, because it is wireless and extends beyond the body in its range of action. The gross prana flows over the wires of the nervous system, and is the physical life prana in its airy quality.

Throughout all Creation, it is natural for the above or finer to rule the lower energies and functions. It is only man who is swayed by and succumbs to the lower tendencies; and not until he himself becomes aware of this fallacy and makes an effort to extricate himself, can he start on the return journey to his Divine Source of Eternal Bliss.

When the lower fields become dense, they often accumulate foreign matter which crystallizes as blocks and resists the normal influx of energy and motion. All energy blocks are expressed as pain, because the current is resisted or interrupted there. Then the temple needs housecleaning and intelligent guidance in order to re-establish its own energy polarity current flow. This is a brief description of energy involution in the building of the miniature universe, the human body, which houses the soul. As the soul is a particle of the Supreme Being Himself, the body is rightly called the house of God and we should regard it as such.

With the description given thus far, it will be easier to understand the brief account of Creation as given in the Bible. Creation took place on various different levels and planes. For instance, it is mentioned in the Bible that man was created prior to the creation of Paradise; yet later, it is mentioned that there was no man to till the ground. It is obvious that the mental creation of the pattern must come first, even as we draw blueprints and call them real.

Then comes the stage of gathering and precipitating the material with which to build according to the pattern design or blueprint. This is the Etheric or Astral stage and its enlivening with the vital currents of Prana. From there on down follows the physical stage and its specific physical currents, needed as physical prana or physiological energy to move the media of substance, to assemble parts and functions such as blood and lymph, serum, fibrin and albumen, over and through the fields of organs and tissues. This is a practical description which can be proven in therapeutics, as it was in Ayurvedic Medicine over six thousand years ago.

The writer would like to state here that Saints of the highest order or True Mystics are not interested in the material conditions at all; that is, they do not come to right the wrongs in this world, but to guide and take with them the souls who realize that this is not their true home and who wish to return to the Father's House. The True Mystics or Masters do not concern themselves with any functions below the point of consciousness located between the eyes. There are others in this world whose duty it is to attend to such affairs, while the Masters are interested only in the welfare of souls. Neither will the Masters make any assertion as to Ayurvedic or any other type of therapy. Mysticism deals with the soul and the spirit only, and its way **out** of matter instead of into it.

The Kabbala calls the region beyond the mind, 'the Great Abyss', and they give no further stations or regions above Atziluth, Yesod or Trikuti. Other Sacred Scriptures also stop here in their ascent and description of regions. Only the True Saints, Masters and Mystics go higher.

In the philosophic system of the Kabbalistic Tree of Life, the three gunas become the three mothers, or the three mother letters of the Hebrew alphabet; Aleph, Mem and Shin. These are the air, the water and the fire elements of the ancient systems, and the three energies in the blood stream. They are spoken of as the three Doshas in the Ayurvedic system.

The Kabbalistic system has seven double letters and twelve singles which are placed on the Tree of Life, the Adam Kadmon, the one universal man in whom and out of whom all creation was formed below that region. It is based upon the idea of reflection, where the 'Ancient One' looks into space and beholds his image, and puts life into that man made in the image and likeness of himself, the Universal Adam.

It is similar to the myth of the Universal Giant who was slain by the Titans, the universal energies, and out of his body all the other creations were made. This is also the Universal Man who was a problem to the great seer, Emanuel Swedenborg.

It probably would be more nearly correct to state that **in** the One Universal Being called Adam, all lesser creations were formed and brought up before him to name them each. This he did, as he knew them to be of his own substance, or he could not have given them their names. All systems have a way of duplicating a process which **is** and telling it in a little different way.

The Vedas, in their sacerdotal language of Sanskrit, have probably the most lengthy and accurate of all systems on the account of the Creation. Our own alphabet has only twenty-six letters, and that of the Hebrew has twenty-two letters, while the sacerdotal Sanskrit has fifty-two letters. These fifty-two letters are each carefully and specifically placed on the chakras of the Tree of Life in the human body, apportioning to each their number of petals, as rays of potential energy. In their symbolic beauty of description, they use the lotus plant as the Tree of Life; and each chakra or psychic whirling center of energy is given its number in petals of the flower. Naturally it can and does more readily and clearly explain the gap between the spiritual and the physical, because it has the wherewithal in the language with which to explain it. We cannot find, nor do we have the words and expressions for these explanations, in the English language.

The whole Vedic system is very comprehensive. It begins with the Sound Current or the Word of God as the first emanation. This forms the central core and axis of the

Universe and of the cerebrospinal nervous system of the human body, and distributes the energy impulses upon that central axis as the motive power of the finer energies in man, from within outward, as the Life flows. First it is the psychic wireless energy and then precipitates into the physical life energy and currents.

Looking from above downward, the mind has four petals or constituents through which it functions: 'Manas, Chis, Buddhi and Ahankar'. These are reddish in color, and are placed in the brain and faculties of the mind.

The center of consciousness, where mind and gross matter meet is between the eyes. Here is the narrow gate, spoken of in the Bible as "the narrow door which leadeth unto Life Eternal". It is also called the 'third eye' or 'Tisra Til'. Two petals of color value are placed here, as their Psychic Centre. One is gray, for the material energy, and the other is white, for the finer or psychic energy of Prana. This is very much like the gray and white matter in the human cerebrospinal nervous system, over which gross Prana or Life currents flow.

On the throat, at the center of speech which is the Akash or etheric representative oval of the body, are placed sixteen petals or letters. This represents four times four of the mind energy petals, for its full expression in action of speech and sensation. The throat has many psychic sensory reactions in addition to the physiological ones from the sympathetic nervous system.

In the airy center of the heart are placed twelve petals or letters, or three times four, which permits less complete expression at this center than at the one above it. The mind often says, "I cannot express myself completely" or "How can I say it?"

The navel is the fiery center of digestion. Here are places ten petals or letters, equivalent to two times and a half-time of energy distribution from the central beam. The "times and a half-time", etc. mentioned in the Bible, refers to quantum of time or energy at a given area or period.

In the generative or water center are placed six petals or letters. This amounts to "times and a half-time" measure of the energy volume of the axis current flow.

And the rectum, the Muladhara Chakra and outlet of the gross energy, the four petals of the mind are equally represented as four red petals, the essence of which is the red earth or red clay spoken of in the Zepher Yetzirah and other occult writings.

"As above, so below". The four petals above in the mind substance, are reflected below, in the Muladhara Chakra, as a red clay energy center. Mind as sound and speech, is multiplied in its full measure in the astral light of the voice in the throat, and is balanced below as an expression of thought and matter substance in various functions of Nature.

The Kabbalistic account of creation is an interpretation of the Zohar, which is very old. The instructions were legendary and were supposed to have been given by the angels in Paradise to Adam, before the Fall. Similar mystic information was handed down from mouth to ear especially in the Middle East and by many races and nations for thousands of years. This was only for the initiates or the elect, and many tests and hardships had to be undergone before such initiation was granted. Those who received such instructions were usually the priests and teachers of the people, and a few chosen ones who were considered ready to be taught the Secret of THE WORD.

It was the impact of such knowledge and faith which built the Great Pyramids, the huge temples, etc. like the Temple of Bel Marduk in Babylon, also called the Tower of Babel. Pyramid and Mound builders all had a fraction of this mystic information, which they concealed in stones or earth, as a hidden secret message to those who could read the cryptic writings and understand at least a part thereof.

The symbolism is very much like the fiery message of Jehovah's, written by His holy fingers of Life upon the tables of the heart of humanity, which were forgotten and broken by mankind. Symbolically, Moses broke the two tables in wrath when he saw the idolatry of Israel at the base of Mount Sinai.

When the people of Israel turned their attention to worldly things, they turned their back on Jehovah, so His Vital Spirit was not among them. And that made an external substitute necessary. Whenever the ONE WORD is not the **Supreme Value** in life, then the mind sets up its own patterns. That is idolatry. When the spirit of understanding is not within, then the Great Love of that Holy Spirit of Shabd is absent. Consequently, other forms and patterns are set up by the mind and the emotions of the majority. These, then, become a physical reality to the uninformed peoples of the earth.

Anything which does not turn our attention to God, could be termed as idolatry if worshiped or held in high esteem, or as being of the greatest value in life. This is idolatry because it leads the mind and heart astray from THE ONE WORD which is the secret and the Life of all creation. It is the very light of the soul, which lighted every man into this world (John 1:9), and by God's Grace will show him the way out of this world, back to the Supreme Father's abode of Love, Bliss and all Knowledge and Truth.

From the historic information available, it seems that in about the twelfth century the Kabbalistic doctrine was formulated into a marvelous philosophic system. The Tree of Life was used as its keynote and patterns to lead the soul back to God, through Kether, the Crown of Creation locked in the secret chambers of the human brain, as the highest inner temple of Life, and Mysticism. Ten fiery centers of virtues or powers, or called Sephiroths, were the pivots of Energy Whirls, or Chakras of Life in the finer etheric or Edenic Essence of Man's astral body. Thirty-two paths lead the way to and from the Source. This symbolism corresponded to the thirty-two vertebrae of the human spine and the thirty-two teeth in the skull. It was explained by the Major Arcana of the twenty-two Tarot Cards, placed in definite arrangements along the paths.

The brilliant Hebrew Scholar and Mystic, Moses Mimonidies, was supposed to have written and formulated this Kabbalistic system, as we have it today. No doubt other great scholars collaborated in this highly specialized philosophic system. Its survival and depth seems to verify this. For only that lives or survives in Nature which has at least a spark of Truth in it.

A similar system was taught as the secret of the East, in the Vedas and other Sacred Writings, thousands of years ago. The One Word of God is the Essence and Secret of it all, expressed through centers and channels of intelligence. As the One Life, the Soul, animates the body, so is the One knowledge thereof.

The very height of all the wonderful writings and teachings reaches up to the region of Trikuti, which is still within the realm of mind and matter; and while it may endure for millions or billions of years, it is subject to dissolution or 'pralaya'. The Saints tell us of pure Spiritual Regions above this, and even they are subject to change, but after much greater periods; namely, at the time of Grand Dissolution, called 'Maha Pralaya'. Therefore, the Saints tell us of still higher regions, known as Pure Spiritual **and which are Eternal**.

The whole creation actually began from the very highest, and each one of the higher regions supports the one below it, and so on down to the physical one with which we are familiar. Therefore, the chapter on Stages in Creation begins with that which is familiar to us, and leads on up to the highest as revealed to mankind by the Saints. They actually look at this creation from the top, down; whereas we are at the bottom, looking up.

The region above Trikuti is called Daswandwar or the Realm of Silvery Light. The sweet sound of the Kingri or the Zittar is heard here. It is a Spiritual Region, but not an eternal one. The mystic who reaches this realm in his upward journey is called a real *sadh* or *sadhu*. The light of the soul at that stage is equal to that of twelve suns, comparatively speaking. The souls inhabiting that region are referred to as *hansas* or swans, and the joy experienced there is said to be indescribable.

Above this realm there is described a Sunna Region, which is not counted as a realm because it is a Great Void or Abyss, like space itself. Guru Swami Ji reported going through such vast density of darkness in this region, that He could find no end and returned. It is called the Maha Sunna or the Great Void.

The next region above, is still below the Eternal realm, and is called Bhanwar Gupha or the region of whirling vortices which appear like caves, where the first essence of Maya or illusion is formed or precipitates as energy whirls. This realm is the gateway to the Eternal Region, just as Trikuti is the gateway to the pure spiritual regions. It is a high spiritual region, with essences at work for creating and sustaining the regions below it. Bright light and swinging rhythmic motions form the keynote of that stage. A heavenly sweet sound of the flute is heard by the mystic when he approaches that realm. There is also a wonderful fragrance in the atmosphere, and an inner uplift when the soul comes from the regions below, upward.

In Sat Lok, also called Sach Khand, dwells the Lord Sat Purush Who is the Creator of all regions and substance below the Eternal Essence. This is the first of the Eternal Regions, when coming from below. That is where the true Spiritual and Eternal Union of the soul with God can take place and from which the soul need never again be separated. It is the fifth region, when coming from below, not including the physical one.

Creation in the four Eternal Regions was a process of extension in consciousness and a greater intensity in Bliss for all beings in it, through an upraising in vibratory velocity, closer to the Unknown Center of the Eternal One.

It may be well to again call to the reader's attention that the Bible and other Sacred Scriptures indicate that there are many planes, levels or stages in heaven.

Jesus said, "In my Father's House there are many mansions" (John. 14:2) According to the teachings of the Saints, the regions in the *Eternal* Realm, from the topmost on down, are:

ANAMI, the Nameless, the Absolute, also called Radha Swami Lok

AGAM LOK, the Inaccessible

ALAKH LOK, the Invisible, or Unseen

SACH KHAND or SAT LOK, the first True Region, when ascending from below.

Sant Sat Guru Swami Ji of Agra mentioned the highest Eternal Region of Anami, as well as the intermediate Eternal regions of Alakh and Agam, and He taught His followers the method by which the Anami, Radha Swami Region could be reached. Prior to that, Kabir Sahib, Guru Nanak, Paltu Sahib and a few other great Saints mentioned Sat Lok and the three regions above it. Their method of teaching the true seekers how to reach Sach Khand was also by means of the Five Holy Names and the Five Holy Sounds — THE WORD — the same as it is taught by the True Masters of today.

The individual's Master will Himself see that the soul under His care reaches the Eternal Spiritual Region of Sach Khand.

CHAPTER VI
CREATION AND THE MYSTIC WAY

Creation, as we see it and know it through our mortal eyes, mind and senses, is but a speck on the horizon of the process of Creation on all planes. There are realms upon realms of finer essences in various gradations of vibratory intensity, which teem with animation and life. True, this is not all organic life and form such as we see on earth externally, but each region has a beauty of its own which is far beyond mortal comprehension.

In the thirty-sixth stanza of the Japji, the morning prayer in the Granth Sahib, Guru Nanak wrote:

"As in the realm of knowledge reason is triumphant
And yields a myriad joys,
So in the realm of bliss is beauty resplendent.
There are fashioned forms of great loveliness;
Of them it is best to remain silent
Than hazard guesses and then repent."

St. Paul intimated that eye hath not seen, ear hath not heard, nor can the mind conceive the glory of the Almighty. In order to comprehend and enjoy the Spiritual, it is necessary for us to develop the spiritual faculties of sight, hearing and inner consciousness. This is automatically done by following the instructions as given in the Bible and other Sacred Writings, under the guidance of a living Master or Mystic. St. Paul also said that spiritual things must be spiritually discerned. Most Sacred Writings mention the Sound Current, the Holy Word, in one form or another. One such example is the following poem by Shams-i-Tabriz, translated from the Persian by Rai Sahib Lala Munshi Ram, Retired Distt. & Sessions Judge, who is Secretary of Dera Baba Jaimal Singh:

1. "A sound without parallel is coming; It is not from inside, neither from outside, nor from left or right or alongside.
2. "Thou asketh from which direction then? The same direction as we are in search of;

To which side shall I turn my face? thou asketh.
The same side from where that Lord proceedeth.

3. "The same direction from which comes the life-giving nectar to put life into the parched fish.

4. "The same direction which made the hand of Moses
shine like a full moon.

5. "The same direction from which cometh ripeness
into fruit.
The same direction which imparts the quality of
precious stones to pebbles.

6. "It is not permitted to give details;
Otherwise every non-believer, wherever he were,
would be released from denial.

7. "In time of adversity even a non-believer turneth
his mind to that direction;
When he sees pain in this direction he turns his feet
to that direction.

8. "Be in pain (of longing for Him) so that the pain
may lead thee to that side,
Which is seen by him who is overcome with pain.

9. "That great Lord had shut the door tight; Then He
put on Adam's garb, (meaning that He is at the
door to open it).

10. "Hush; hear five sounds from heaven,
The heaven which is beyond the five senses and six
directions."

The following explanatory notes on this poem were
given by Professor Jagmohan Lal of Dera Baba Jaimal
Singh:

1&2. The Sound without parallel is the Shabd, the Divine Sound that really comes from Sach Khand and
is the quintessence of all life and development. It
is the Word that proceedeth from God and is One
with God.

3. Poets and mystic have compared souls not connected with the Word and deprived of the Divine Grace, to a fish out of water. "parched fish"

represents the '*manmukh*', the soul without the Divine Grace. In stanzas 3 to 5 the poet emphasizes the life-giving power of This Sound.

6. Refers to the mystic discipline which enjoins silence and strictly forbids talking about inner delights and experiences.

8. This is the pain of love, suffering of separation, which ultimately leads to union.

9. He sent us into the world and shut the door upon us, so to say, but then Himself descended in the human form or garb to open the door. This is the Grand Mystery. At the Tisra Til, or the eye center, behind the eyes, He stands in the form of Sat Guru to open the door to those who, following the instructions of the Master in the flesh, reach that center. In fact, Saints are incarnations of God—The Word made flesh.

10. This sound is heard when we rise above the five senses. It is referred to as the five Sounds because in passing through the Five Regions it is heard as such, though it is really One.

It is obvious that in the brief account of about four chapters in Genesis, little could be told to cover the immensity of Creation and its process. The days and nights mentioned therein are cosmic time, not the earthly twelve and twenty-four hour periods. They are '*Manwantaras*' or cycles of four million, three hundred and twenty thousand **years** each. The nights refer to the '*Pralayas*' or dissolutions, the cessation of creation in one cycle of the essence in one energy realm. The bible also mentions that a day of the Lord is as a thousand years. This figure of speech may be truly expressed as light-years, since it deals with the energy of Light and Sound, and universal creations of stars, planets and orbits of energy travel.

The sun and moon of this particular universe, and the vegetative process produced by their action, are only an outward manifestation of an inward extension of an eternal principle in action. For it was in the inner, psychic energy field that Joshua made the sun and the moon stand still, indicating that he had ascended up to that region within and had become one with it. The material forces **within** him were the enemies which tried to block the progress of that mystic hero to the Promised Land of the Spirit and its nectar of Milk and Honey. It was upon these enemies that he was revenged by ascending above them and conquering them.

This is an actual experience in the life of every mystic, as he reaches the state of inner transport and consciously leaves the physical body, *'the land of Egypt'* and its slavery and bondage of self-indulgence and enters the *'Promised Land'* mentioned in Holy Scriptures. It is said in the Quran that *'Mohammed split the moon in twain'*. Naturally, this was also an inner experience and not a material one. He ascended on the attention current, to that inner region, as all mystics do.

The promise that was made by Jehovah to the true seed of the essence of Abraham, who had his faith and devotion and lived after the manner of the saintly Patriarch, also did not pertain to the physical earth. It was a promise like the salvation of the soul prophesied to the followers of Jesus the Christ in His lifetime. Jesus made it very clear in His private talk with Nicodemus at night, that His mission was for the salvation of the soul and that flesh and blood could not inherit the kingdom of heaven. (JOHN 3)

Earthly possessions are for the body only and can be granted by a mortal monarch or ruler. No spirituality is necessary for such earthly acquisitions. Why should the temporal be exalted over the spiritual value in any Sacred Writings? So, it is quite obvious that all these references pertained to inner, spiritual kingdoms and values.

The soul cannot serve two masters. It is stated in the Bible:

"Ye cannot serve God and mammon."   (MAT. 6:24)

Heaven and earth are opposites, and their energies flow in opposite directions. The soul cannot rise to the spiritual realms as long as it is anchored, bound and covered over by the filth of ego and earthly attachments. The spirit must be cleansed of all this filth, down to the very last desire, before it can return to the Father's House.

"When the unclean spirit is gone out of a man, he walketh through dry places, seeking rest, and findeth none." (MAT. 12:43)

"Because it is given unto you to know the mysteries of the kingdom of heaven, but to them it is not given. For whosoever hath, to him shall be given, and he shall have more abundance: But whosoever hath not, from abundance: But whosoever hath not, from him shall be taken away, even that he hath."

(MAT. 13:11-12)

The above was another hard-to-understand saying of Jesus, as a parable, and a puzzle to many. But spiritual values make it very plain: Whosoever hath not inner faith and Life and who hath not wisely used God's gifts, from him shall be taken away even that which he hath. It is even so in nature. Only that survives which is fit or useful somewhere.

Heaven gives and earth receives. The temporal cannot inherit the Inner Essence of energy realms, because it hath nothing in it to make it akin to this finer, vibratory life. It would only be miserable and out of place if such a privilege were granted even for a moment; just as beasts of the jungle would not be helped by living in palaces or in human abodes.

In Nature everything has its place and time, as cycles of life, and days and nights on earth. The energy in the sap of all vegetation is drawn up by the sun's *prana* into the upper part and foliage for oxidation in the daytime and in the spring and summer seasons. It recedes to the root system at night for assimilation and distribution of that heavenly energy, as a real digestive process in vegetation. This is also true of the fall and winter seasons which are brought about by the travel of the energy currents locally and in the cosmos.

The soul is of an eternal essence. It is actually a particle of the Supreme Being, and its very nature is to ascend and return to its Source; while it is the nature of the grosser energies to descend. Therefore, which would be the logical path to point out in the Holy Scriptures and in all Sacred Writings? The physical and mental? Or appeal to the higher mind and point out the Heavenly Path? First comes the desire or motive and then the deed; for where our attention is, there our heart is also.

"for where your treasure is, there will your heart be also."

(MAT. 6:21)

When we once become aware of the idea of an inner direction of Life and its energy paths, bubbling like a fountain from within outwards, then confusion vanishes, and we have a clear indication of direction of the lines of force and energy waves. But the lower mind does not penetrate into essences. It cannot enter into the inner court of the Temple of Life; therefore, as long as the mind is swayed by the senses instead of by the soul, it wants its way and uses force to rule outside in matter, it further binds and buries the soul in the mire by these desires, actions and reactions.

The pity of it that man does not realize that he must reap the rewards as well as pay the penalties for all his **thoughts, words** and deeds and when he has the opportunity to pay some these debts through the sufferings and afflictions that come his way so that he may learn humility and love, instead of being grateful and patiently doing his best under the circumstances, he begins to grumble and blame others, which only further entangles him in this valley of tears.

"Be not deceived; God is not mocked: for whatsoever a man soweth, that shall he also reap. For he that soweth to this flesh shall of the flesh reap corruption; but he that soweth to the Spirit shall of the Spirit reap life everlasting.

(GAL. 6:7-8)

"Many are the afflictions of the righteous;"

(PSM. 34:19)

"Behold, I have refined thee, but not with silver; I have chosen thee in the furnace of affliction."

(ISA. 48:10)

"For which cause we faint not; but though our outward man perish, yet the inward man is renewed day by day. For our light affliction, which is but for the moment, worketh for us afar more exceeding and eternal weight of glory; While we look not at the things which are seen, but at the things which are not seen; for the things which are seen are temporal; but the things which are not seen are eternal."   (II COR. 4:16-18)

"Wherefore we labour, that whether present or absent, we may be accepted of Him. For we must all appear before the judgment seat of Christ; that every one may receive the things **done in his body**, according to that he hath done, whether it be good or bad."

(II COR. 5:9-10)

"Dearly beloved, I beseech you as strangers and pilgrims, abstain from fleshly lusts, which war against the soul; having your conversation honest among the Gentiles; that, whereas they speak against you as evil-doers, they may by **your** good works, which they shall behold, glorify God in the day of visitation."

(I PETER 2:11, 12)

The above are only a few quotations from the Bible to indicate that we should be grateful for the vicissitudes. Even in our material pressures, we should never forget the Giver. We think we are doing things, but in reality we are only children who move things around and build toy houses and empires which crumble and decay. Then the dust or sands of time cover all. Yet we cry constantly for more such temporal dominions and possessions.

The Mystic Way is above this childish play and its toys. The Mystic is a hero in an inner sense, like all the heroes in the various Scriptures, who start out definitely to find the Kingdom of the Father in Heaven and to become One with the Father in thought and in deeds of Truth, and in

Life itself. No pelf, no bribery will interest a sincere seeker of the mystery of the Source of the soul and the Truth Eternal. There the Source of the soul and the Truth Eternal. There is a gulf, like a firmament, between the life as the essence and the life as the form which is matter and merely the abode for the living Intelligence of the soul.

There were creations and days of manifestation, called *Manwantaras*, of the positive, centrifugal energy, long before this time and before they were recorded on earth. In fact, creation and dissolution, in one form or another, happen all around us on earth daily and we think nothing of it. The same occurs in all lower regions. The lower the region, the shorter is the life span. Whole regions of Brahmands or Universes undergo this cycle constantly, and planets grow old and die. In the higher and vaster regions, this process is progressively slower and less obvious than in our short time of mortal existence.

If we could only stand aside and see this grand Cinema of life in its Reality, we would become a most absorbed observer, in astonishment over the wonders that have been created for our use. We would then become the **witness** and the **viewer** instead of the idea that we are the **doer**. If we could do this, our "toil would cease, our yoke would be easy and out burden light." Then faith and love would rule in appreciation rather than the agitation of constantly desiring things and wanting to push them around according to the dictates of the mind and senses and rule them for personal gain.

"The mind is the slayer of the Real."

(Voice of the Silence)

God is the wonderful Giver and always gives in abundance. But material things alone are not for the benefit of the soul's progress. In most cases, material success immediately puffs up the ego and hardens the heart, like Pharaoh's. Then the Giver and the inner appreciation of God's gifts, also gratitude and humility are forgotten, and the soul is helpless, because self will and the ego rule. It is difficult to talk to a materially successful Man about the deeper essence of soul life; but it is easy to talk to a great man about such things. Only the great are truly humble.

When the lower mind is puffed up with material success, it crystallizes on things material and seeks for deeper things no more. Mysticism is not possible in that life, so it goes the way of all mortal things. The mind is a real slave driver and gives us no rest. It continually goads us on to more and more and more. We become mere watchdogs over that which we have accumulated. Except for the few occasions of giving gifts where the ego can shine, the mind cannot let go, no matter how much it possesses. Its cleverness must rule, and it pinches pennies even in honest deals. The habit of getting the best of any deal survives. The few philanthropic deeds or other acts of charity which expand the ego are not enough to resurrect the soul as 'Hiram Abiff' the Grand Architect of the Universe, after he is buried. The **cosmic** way of the simple life has lost value and attraction for that individual.

The mortal nature must die that the mystic soul essence may shine forth, even while in the physical body. Jesus said:

"Verily, verily I say unto you except a corn of wheat fall into the ground and die, it abideth alone; but if it die, it bringeth forth much fruit.

He that loveth his life shall lose it; and he that hateth his life in this world shall keep it unto life eternal. If any man serve me, let him follow me; and where I am there shall also my servant be; if any man serve me, him will the Father honour." (JOHN 12:24-26)

St. Paul said:

"I die daily" (I COR. 15:31)

The true mystic practice consists of actually **dying while living**. The real mystic accomplishes this by Spiritual Transport; that is, he does not sever connections with life on this earth, but properly uses the energies for Inner Liberation. The mystic withdraws all his interest and

sensory energy and mind from the surface and extremi-
ties and brings them up to the center of consciousness between the eyes, called the Ajna Chakra or Tisra Til, and
returns at will to perform his daily duties on this earth.
In the early morning hours, while others are asleep, he
climbs the heavenly ladder, rung by rung.

It is at this center of consciousness that the crossroad of
the inner and the outer interests meet. This is where renunciation takes place. Then the Master within meets the disciple whose feet have been washed in the life blood of his
heart (as mentioned in the *Light on the Path*) and whose desire body has been cleansed that far. From here the Master
within lovingly guides the devoted soul onward to greater
heights in inner regions. This is the Pathway of the Inner
Life of the true devotee of the Lord. The mystic always re-
gards himself as the humble servant of God.

CHAPTER VII
CREATION OF ADAM AND EVE

Through an unfortunate misinterpretation and misunderstanding of the brief mystic text in the Old Testament on the Creation of Eve, the women of the world have suffered much. Giving a cosmic event personal and individual interpretation made life difficult and miserable for the feminine species. It is only in this century that women were given statutory rights, equal to that of men: although there were a few exceptions in other countries previous to this time.

The account of the Creation, as given in the four brief chapters of Genesis, was based upon the older text of the Zohar and the Talmud. The principle of reflection and emanation was the foundation of this presentation of the cosmic Adam, called Adam Kadmon in the Kabbala. The Creator, in that essence and realm, was called the Ancient One in the writings of the Kabbalists. By His Light and by the means of the Sound Current in that region, He beheld His image in space and breathed the breath of life into that image. Thus Adam became a living being, after the image and likeness of the Creator, first as a cosmic creation. All other creations on that plane were included in that huge cosmic man, and all things below were taken out of him as units of life; yet they continue to live in him as the Universal Whole of creation, the same as mankind lives and breathes the air in the universe or on earth.

Just as the male principle was present in the very first manifestation of creation, in the same manner was the feminine essence of 'Prakriti' or matter present but latent in the first centrifugal, outpouring energy. The neuter pole or the Source manifests first as a positive (male) outward current, in order to create that which is not yet, by bringing all things out of himself. When the outpouring is finished, then the precipitation and crystallization of forms, and sprouting and reproduction is in order, like after a refreshing rain.

Forms are of the feminine pattern, out of the substance of Prakriti. Life itself is the masculine pole of energy, which precipitates as a substance, into forms on the return current to the center, from the opposite pole or direction. As the energy rises from the center or heart of life, which is its Source and neuter essence, it rises like the sign of Aries to the head region, the positive pole, and splits into two currents, like horns, to complete the oval as it descends. This oval, when formed, is the female symbol of life. It can be a planet, a human being, a cell, a magnet with its currents, a molecule or an atom.

The neuter center plus the positive protons and the negative electrons are still the essential ingredients of energy forms in matter. The outer energies, which form the shell of the oval shaped forms are usually the negative, dancing electrons. These are like the **ribs** of the structure which hold it bound and form its limits. If one of these units were extracted, it would be a feminine electron in action.

This process goes on everywhere in the universe, even in the minutest structure or whirl of energy. This dual polarity was present, from the very beginning, even in the mind energy field as well as in the formative astral region. Genesis 1:27 plainly states:

"Male and female created He them"

and that was prior to the account of the physical creation.

In the cosmic man or outpouring of energy, in the form of the sign of Aries (γ) as the beginning of the oval, there are two positive or male currents, like father and son. At the center of the upper half of the oval, the expanded portion of the egg, the masculine energy has expended most of its energy and must return to its Source or it would be lost in space. Then the attractive power of the neuter center draws the current from the other end of its central pole where the current flows **in** on its return circuits, creating an upward and inward vortex from the lower center where the oval joins, forming the upward indentation. The outer lines flow into the center by attraction as a return current.

The negative or feminine was in the positive or masculine energy from the beginning, and the positive and negative currents cross over at every joint in the human body as they do in the very pattern of form, like alternating currents, to carry on, else there would be no motion or perpetuation of form.

In the cosmic process, mentioned in Genesis 1:6, 7, the first dividing of the upper half of the arc of the circle from the lower half, by the firmament, confirms the idea of the Kabbalistic system of two positive polarized currents above and two negative polarized currents below, in the creation of energy fields of elements which are called Tattwas in the Vedas. It is the 'Yod He' above, and the 'Vau He' below the central line. The ancient Chinese called it the 'Yang' or active male principle above, and the 'Yin' or negative female principle below.

In the human body, which is a microfilm of the cosmos, the diaphragm is the firmament which divides the fiery and airy regions above, from the earthy regions and watery regions below. Again, the composite is male and female, while the below or watery and earthy regions represent the feminine half. The diaphragm functions as the neuter stabilizer and activator of the fire of life and pranic breath from above, and for nourishment and reproduction in the lower half of the human body.

This separation of the male elements as the superior pole, from the female as the inferior in the cosmos, was established in the pattern world of mind, right in the beginning of creation or nothing could have been fructified and reproduced in all the lower regions of creation.

The same was established in the astral sky as the list of the positive sun energy, which is the pranic generator in our solar system. The negative or moon energy of the watery and earthy essences acts as conveyors of life and form in the etheric principle of the cosmos. The sun force expands energies, as heat; and the moon contracts them as cold. This Principle of Polarity is present everywhere in nature.

In the second chapter of Genesis, verse 5, is plainly stated:

"And every plant of the field before it was in the earth, and every herb of the field before it grew: for the LORD GOD had not caused it to rain upon the earth, and there was not a man to till the ground."

Creation from top down, up to that time, had taken place in the pattern energy field and in the astral light of the pattern energy substance, as Tattwas or essences of matter.

According to Genesis 2:7, the microcosmic man, as we know man, was formed out of the essence of the four elements, the dust of the ground representing the four polarized Tattwas of matter, since air and earth form dust. This is the substance spoke of in the Sepher Yetzirah as the red clay out of which Adam was made. The red, earthy principle mentioned here represents the four polarized elements or Tattwas of matter; namely, the air and fire as the dual positive poles, and the dust or earth and water as the two negative poles. This creation furnishes the composite body with the four cosmic earthy Tattwic qualities to complete his complex make-up as a human being and a perfect replica of the great Cosmic Being or the Universal Adam and its universal forces.

The Hebrew Yod-He-Vau-He is the sacred Name or Word of the Creator called Jehovah God in the Bible. He Himself is the fifth Neuter Essence out of which the other four flow and return to constantly. He is the first and the last, the beginning and the end.

The brief allusion and description in Genesis, of the entire process of creating the various bodies and stepped-down energy fields of man, could not be understood except by a deep study of the Zohar and the Talmud, from which the ideas were extracted. Later the Kabbalist formulated this into a system with a Philosophic Tree of Life.

Prior to this, all these processes had been explained at great length in the Vedas. In the light of these older writings, the account given in Genesis can be deciphered intelligently. The Ayurvedic medical practice of India, founded about six thousand years ago, was based upon the understanding of these finer energy constituents as bodies and forces within the form of the physical frame, which were the real factors of the soul to express itself in form as well as in its finer atomic energy constituents.

It may be well to explain here that man has three bodies within and through which he functions namely, the causal, the astral and the physical. This coincides with the three separate accounts given in the Bible and other Sacred Writings on the creation of man as Adam. If this idea is not accepted, then the biblical account of creation and much of its other deeper significance amounts to unintelligible repetition, because it has no bearing on the gross physical body of man as we understand it from the standpoint of merely physiological, chemical and anatomical construction.

Materialists insist that all must be matter or it could not be real and accepted as scientific data. Yet how much of real solid matter is there in the energy field of one single atom? However, the existence of energy in the atom is accepted by material science while it rejects the idea of extending it to the composite whole of man's energy fields, and seeing the whirling spinning wheels or *Chakras* as finer centers within the gross form. Yet the physical form is the result of spinning, finer energies which precipitated into grosser ones.

"There is nothing new under the sun", said Solomon, the wise king. This is truly spoken when we see how the old becomes new by a new aspect and approach discovered through man's research in another cyclic round of time. When **he** finds it, then it exists to his mind; not before can he accept it or know it except the physical methods of external research and proof. And this accepted material standard has proven a great handicap to man's understanding of the deeper concepts of Life.

Man, as a genius of intellect and a good mechanic, makes all his instruments for his scientific research and then depends solely upon these man-made instruments and their recordings. That is the accepted proof today. But man has faculties **within himself**, which if trained and given only a fraction of the time and attention that the machines and instruments require, would prove far more sensitive and penetrating into the depth of the mystery of Life, and open up his own inner capacity of thought and observation in the realm of essences far beyond mortal ken. Nevertheless, this idea is too startling and not scientific from the accepted external point of research, even though every human being has the capacity to prove it in God-given laboratory within himself. And no matter how many others may have found it, it is up to each individual to discover and prove it to himself. Each soul must find his Savior. Every man must light the lamp of his inner intelligence and love to find the way of life.

Matter, as the one substance and reality, is uppermost in the minds of the people in this Iron Age. However, a greater vision and a longing for **depth** rather than merely material gains and comforts can still usher sincere souls and minds into a deeper concept of Life and understanding, as one lamp can light another.

Mind and its function in man is an accepted fact. But in order for the mind energy to function intelligently, it must reach, govern and influence every atom and sensory cell in the body. How else is this possible but through a mind body which is the pattern energy of the physical body? The pattern energy which formed this physical frame by precipitation of its energies, is a finer substance of matter.

The same holds true of man's emotions and sensory ability and activity. The finer energies first worked to precipitate, build and function through the grosser form which we call the body and senses of man. These two ideas are the factors described here in the story of Creation, in their process of condensation **before** they became the gross material body and functions.

The negative pole as matter in its magnetic desire body, was called the feminine form, which had not yet been precipitated out of the positive, active centrifugal cycle, and so was not bent upon its return journey, inward. In the Bible, Eve is referred to as the mother of all living. This essence existed in the very beginning in the highest spiritual plane situated below Sach Khand, the Eternal Realm.

Male was the energy **essence**, and female was the energy **substance**. The latter was latent in the essence, or it could not have been extracted or precipitated out of it. Without the **substance** or the **Light** principle there could be no form, no refraction, as the microfilm of the macrocosm. **Sound** energy is the **essence** and the life principle. LIGHT PROCEEDS **OUT** OF THIS PRIMAL SOUND ENERGY. It lighteth every man into this physical world, as **Light substance** from the **Sound essence**.

"That was the true light, which lighteth every man that cometh into the world."　　　　　　　　(JOHN 1:9)

"The light of the body is the eye: Therefore when thine eye is single, thy whole body also is full of light; but when thine eye is evil, thy body also is full of darkness. Take heed therefore that the light which is in thee be not darkness. If thy whole body therefore be full of light, having no part dark, the whole shall be full of light, as when the bright shining of a candle doth give thee light."

(LUKE 11:34-37; and similarly stated in MAT. 6:22, 23)

It is by this same Light and Sound that we are to again return to the Father's House. But most of us have so completely covered this Light with the filth of egotism that we see nothing but darkness when we close our physical eyes. Naturally, we need a living Guide in the human form to show us the way until we have reached that state within where we can consciously contact the True Light and Sound, and the Guide in that resplendent Light and Sound or Shabd Form.

Now to get back to the creation of Adam and Eve: Both male and female energy existed in the very beginning of every place and realm of creation. That does not imply two beings, as man and woman, but rather the two currents or energies. Woman was not a brand new creation when she was drawn out of the essence of Adam, the male principle, as all energies were so precipitated.

Heaven, the above, gives. The deep sleep which fell on Adam (Gen. 2:21-22) was a sinking into a lower level of consciousness in his energy fields or *chakras*, where the negative pole of energy as the lower half of the oval of energy was extracted in the form of the desire body, and presented to the composite beings called Adam or the Adamic Race, as a new vehicle through which each could function on a lower vibratory key. Geometrically, in the lines of energy travel in the cosmos, it is the sinking down of the centrifugal waves below the straight line or in the lower half of the oval travel, in an exhaustion of the positive qualities of the outward flow, as previously described. The return flow gravitates inward and sets the limits of the outward-bound currents.

As stated before, myriads of male and female beings existed in individual forms on higher regions and planes, long before the creation of this material world. The shells or forms constituted the feminine principle or substance, while the life and energy — which is the soul — was the masculine essence. All human beings have both principles within themselves in order to polarize, but one or the other is predominant in each individual, resulting in one being male and the other female. Souls may take either a male or a female body, as their *karma* directs.

All that was mentioned in Genesis thus far took place on the astral plane and its substratas of energies nearer to the physical plane. However, the actual descent into the gross physical plane, as we know it, did not occur until **after the fall** and expulsion out of Paradise.

"And Jehovah God made for Adam and for his wife coats of skins, and clothed them."

(GEN. 3:21, American edition.)

"Unto Adam also and to his wife did the Lord God make coats of skins, and clothed them."

(GEN. 3:21)

When Jehovah made the *'coats of skins'*; He gave them bodies of flesh, bone and blood. Then they were clothed. This was an entirely new field of life on earth, and a physical body was necessary to protect them from the elements and enable them to function as human beings.

In Gen. 3:16-19, new conditions and rules were also given in the new environment, which may sound like a curse, but are the natural consequences of life in a grossed media and density of matter. It is all a part of the plan of involution for experience and ultimate emancipation.

In Genesis 3:13, 14, 15, the desire principle is referred to as the serpent in Paradise. The desire body is the sphere in which it operates, and is called woman. "Desire, they name is woman". The lower, sensory and sensuous part of the mind is like a serpent. It entices and promises so much in sensory pleasures but, acted upon, they result only in pain and misery. This part of the mind ever grovels and cringes and crawls in the dust of desire and wanting. It is evasive and winds and winds and craves to get what it wants, but is never satisfied in this downward trend.

Substance attracts energy unto itself. This attractive field is centered within the female principle and identified with her. Hence, women get all the blame for man's fall. The fact that this feminine aspect was also a part of man **before** the separation of the sexes, is entirely forgotten. No mate was found for Adam until Eve was extracted out of his energy which included this desire body. Without his latent desire, there could have been no such creation out of his own essence.

The upward and inward current of Love and Devotion, which this same desire body is capable of will ultimately crush the head of the serpent after it has bruised the heel of the desire principle and lead it through dire experience and suffering. This is the fulfillment of the prophecy in Gen. 3:14-15, the promise of raising up the soul beyond the realm of desire. It is truly a promise of Salvation for incarnated souls. Jesus fulfilled it in Himself, and so must all His followers and every individual who desires Liberation.

According to Gen. 3:22, in order to ascend to the spiritual heights, man must learn to govern the mind and all its lower energies. Otherwise sensation runs wild and become evil and destructive. It was necessary for man to come to earth and learn this lesson through bitter experience in a denser media, where the mind could register resistance and reaction in all levels of matter and sensation. Only thus could it become aware of its doings. And that is a slow process.

Genesis 3:24 confirms the expulsion of man and his consciousness out of the Paradisical state of Eden, and the placing of a Cherubim before its gates to guard them. The Cherubim is the dweller of the threshold, and is symbolized by the Egyptians as a Sphynx which must be conquered before entering its gates. **Its riddle** must be answered and understood.

The special emphasis on the creation of a new desire body for man to function through in a new sphere of action was a major event and much misinterpreted as an external, brand new being in creation. That this is not so is proven in all the writings of cosmic events, of separation and extraction of the below from the above, as in the case of creating the firmament; also in creating the sun and the moon **as two polarity forces** of male and female; also the myriads of animals, birds, fishes, beasts and vegetation which were created en masse and told to be fruitful and multiply.

Neither was the extracting of a lower, feminine principle from the higher, masculine one a new process. It was the standard procedure, as shown above; but it is unduly emphasized and misunderstood in the case of Adam and

Eve. Hosts of male and female beings existed on planes of essences and energy fields, prior to the time that the new creation was formed for them. According to Job 38:7.

"When the morning stars sang together,
And all the sons of God shouted for joy?"

In connection with this process of creation on every plane and level of vibratory intensity we find repeated references to "Male and female made He them." And yet, after all this, there was no mate for Adam. How can that be interpreted to make sense?

When we realize that an involution of energy on a new sphere of action formed the creation on that new, lower sphere, and that hosts of beings have been termed as Adam all through this account thus far, we can see that all the other creatures in the newly formed sphere **had new shells or bodies, but** that **the race of Adams** had none as yet. It was then that the deep sleep of involution fell on Adam, and a new desire body was extracted from his rib or external energy whirl which was on the surface of his being and condensed like a mass of electrons to form a new vehicle, inversely in action and polarity to the one above, which he had on the higher plane and with which he was not able to function on this new sphere. It was a new edition to his equipment of vehicles or soul coverings, which was presented to him as the keynote of the feminine pole on this plane of substance, while he remained the positive pole in consciousness. The extension of the desire principle from man made it possible for him to incarnate into that vehicle and live in it as a new edition, "flesh of his flesh", or half of himself, and express himself or rid himself of those hidden creative desires which kept him stationary where he was before he became a human being.

Creation is involution from the higher to the lower, and experience in form. The essence or vital body is always positive to the form because it is the moving dynamic energy field. The form must have a static factor for gestation, or it cannot reproduce in this sphere. 'The Fall' was not in the involution and reproduction, but in the **lack of control** of this desire body, newly acquired in Paradise.

'The Fall' occurred in Paradise before the expulsion. It was all in the design and purpose of the Creator, so man may know both sides of his being—the dynamic and the static natures. Socrates said, "Man, know thyself". But up to the present time man has already accumulated so many desires to be fulfilled—and in trying to fulfill them encumbers himself with still more entanglements—that he has completely neglected and forgotten the very purpose of creation.

Desire to experience and sense things, to create and rule, was the inherent downward pull for incarnation in human form. This primary desire formed a chain of reactions; that is, each succeeding desire led to many more, and all the good and bad deeds—intentional or unintentional—yield their fruits in turn, until we are hopelessly entangled and lost in a maze. But once we realize this, then it is possible to find a Guide who will instruct us and show us how to obtain Eternal Salvation and freedom from the gnawing worm of desire.

"for their worm shall not die, neither shall
their fire be quenched;"   (ISAIAH 66:24)

Natural desire has its roots in the sensory consciousness of the mind and the ego. Experience is the remedy and makes the soul richer for having traveled in the outer boundaries of the substance of space. In that 'otherness' man discovers his lonesomeness and emptiness, and longs to return Home. Self-realization is essential before God-Realization is possible. Man must see his need, become humble and seek a Teacher who can instruct him in the way back to God.

All the shining promises of the serpent of desire in the mind, about sensations, possessions, sensory pleasures and powers become ashes and pain. And all the glory of seeming independence, knowledge and rulership becomes a chore and responsibility along with grief and loss. "All is vanity" said Solomon, and so says every soul who has gone through it all and learned the lesson.

CHAPTER VIII
CREATIONS IN EDEN

1. Eden, as described in Genesis 2:8, is the etheric or astral plane of finer substance than the physical. The garden is a special, local limitation of that substance. This garden is also called Paradise. It is the individual etheric or astral body created for man at this stage and on this level of involution.

Genesis 2:15 gives us the key and explanation of this mystery: "And the Lord (Jehovah) God took the man, and put him into the garden of Eden to dress it and keep it." This instruction would fit any soul which is literally put into a new body, to dress it and keep it. So we see that our etheric or astral body is just as much our responsibility as are the physical and mental bodies of our being.

According to the Bible, the Garden is planted eastward in Eden, the etheric realm. This would indicate that it is the sensory body and area, because the sun rises in the east. The anterior part of our body is the east, as we face the sun, symbolic of the rising of our sensory currents. The back of the body is the west, of the setting sun, or the outgoing motor currents and their major area. Accordingly, the top of the head is the north pole, and the feet the south pole of the body. All these currents were understood as sun and moon or hot and cold Polarity Principles in the Ayurvedic medicine of old. They have their physical application in therapeutics, Whether known or unknown.

2. Three types of trees are mentioned in Genesis 2:9. These trees are not physical trees in our sense of the word. They represent energies, because all this description is of an energy realm and not a physical one, for this had not yet

appeared in the process of creation and precipitation from the higher energy levels. The **three types of trees** are the **three gunas** or the **three energies** in their mode of motion.

The trees themselves and their locations in the physical design of the body, become the three *Tattwas* or substances which are the most active and important in the material body and in the bloodstream. They also become the three 'doshas' or evils when out of balance and proportion in their function, as mental, emotional and physical action. The heart center in the etheric realm was assigned to Siva, the Destroyer, for that reason.

The first and most important tree in the human body is the **Tree of Life** (Gen. 2:9). The position of the Tree of Life in the human body is the central axis of the brain and spinal cord, down to the second lumbar vertebra. The brain is the root of this tree, from where the higher energies descend. This is an inverted tree, with its branches growing downward and its roots in heaven above. That is why man is not comfortable on earth and always seeks an escape in one form or another. If man were to seek a solution to his problem, by the light of this God-given intelligence, then the answer would be found, because it is engraved in his very being, in definite patterns and characters of geometric design, like on the tablets of Moses on Mount Sinai. The Tree of Life is the airy element, in the finer Tattwas, over which the mind energy travels and gives the intelligent direction for coordination, sensation and motion in the body. Kabbalistically, it is the mother letter 'Aleph' of the Hebrew alphabet. Its position in the human body is the cerebrospinal axis, down to the end of the spinal cord, the second lumbar vertebra.

The **Tree of Knowledge of Good and Evil** is the generative impulse. (Up to that time there was no such thing as good and evil, for all was heavenly bliss; therefore, the need for knowledge of good and evil did not exist.) It is the mother letter 'Mem' in the Hebrew alphabet. It embraces the waters and all watery secretive action. In all accounts of the Creation, it is stated that the earth rose out of the waters where it was generated and floated in the amniotic fluid in the womb of the cosmic mother, much the same as the human embryo develops into the fetus and is born out of the human mother. Brahma, the creator in that realm, was given these attributes and functions in the cosmos. In Greek cosmogony, the name of the one entrusted with this function was Jupiter. The attributes and functions are identical, but each language has a different name for them. So it is in all Sacred writings. The places and functions are the same, only the names differ according to the language used. Energies and regions exist, whether they are described or not in any country or language.

The Tree of Knowledge of Good and Evil, as referred to in Gen. 2:15, 16, 17, is the center of the desire body in man, which has the power of further involution into matter by attraction and craving. Its physiological position in the human body is below the Tree of Life, where the spinal cord ends, at the second lumbar vertebra. These parts of the spinal nerves are called the "*Cauda Equina*" or horse's tail, because of the branched-out appearance. This is the motor area of the generative impulses. The sensory area is in the front, in the external generative center in both, male and female.

Without the bonds of the desire impulse, these would be but fields of reproduction, the same and as natural as in the vegetable kingdom. Man is the only living creature who can **either** degenerate and scatter himself into matter, **or** properly control and use these same energies to return to his Father's House of Eternal Bliss, by directing them upward and inward to the brain, from whence they came. By doing the former only, he is but an animal in human form. But if he makes the proper use of his human body, then he becomes God-like. The central core must eventually have the same expression of fulfillment as the shell or the circumference.

The **Trees Good for Food** represent the fiery energies of the digestive system, which separate the food and extract the fine fiery essence out of it for warmth and nourishment of the body. The deity in charge of this cosmic process is Vishnu, the nourisher and supporter. The Greeks attributed this function to Saturn who devoured his own children, because life lives on life in all lower creation. Even man has not chosen to step out of that category of eating flesh, fish, fowl and eggs, and things containing them. In the Kabbala, the Hebrew mother letter '*Shin*' was applied to this function.

The three classes of tress or principles of air, water and fire, are the etheric energies in the cosmos. They represent the three *guna* essences in the bloodstream, as breath, semen and nourishment; or air, water and fiery substances or warmth. The etheric realm and *prana* are their root and cause. The gross physical body is the end product or precipitation of all these processes.

3. The **One River** of energy is the psychic *prana* which flows out of the etheric realm and becomes the gross physical *prana* which in turn flows over the nervous system in the body of man. The *prana* flows over the five Tattwas as fields and regions in the human body, as wireless energy, before it becomes the gross *prana* of nerve impulses and physical action.

The downward drive for sensation, wastes the precious psychic pranic energy and binds the senses, mind and soul to this earthward pull. There is little chance for this fine sensory energy to be purified and drawn upward and inward by concentration, when it is exhausted in the downward trend. Not only does this waste of energy prevent one from making spiritual progress, but it also robs the rest of the life energy currents necessary for maintaining the physical body in perfect health and vigor, because through this wasting or squandering it uses more than is naturally apportioned to that center by the economy of the pattern essence. Only six petals are allotted to this lotus or chakra, out of the total of fifty-two petals on the Tress of Life in the body. The energy goes either up or down. If up, it enriches the mind function and the consciousness and helps to free the soul from bondage.

"And a river went out of Eden to water the garden and from thence it was parted, and became into four heads. The name of the first is Pison: that is it which compasseth the whole land of Havilah, where there is gold; and the gold of that land is good: there is bdellium and the onyx stone." (GEN. 2:10-12)

The river Pison means 'Current', 'energy'. Havilah, the land over which it flows, means 'sand land'. The gold and onyx stone further complete the definite identification, in the mystical language, of the actual current and where it flows in the little world of the microcosm, our body. This is the energy or element of fire of the ancients, which creates the first sphere or oval — the head, the brain, and the nervous system — and flows over it. The brain is the root of the nervous system, like a tree that is upside-down. This latter is spoken of in the Bible as the symbolic Tree of Life.

'Havilah' (sand land) identifies the pituitary and pineal glands, by their sand-like constituents.

The 'gold' spoken of is the energy current of a yellow color, flowing upward, over the pituitary and pineal bodies and the optic thalamus, and creates a gold-colored light current which is pictured as a halo around the head of saintly persons. The Hindus call this current 'Udana'.

The 'onyx stone' is the stone spoken of in Revelation as being in the center of the foreheads at the third eye, or Tisra Til, the door of the soul, the narrow gateway to the Lost Word and higher realms, symbolized by the Ureus of the Egyptians. Physiologically, we think we cover all this ground by merely calling this the cerebrospinal nervous system.

The name of the second river is Gihon, which means 'gusher' or 'intermittent spring', 'virgin fountain'. This applies well to the heart and its beats, the fountain of life in the body. This energy element was called 'air' by the ancients. It creates and sustains the second oval cavity, the chest with the heart and lungs. Science calls it the respiratory and circulatory system. The diaphragm is the diving line.

This is also mentioned in the Bible:
"And God said, Let there be a firmament in the midst of the waters, and let it divide the waters from the waters."

(GEN. 1:6)

In the human body, the diaphragm is the elastic, functioning firmament which divides the waters or energies — the above from the below: two rivers above (the fire and air elements) from the two below (the earth and water elements) It is upon this important interaction that life depends. Without diaphragmatic function, there can be no respiration nor heartbeat, no proper elimination nor assimilation, nor motion. It is a fixed stabilizer of bodily functions.

Here, also, we find the mystic chalice spoken of as a cup: namely the heart, the mixing bowl of the life principle (Prana) in the air, fire and water elements. Prana or the universal life force, which is the same energy as is in the sun, uses oxygen as a conveyor, and we breathe it in as air. The Bible clearly states that the "life is in the blood".

If the chemical oxygen was the life principle itself, we could prolong life indefinitely under an oxygen tent, which is not the case. Prana is the universal breath of life, called 'Ruach Elohim' by the Hebrews. And when Elohim breathed this breath into the nostrils of the form called man, this form became connected or united with the function of the Soul power within, and man became a **living**, existing soul on this earth. This Prana, Ruach or Energy flows over each nostril alternately, enlivens the sympathetic nervous system, and links the body to Nature in this Energy field.

The third river out of Eden's one river is '*Hiddekel*', '*Tigris*', or '*black*'. This is the earth element of the ancients, which built and operates the third cavity — the abdomen with its digestive, assimilative and eliminative activity. The Hindus call the energy '*Saman*'. We call it the gastro-intestinal tract and its function of digestion, assimilation and elimination.

The fourth river is the Euphrates, the *'great river'* or *'water wheel'*. The ancients called this the water element, it is situated in the fourth cavity of the body — the pelvic cavity. As earth and water landmarks are irregular, so is the space, with the earth element above it. Science calls this the genito-urinary system, including the kidneys, which are post periteneal structures.

The earth is said to have been created out of water; and is surrounded by it, like the embryo is surrounded and floats in the amniotic fluid. The Great Wheel refers to constant birth in this river of life. It is also referred to as the *'wheel of eighty-four'* because it contains eight million, four hundred thousand species of life through which the soul can incarnate. It contains the seed power which is the one evidence of the eternal power of perpetuation in all life, whether human, animal or vegetable. The billionth descendent of any life form or pattern has the power to create, the same as the original pair had. This is the only perpetual motion power we know of; namely the seed power in all created things, sustained by the psychic prana as the energy immediately above the physical plane.

The *'four rivers'* are the same as the four elements of solids, liquids, gases and energy fields of the ancients, and the *'four systems of the body'* of modern science. As long as these four elements or energies flow into and through each other, and support each other in function, all is well. When one or more river of energy is stopped up, or cannot flow, life departs from it and goes back to whence it came. It is then that the good minister, at the funeral service, revives our memory of this mystic lore not now understood, when he picks up a handful of earth and says, as he throws it on the casket. "earth to earth, dust to dust, and ashes to ashes." A doctor wrote out a death certificate which probably stated, *'heart failure'* or *'endocarditis'*. But the minister here tells us the true story as to why this person died, from a real scientific energy standpoint. The earth element in this body could no longer function nor draw energy from the great earth element outside, which is the cosmos, and could not co-operate with the other elements, so now this earth element of the individual body goes back to mother earth.

"and thou shalt eat the herb of the field: In the sweat of thy face shalt thou eat bread, till thou return unto the ground; for out of it wast thou taken: for dust thou art, and unto dust shalt thou return."

(GEN. 3:18, 19)

"Dust to dust". The element of air has dust as its negative symbol, and when the air principle can no longer breathe or flow in rhythm with the universal air principle outside, the individual air or life breath of Prana, the life in the body returns to its universal reservoir.

"Ashes to ashes". This person died because the fire principle of energy could not flow in this body, and be renewed by the universal fire of energy and life. That is why it must return to its source in the Essence. The evidence of fire is ashes.

In the Koran it is stated that when the forms were built, God played beautiful music upon them, and souls entered those forms. It is important to know and understand this process of the involution to know and understand this process of the involution of the soul into matter, because 'this beautiful music' is the Sound Current, THE WORD, or the Holy Shabd. All these finer principles, vehicles and life lines of energy direction are still within us, although buried and covered with mud and rust, the results of our own thoughts, words and deeds. That is the reason we have so much conflict within ourselves and are constantly searching for our lost estate, a 'Lost Chord' or link to Life itself, by seeking out higher essences and trying to discover ourselves.

Every principle or energy field within us, our little world, has a universal plane of being or field of operation. And as our four elements must blend with that greater world outside and draw from its universal supply in order to be well nourished and healthy, even so, all the higher energy principles must be supplied from their own plane.

The Soul itself must constantly be supplied by the Word issuing forth from the Supreme Father who created it. No part is complete in itself "Except it abide in the Whole" and is united with It.

"I am the true vine, and my Father is the husband-man. Every branch in me that beareth not fruit, he taketh it away: and every branch that beareth fruit, he cleanseth it, that it may bear more fruit. Already ye are clean because of the WORD which I have spoken unto you. Abide in me, and I in you. As the branch cannot bear fruit of itself, except abide in the vine; so neither can ye, except ye abide in me. I am the vine, ye are the branches: He that abideth in me, and I in him, the same beareth much fruit: for apart from me ye can do nothing. If a man abideth not in me, he is cast forth as a branch, and is withered; and they gather them, and cast them into the fire, and they are burned. If ye abide in me, and my *words* abide in you, ask whatsoever ye will, and it shall be done unto you." (JOHN 15:1-7)

Why should man be so proud, when everything is but a gift and a loan to him from a gracious, loving Father, the Source of all things and essences?

Communication, contemplation, meditation or concentration by the individual soul within man with its Universal Source, is man's real function, path of travel and well-being. This can be a communication or communion of soul with its Source, during this very lifetime, as Love with the Ocean of Love and Bliss, or Intelligence with the Universal Intelligence and Pattern World of things, creativeness and inventions.

The individual mind also communicates with the Universal Mind in its constant activity, motion, illusion and theories, thoughts and wishing. This gives us the psychology of man in its true scope and path of travel. Like any one of the four elements, when one stops flowing, having lost its rhythm or tuning with the Whole and its Source of supply, it has a tendency to lock itself in, turn upon itself and disintegrate. There is pain, sorrow, etc. If this balance can be restored, there is well-being and free flow of energy.

The Universal Energy, like air, is all around us, and we can benefit thereby if we do not choke ourselves up with too much at once or try to retain used material. In fact, we, like a bubble in an Infinite Ocean, live, move and have our being in this Source of all, at all times. It is merely a matter of what we are seeking, and at what level we tune in. This is what actually takes place and needs no other psychology, for it is the breath and movement of the Soul itself.

All dramas are based upon the story of the tragedy of the Soul being bound by matter, as with chains. '*Prometheus Bound*' is one of these dramas, telling much of the Greeks' understanding of psychology.

Every life is but the relationship of the unit to its source; and the only possible path of travel is the flow between the two—the microcosm (man) and the macrocosm (the universe)—in its various degrees of fineness and density of energy and matter, as crystallized, fixed, static fields. The outer relationship is the form relationship of the unit to the storehouse or the whole in which it lives. The True Inner Relationship is of the soul or spark of the Eternal Essence to its Divine Source, the Creator Himself, and His Breath of Eternal Life which is the Holy Shabd. It is the Truth that was before creation, and the Love and Wisdom which enfolds all in a perfect state of Eternal Bliss.

A centrifugal force, out from the center of The All—Being Essence, causes creation, as myriads of sparks from a central hearth fire. And the return flow of this energy, as the centripetal, attractive force, links it and makes it seek its Source in an effort to become unified again in its Rhythm, Essence and Bliss. That explains the hunger of the Soul and the constant will and desire within the Soul as unrealized longings and yearnings. The whole mystery of destiny and pre-destination lies here.

The Soul, in turn, steps down its energy, is influenced by the mind, and expresses itself through the senses. These relate to the mind as units to the Whole; a positive pole above, as the Source; the negative pole or units below, seeking experience in multiplicity and outward expenditure of energy. Mind is the negative pole of the soul, for expression in the denser states of matter. All things are suspended from a Universal Source or Center and travel in that orbit; like the planets around our sun, the electrons around the neutron, etc. It is one grand story, in endless variety of spinning energies and finer particles, clear up to the Essence.

CHAPTER IX
A REVIEW AND BRIEF EXPLANATION

All Sacred Mystic writings have only one main objective; namely, to inform or remind the soul consciousness, the spiritual Adam, how to wisely use his various tools or bodies and their energy currents so he may rise above them in liberation or freedom of the soul. This state of freedom during life on this earth is called '*Moksha*' by the Hindus, and is the '*Nirvana*' of the Buddhists.

Instructions were given in the Vedas, the Uttara Gita, the Upanishads, Yogic Sadhan, etc., as to how to use the four faculties of the mental body, and the will, for liberation; when to use passivity of the mind substance and the understanding while the will acts, etc., etc.

These writings throw additional light on the creation of the Sukshm Prana, the fine psychic prana, **out of the mind** substance known as Chit Akash. This is referred to in Genesis as woman, called Eve, drawn out of Adam, as flesh or substance from his substance or flesh.

The Sukshm Prana is the seat of desire, and its Purification is of the utmost importance to the yogi or the mystic. Until we have gotten rid of or at least purified our desire, we have accomplished nothing permanent.

"The prana forms the link between the physical and the mental man."

(from Chapter VII of Yogic Sadhan)

These instructions further state that we should detach ourselves as much as possible from the body, think of it as a mere case and leave it to the care of God and His Shakti; that is, His Radiant Will and Power. The Saints call it God's *Mauj*, which, however, goes far beyond this limited application. God's Supreme Will governs all. Nothing can happen without it. Not even a sparrow can fall off the roof without the Father's Will.

(MAT. 10:29, 30, 31)

This is sufficient to show a complete science of the soul and mind, similar to the very essence of the Old and the

New Testaments of the Bible; that is, to be in the world but not of it; to rise above temptation. True, trials, tribulations and temptations there will be, but we should become so firmly fixed in His Love that we do not fall nor can they make any impression upon us. Jesus said:

"Therefore whosoever heareth these sayings of mine, **and doeth them**, I will liken unto a wise man which built his house upon a rock: And the rain descended and the floods came, and the winds blew, and beat upon that house; and it fell not; for it was founded upon a rock.

And

"everyone that heareth these sayings of mine, and doeth them not, shall be likened unto a foolish man, which built his house upon the sand; and the rain descended, and the floods came, and the winds blew, and beat upon that house; and it fell: and great was the fall of it."

(MAT. 7:24-27)

When St. Paul said, ...75-Right

"I die daily" (I COR. 15:31)

that indicated not only the unconditional surrender of the physical body, but of the mind and all its desires as well. This is the keynote in the New Testament; namely, the path of faith in and love for the Supreme Being, and the perseverance in the Great Work of ascending and uniting with Him, by freeing the soul of its material and psychic attachments and desires, the very foundation of which is the ego. It is not only the daily dying, overcoming or sublimating of the physical senses, but of the ego as well, which is absolutely necessary before we can obtain Eternal Salvation or Liberation. No strange thing or 'otherness' can enter the Eternal Essence.

The Saints give definite instructions to their disciples, telling them how to withdraw all the attention from the sensory fields below the eye level and bring the consciousness into the center between the eyes, called Tisra Til. When this is duly accomplished, all feeling and sensation is withdrawn from the body and gathered in this center. This is the process of which St. Paul spoke when he said, "I die daily". It is the completion of the first step for ascension inward and upward into the higher spiritual regions. In such a state one is dead to the world but alive inside, in the center of consciousness, by the Lord's Grace of the Eternal Sound Current, His Word, His Truth and His Love which sustains all.

The five prana currents in the body are not interfered with nor used in this process of withdrawal, as in other types of yoga. Only the five currents of energy which flow through the five senses and cause desires and thoughts are withdrawn and lifted up to higher states of awareness. When this is done according to the instructions of the Saints, the consciousness can return to the body at will, without harm or strain anywhere.

In the New Testament, Jesus definitely points out the necessity of purifying the desire principle:

"Ye have heard that it was said by them of old time, Thou shalt not commit adultery: but I say unto you, that whosoever looketh on a woman to lust after her hath committed adultery with her already in his heart."
(MAT. 5:27, 28)

Accordingly, Jesus clearly indicated that the very thought or desire in the wrong direction is a sin even without the Physical deed or motor expression of the act. This also explains the fall of Adam and Eve in the garden of Paradise, before they were expelled from it into the human form.

The same idea of purifying the 'desire body', the Sukshm Prana, is clearly brought out in the following quotation from the Bible:

"And if thy right eye offend thee, pluck it out, and cast it from thee," etc.   (MAT. 5:29)

Of course, this does not mean that we should remove the physical eye, but that we should REMOVE THE SENSORY OBJECT AND CURRENT FROM THE FOCUS OF

THE MIND. That temptations and trials will continue to come our way, we may be sure, and that in itself is not a sin. The sin is committed **when we dwell on them** and continue to focus our attention on them, either **with** or **without** acting upon them.

Beholding, coupled with a feeling of desire, is an involuntary attraction or concertation which calls for motor energy to fulfill the desire and sensation which, if not acted upon or sublimated, remains in the background as an unfulfilled craving and will rear its ugly head during our unguarded moments, the most opportune time for its victory.

People have been known to physically blind themselves or to put on physical blinders because of this admonition in the Bible, simply because they did not realize that it was the '*desire*' and the **thought behind it that had to be plucked out**, while **retaining the organs of sight**, etc. Destruction of the physical organs only adds insult to injury and still does not eradicate the desire or craving. In fact, by so doing, the evil is intensified. Neither does one become saintly by not having physical sight.

"And if thy right hand offend thee cut it off, and cast it from thee," etc.   (MAT. 5:30)

Here, the motor energy current of action is implied. Whatever action is wrong, do not dwell on it. Renounce it, clear it out of your mind, cut it off from further energy supply by discontinuing the action of wrong-doing and sublimating it into proper channels, which can be done only under the proper guidance of a True Master or Mystic.

That makes sense as excellent advice and good psychology; but, to become a cripple through the physical application of this admonition, solves nothing, as many have learned to their great sorrow and disappointment. Again, the physical is not the cause; it is only the agent through which these mental and emotional currents are expressed as sensory motor action. And that desire continues to gnaw and increase more so without the vehicles of expression than with them. So the physical maiming and crippling solves nothing.

This further proves that the statements and parables of Jesus need the mystic interpretation in order to find the real inner message of value in these Jewels. Jesus personally spoke to the multitude in parables only; but gave the full explanation to His disciples, in private:

"And when he was entered into the house from the people, his disciples asked him concerning the parable. And he saith unto them, Are ye so without understand also? Do ye not perceive that whatsoever thing from without entereth into the man, **it** cannot defile him; because it entereth not into his heart, but into his belly, and goeth out into the draught?" (MARK 7:17-19)
"And he said that which cometh out of the man, that defileth the man. For from within, out of the heart of men proceed evil thoughts, adulteries, fornications, murders, thefts, covetousness, wickedness, deceit, lasciviousness, an evil eye, blasphemy, pride, foolishness. All these evil things come from within, and defile the man."

(MARK 7:20-24)

The following statement of Jesus shows how faith in God, such as Abraham had, is not only righteousness but also the means of Salvation:

"How hardly shall they that have riches enter into the kingdom of God! And the disciples were astonished at His words, But Jesus answereth again, and saith unto them, Children, how hard is it for them that trust in riches to enter into the kingdom of God! It is easier for a camel to go through the eye of a needle than for a rich man to enter into the kingdom of God."

(MARK 10:23-25)

This does not mean the riches in themselves, but rather the attachment for and **faith in them** or anything transitory. It is our own attitude toward a thing that makes it good or bad for us. Of itself it is neither good nor bad, but our abuse of it makes it so. It is the desires and indulgences which constitute the evil.

"(Be ye free from the love of money;) Let your conversation be without covetousness; and be content with such things as ye have: for he hath said, I will never leave thee, nor forsake thee. So that (with good courage we say) we may boldly say, The Lord is my helper, and I will not fear what man shall do unto me."

(HEB. 13:5-6)

"Circumcision is nothing, and uncircumcision is nothing, but the **keeping** of the Commandments of God. Let every man abide in the same calling wherein he was called."

(I COR. 7:19-20)

"But he is a Jew, which is one **inwardly**; and circumcision is that of the heart, **in the spirit** and not in the letter; whose praise is not of men, but of God."

(Rom. 2:29)

"For we are the circumcision which worship God in the **Spirit**, and rejoice in Christ Jesus, and have no confidence in the flesh." (PHIL. 3:3)

"in whom also ye are circumcised with the circumcision made without hands, in putting off the body of the sins of the flesh, by the circumcision of Christ."

(COL. 2:11)

It is the *desire* and the lower mind which must be circumcised in the consciousness of Christ Jesus, as He surrendered all even unto the death on the Cross.

"Cometh this blessedness then upon the circumcision only, or upon the uncircumcision also? for we say that faith was reckoned to Abraham for righteousness. How was it then reckoned? when he was in circumcision, or in uncircumcision? Not in circumcision, but in uncircumcision. And he received the sign of circumcision, a seal of the righteousness of the faith which **he had yet** being uncircumcised; that he might be the father of all them that believe, though they be not circumcised; that righteousness might be imputed unto them also; And the father of circumcision to them who are not of the circumcision only, but who also walk in the steps of that faith of our father Abraham, which **he had** being **yet** uncircumcised."

"For the promise, that he should be the heir of the world, was not to Abraham, or to his seed, through the law, but through the righteousness of faith. For if they which are of the law be heirs, faith is made void, and the promise made of none effect: Because the law worketh wrath: for where no law is, there is no transgression. Therefore it is of faith, that it might be by grace; to the end the promise might be sure to all the seed; not to that only which is of the law, but to that also which is of the faith of Abraham; who is the father of us all, (As it is written, I have made thee a father of many nations,) before him whom he believed, even God, who quickeneth the dead, and calleth those things which be not as though they were."

"Who against hope believed in hope, that he might become the father of many nations, according to that which was spoken, So shall thy seed be. And being not weak in faith, he considered not his own body now dead, when he was about an hundred years old, neither yet the deadness of Sarah's womb; He staggered not at the promise of God through unbelief; but was strong in faith, giving glory to God; And that, being fully persuaded that, what he had promised, he was able also to perform. And therefore it was imputed to him for righteousness. Now it was not written for his sake alone, that it was imputed to him; But for us also, to whom it shall be imputed, if we believe on him that raised up Jesus our Lord from the dead;"

(ROMANS 4:9-24)

These quotations show definitely how the Inner Life of Devotion and Faith is the essence of all Mystic Writings, and the **actual practice** of these qualities was once taught in every religion. It is not the form, but **living the life** which yields results. Mind and emotions must both be purified and co-operate with the soul in following the Path that leadeth unto Life Eternal.

The teachings of the Saints of the past and present put all emphasis on faith, devotion and love as the best method of controlling the mind and senses. Mere blind faith does not do it, but **faith coupled with effort** through devotion to the Supreme Being, through the Beloved Master on this earth who is already in Mystic Union with Him in the unheard of heights of inner penetration and Realization.

Under the able guidance of a true living Saint, disciples are able to proceed directly from the center of consciousness between the eyes instead of first taking the consciousness to the lower centers and proceeding upward from there. The Saints do not advocate suppression, but rather facing and understanding a situation. Suppression never solves anything but merely postpones the solving of a problem, and it only increases in size and becomes more involved in the meantime. Saints make it possible for us to tread the Path by constantly calling our attention to the Goal. And when our attention is on that which is more desirable, the lesser or lower is automatically conquered.

The energy is centered wherever the attention is fixed. That is why the Psalmist calls upon all followers to:

"Lift up your heads, O ye gates; and be ye lift up, ye everlasting doors; and the King of glory shall come in."

(PSALMS 24:7)

This refers to the mind current and the attention current of the soul, until they blend with the Shabd Current.

Most methods of practice start with the lowest of the six chakras in the body. Even in the time of Saint Kabir, this method was still used. By Concentration, the energy of the soul's sensory currents, the psychic prana, was to be collected first in the lowest or Muladhara chakra, then taken up, step by step — after many years of hard labor and suffering to the Ajna chakra referred to as the Tisra Til by the Saints.

This center between the eyes is where the consciousness normally dwells when the individual is in the wakeful state. According to the teachings of the Saints, it is also the link into the super-conscious realms. In fact, the Saints refer to the body as being made up of two parts — the conscious and the unconscious. Everything below the eyes is unconscious, and what is above the eyes is conscious. Therefore, the Saints teach us how to proceed from this first center of consciousness (between the eyes) without first wasting time and energy on the lower centers.

This first center of consciousness, the Tisra Til, which was the final goal in some methods, is spoken of by Jesus as the narrow gate, as fine as a camel's hair. Our consciousness dwells at this lotus center of the white and gray petals. In sleep the consciousness descends to the throat center and below this point into the subconscious regions of the lower chakras. In deep sleep it sinks down to the heart or abdominal center, and that individual is hard to rouse.

Nothing is learned or controlled by unconsciousness. The yogi tries to bring consciousness into these lower centers by concentrating the mind energy and attention there consciously. Some spend hundreds of years at it, and some thousands. This is only a method of control, and the mind has a way of reverting to old tracks under stress of temptation or in fits of anger. Nothing lasting is gained spiritually by concentrating on the lower centers. Besides, the practice is too severe and drastic to be attempted in this age, and it is utterly unsuited for the western mind and body. Until the center between the eyes is crossed **consciously**, the Narrow Way is not found, and the real upward Spiritual Journey has not yet started.

In the year 1861 the Great Saint, Swami Ji of Agra, began to teach a system of release for the soul, by starting all concentration at this Tisra Til center of consciousness,

and going in and up from there. He taught His followers how to go in and up at the very center which was the
final goal for those who practiced concentration at the
lower, centers. He said, why go down first from the center
of consciousness, when you can draw the energy up to it
from all the lower centers by the method of concentration
taught by the Saints. In this way not only much time and
effort are saved, but the Goal is also much higher than that
reached by previous methods and revelations.

The Saints and True Masters or Mystics are the only
living authority for this sublime Mystic Road of the Inward and Upward Journey of the Soul. This Journey is
known as Spiritual Transport. When, out of their great
love and mercy, They take on a disciple, They assume the
responsibility of guiding and protecting that soul until
it has attained God-Realization in the Eternal Region of
Sach Khand. The soul may become wayward and forget
the Master, but the Master never leaves the soul.

The progress of the soul is made in proportion to his
past *karmas*, coupled with the Lord's Grace, and through
his faith and devotion in the effort made during concentration, as he has been taught, to raise his consciousness
internally to highest regions, as well as the degree of humility and service to mankind in his daily life. His outer
conduct in his dealings with others also improves in proportion to his inner progress.

The present or Kriyaman karma of the soul is also a
factor which must be fulfilled; that is, through the help of
the Master, all accounts are to be settled and all debts paid.
From the time of Initiation, the Master takes full charge of
the karma of the disciple. If the disciple surrenders himself to the Master, He sees to it that at no time is the load
greater than he can bear, but enough to pay the debt and
learn the lesson of humility and love. That is the main objective in paying off karma. And only with the help of a
living Master can we do so without at the same time in-
curring new debts.

Karma is not really a punishment, but rather a necessary remedy and measure to re-establish the balance of justice and the equilibrium of forces at work. The Master takes care of the disciple and balances and apportions all his *karma* to suit his needs, so that he can make the fastest progress possible in any one life if the love for the Master is great.

Some souls still have latent desires and attachments which they cannot as yet **willingly** surrender. The Saints never use force, nor do They speed the pace any more than the disciple is ready and willing to travel. The Great Master, Sawan Singh Maharaj ji used to say, "Slow and steady wins the race."

It may take three life-times, but never more than four, to reach the Goal of God-Realization. Each soul sets the measure of his own progress by the degree of surrender to the Will of God in all things and his effort at devotional practice, together with his love and service to his Master or Guru.

Some minds are less pliable and co-operative than others. And the great love of a few sincere followers is also by the Grace and Compassion of the Guru. Mush can be forgiven *when they love much*, for love fulfills all laws and all measures. Love lights the lamp of final understanding or real knowledge. Love is a consuming fire of all lesser things. It is a vortex of attraction which raises all into its own center of being and Reality. It is beyond the mind and all temporal measures. It is beyond the mind and all temporal measures. It is the Essence out of which all things were created, and it is the finality of Home, Peace and Bliss in the Eternal Regions.

CHAPTER X
THE STORIES OF JONAH AND THE WHALE AND OF JOB, THE BEHEMOTH AND THE LEVIATHAN

The story of Jonah and the Whale has probably raised more controversy in the world than any other story ever written. It has also tested many a person's faith in the Bible. The descriptions of the Behemoth and the Leviathan have also been a seventh wonder, hard to place and understand in any literal, physical interpretation of a Sacred Text. Similar is the experience of Job, and God's way with him through agency of Satan.

Both, Jonah and Job were righteous men who feared God and served Him. Their experiences were almost like those of Odysseus, the Greek leader in the Trojan War, on his homeward journey after the war. These and similar stories all have much inner meaning and value in the journey of the soul, **lost on earth**.

To interpret these stories as mere physical, historic, accounts misses the point they intend to convey to the students of the deeper aspects in Life, which deals not merely with forms and objects in time and space. To ask someone to translate and interpret music when he has no experience in it nor love for it, would be a similar situation. Even written works on arts, mechanics or chemistry can be properly translated only by someone who knows the art with which it deals, through personal experience. Words can only convey what they mean to us.

The same holds true in the study of the Inner Life and the translations of all the Sacred and Mystic writings. Also, it should not be forgotten that the **secrets were meant to be guarded**, and were deliberately covered up when written about, for the sake of safety and security. These things were live topics in olden days and mush discussed. Yet they could not be openly discussed nor written about because those doing so were liable to severe punishment if what they propounded did not fit into the scope of understanding of the ruling powers.

Parables, myths, fables, fairy tales and stories with a hidden inner meaning were the accepted ways of teaching and writing Spiritual Truth is the days of old. Jesus Himself taught in parables. Even today, teaching in similes, metaphors, or by comparison with things men know and understand, is a favorite method of the Saints and Mystics of the East.

"Now the word of (Jehovah) the Lord came unto Jonah."
(JONAH 1:1)

This clearly indicates that Jonah was not an ordinary man, but a prophet who could talk with Jehovah. He was a mystic who had inner work to do in the Father's House, as Jesus also spoke of His work, according to the four gospels.

"Arise, go to Nineveh, that great city, and cry against it."
(JONAH 1:2)

In Biblical times there was a city called Nineveh, a town called Joppa, and a city called Tarshish, to which Jonah fled. But how could a prophet escape from Jehovah's order by merely going to another place on earth? It is evident that some deeper meaning was implied in Jehovah's command. Jonah understood this, but instead of going up as ordered, he went down to Joppa, in the opposite direction.

The names of these cities have a value and meaning similar to the places mentioned in Revelations by St. John, when he described the seven centers in the ethereal body of man as the seven churches. When these are read in that light of understanding, as a message or mystic method of going from one to the next higher and taking the consciousness there, it is a literal conquering of those places and becoming a ruler of that station of Life in one's own house, and of that same energy in the universe.

Jehovah was not only the Deity, but also the Initiator and Hierophant of Jonah, the disciple. He had told Jonah to go up one station further in this consciousness of

development on the tree of his Inner Life. Nineveh represented the fiery, navel chakra, called the Manipura Chakra
in the system of Yoga. Jonah was to "cry out against it"
meaning that Jehovah gave him the *matra* or words to re-
peat in order to conquer that citadel. This order is similar to
the instruction Joshua gave to the children of Israel when
they were marching around Jericho, and he told them to
shout with a great shout at the sound of the trumpet, as
he had been previously told by Jehovah, and the city fell
when they did as instructed. (JOSHUA 6)

Again, it is the mystic way of conquering the mind and
its lower emotional stages or stations of function, which is
referred to in such quotations. Actually, the repetition is
done mentally, with the **attention** of the mind. When this is
done under the guidance of a living, true Master, then conquest and control are assured. It is the concentration of the
mind energy at a given point that is the heavy armament
which conquers the citadel of the lower emotional phases of
the mind and their etheric centers or chakras, the whirling
energies in that area; also the city of the Giants (the egos)
when the inner reach is high enough to conquer the self.

But Jonah fled from the presence of Jehovah and went
down to Joppa to take a ship to Tarshish: In other words,
Jonah retreated to the next lower chakra, the Swadishtana
or Brahma Chakra, which is watery in its essence. *Taking
a ship* means riding on those watery energy currents. He
must have been frightened, like the Children of Israel were
by the Giants in the Promised Land. So Jonah set out for
further retreat to Tarshish, the Muladhara Chakra.

Jonah 1:4-16 describes the storm at sea and how Jonah
was cast overboard. Each energy current of the body carries or conducts the consciousness of the mind, much the
same as a ship carries passengers or cargo.

"Now the Lord (Jehovah) had prepared a great fish to
swallow up Jonah. And Jonah was in the belly of the
fish three days and three nights."

(JONAH 1:17)

The twelve signs of the zodiac symbolize the finer energy currents which flow over the main body areas and centers. The Brahma chakra is in the pelvis, and the currents of the sign of Pisces, the negative pole of the Brahma chakra, are represented by the feet and are pictured as two fishes, one swimming upward and one downward. It was this downward, sensory current which became huge and powerful like a monster, and swallowed up the fleeing, sinking Jonah. Having loss his own control of that energy wave, it was powerful beyond all normal proportions, and he could not extricate himself for three days.

"Then Jonah prayed unto the Lord (Jehovah) his God out of the fish's belly." (JONAH 2:1)

"Out of the belly of Sheol" is also mentioned in the text, *Sheol* meaning depth, pit or hell. And Jonah's prayer was heard. Jehovah extricated him from the clutches of this huge watery every monster or fish, which was the downward current in Jonah's flight of consciousness on his Tree of Life within himself.

"And **the word** of the Lord (Jehovah) came unto Jonah the second time, saying, Arise, go unto Nineveh." (JONAH 3:1-2)

Then Jonah arose or rose up on the upward attention current and arrived at Nineveh. The people or the energies in the city of Nineveh, the Manipura Chakra, did not oppose Jonah as he had feared. Instead, they repented and fasted (3:5-10). Therefore, the city was not destroyed nor conquered by Jonah as Jehovah had commanded him to prophesy. And Jonah was displeased and practically told his Hierophant that was what he had expected it would all amount to when he was yet in his own country before he fled to Tarshish (JONAH 4:1-4).

"So Jonah went out of the city, and sat on the east side of the city." (JONAH 4:5)

"Sitting on the east side" explains his position—his attention—in the sensory currents on the anterior sensory part or side of his body. There he sat in consciousness and meditated on the fate of the city, his own chakra.

"And the Lord (Jehovah) God prepared a gourd, and made it to come up over Jonah, that it might be a shadow over his head, to deliver him from his grief."

(JONAH 4:6)

Jehovah, in His kindness, taught Jonah a lesson, by shading him from the burning sun in this fiery chakra within the body.

"But God prepared a worm when the morning rose the next day, and it smote the gourd, that it withered."

(JONAH 4:7)

The Hierophant withdrew this protection of Grace from Jonah, from the fiery heat of the solar plexus, the sun in Nineveh, the fiery chakra of the digestive energy, the Manipura Chakra. Yogis who concentrate on the five lower chakras of the body, usually sit immersed in water when they get to that stage because of the heat that is developed there. Jonah had to be made to feel this extreme heat because he did not act with implicit faith at the first command of Jehovah to go up and conquer Nineveh, the next higher center of consciousness. Instead, Jonah doubted Jehovah and fled. So he fell lower into the clutches of the negative power of that region. Even then, he doubted and watched while he attempted to concentrate. His concentration and devotion were neither steadfast nor complete.

The symbol of the ruling nature at the watery Brahma chakra is always a huge water animal with a snout. This is the mystery of the whale of emotions which swallows up humans in its passion and spews them out again, when the finer current of devotion raises and lifts up the soul, in answer to its cries unto God. In Hindu symbolism, the whale is referred to as *Makra*, the great fish. The Muladhara or earthy chakra, situated below the watery chakra, is always pictured as an elephant, and is symbolically called *Ganesh*.

This brings to light the fact that God Himself does not extricate us from the mire nor does He prevent us from further descending into it until we ourselves wish to be liberated, and by so doing direct our consciousness upward by thinking of Him. If God in His infinite mercy does so much for us when we merely think of Him long enough to cry unto Him for help, how much more help He would give us if we could keep Him in mind always, in gratitude and thanksgiving for His blessings as well as when we finally realize the need of His help!

When we realize that by our own thoughts, words and deeds, most of us have forfeited every right of happiness before we came to this earth, then we can begin to comprehend to some extent the scope of His boundless Mercy and Love in showing us the way to return to the realm of Eternal Bliss. That in turn instills in us the feeling of gratitude and devotion, which ultimately leads to true love.

Because Jonah doubted Jehovah's Word, he was taught a severe lesson and did not conquer Nineveh to live in it, but he sat outside of it in meditation until a future time, when he would have sufficient faith and devotion to turn to the Lord instead of attempting to do everything with his own mind, will and ego.

The account of Jonah in the Bible is a story of Initiation. In this case the disciple was swallowed by the dragon of the threshold, symbolized by the whale. He was saved by Jehovah who was his Guru and who initiated him. The Holy Spirit of the Lord, also called the Holy Shabd, the Holy Ghost, etc. is always the real Redeemer regardless who the Master, High Priest or Initiator may be.

The reason for Jonah's fall is given in the book of Jonah, chapter 4. In a fit of anger, he listed to his own mind and was convinced beforehand of **his** way. Whenever one deems the mind above God's implicit instructions, that disciple has already fallen from grace and is caught in the meshes of his own **mind, the Behemoth of old.** Faith in the Master and love for Him are the only safeguards on the Spiritual Journey.

CHAPTER XI
THE STORY OF JOB

The reason for referring to the two stories in the title of the previous chapter was to point out the similarity in character of both righteous men, but mainly because of the symbolism of the beasts mentioned therein. The beasts represent the energies in the **psychic** prana, cosmically, and in the individual whirl and flow of prana as chakras in the composite human makeup. The whale which swallowed up Jonah, compares with the *Dragons of the Threshold* or *Makra* the great fish, in other Sacred Writings.

Chapter 41 in the book of Job gives a description of the Leviathan, a similar principle to the Whale in the story of Jonah. It symbolizes the psychic prana, or sex energy of the Brahma Chakra, in the Apan Tattwa of Water as its field of action. Jonah's Whale is a mild description when compared to this tremendous force, as the Dweller at the Threshold of Life, who guards the Tree of Life; the same as the Cherubim guard the gates of Paradise against all who would enter. In the book of Job, Jehovah Himself gives a good description of this energy, as a beast called the Leviathan. (Job 41)

The interpreters make a plain crocodile out of Job's Leviathan, and hope to draw it out with a fish hook or pierce through the jaws in external prowess as a physical feat. Eternal values lie within us; so also the real dramas of life take place within. Externally, they are but passing incidents of accomplishment.

In this account of the story of Job we began with the end in order to clarify the mystery of the beasts. The first chapter in the book of Job indicates that he also was an upright man, feared God and could converse with Jehovah. He was very rich in the possession of animals and other material wealth. His spiritual stature of advancement was seven sons and three daughters—meaning seven positive gains in consciousness through inner meditation, minus three negative ones, as unconquered chakras. That brought

Job up to the heart chakra, through his great devotion. But the Manipura Chakra was not entirely conquered, as is inferred by the many feasts his sons and daughters gave, which worried Job (JOB 1:4-5).

The subsequent test he went through confirmed his faith and gave him back his seven sons and three daughters, on a higher octave, as the fairest in the land. Then all efforts in his concentration were more spiritually inclined than before, because of his experience in patience and humility. His steadfast faith, devotion and humility carried him through all of it. He then became twice as strong in the lower chakras, symbolized by the number of oxen, camels, sheep and she asses he was given. It is all symbolism, which endures longer than the accounts of any physical happening, because it is beyond the physical happening, because it is beyond the physical realm and symbolizes the conquest of the soul in a greater field of consciousness.

"As many as I love, I rebuke and chasten: be zealous, therefore, and repent." (REV. 3:19)

A curious statement is made in chapter 1:6 to 13, which has puzzled many a firm believer and made him wonder; namely, that Satan presents himself among the sons of God, to Jehovah, and Jehovah talks to him and allows him to test and plague Job, His righteous devotee. Nothing is written in the entire Bible which could explain or clarify this action of Jehovah God. Only the teachings of the True Saints can throw light on this veiled mystery, to enrich the understanding of the Bible as a Mystic Text. This will be taken up in the next chapter, but it might be well to mention here that Satan doesn't have to pay much attention to the masses in order to keep them within his prison, because they do such a good job of it themselves by allowing the mind and senses to keep them enslaved and imprisoned; however, once the soul has cried out unto God and made the effort to literally work its way out, and has reached the threshold from where it may consciously tread the Path to Liberation, then Satan really gets to work, and only those who pass this test are actually ready to go up to the next step.

"Then entered Satan into Judas." (LUKE 22:3)

"Simon, Simon, behold, Satan hath desired to have you, that he may sift you as wheat: but I prayed for thee, that faith fail not." (LUKE 22:31-32)

"Take ye heed, watch and pray: for ye know not when the time is." (MARK 13:33)

Similar admonitions are given in I Thes. 5:6-10 as well as in Job 29:23, etc. The struggle of the soul goes on.

To sum up the story of Job, let us state that he was a mystic who was devoted to God, He had done very well in all his progress of raising his consciousness upward on the Tree of Life within himself, and remained humble. But Satan, the mind principle, the tempter, assails all initiates, even as Jesus was tempted in the wilderness. That is when the real weakness shows up, if there is any left at all, whether it is to rule or to enjoy the possessions, or even to glory in good deeds, virtues or ascetic accomplishments. Temptation itself is not a sin, but when we so much as **entertain** the thought, or succumb to it, that is the sin or weak spot which needs to be overcome by sublimation and central attention to Reality, through greater devotion to the Lord, the Savior or the Master in human form.

In the case of Jesus, the temptation proved His greatness, but in the case of Job, there were some old karmic debts to be paid and as a result, he suffered much in his renunciation and preparation for onward progress. His own mind fought him, as is illustrated by his friends who acted as his advisers. Three faculties of his own mind were against him; namely, his *manas* (the thinker or faculty of thinking) his *chit* (mind substance of memory); and his *ahankara* (the ego or "I" faculty) were not yet conquered. Only his *buddhi* remained steadfast in reason and discrimination and lighted his way to the soul energies of humility, devotion, faith and complete surrender of the self. Because of this, he succeeded in his initiation and was rewarded and praised by Jehovah.

This is the true symbolism of a Mystic Initiation. It would fill all the requirements of an ideal devotee of any religion or creed. Of such a universal quality is the Truth of Mysticism. Faith, devotion, humility self-surrender and love make up the keynote. All these qualities are in every person, if he but chooses to use them and work in the Father's Vineyard instead of that of his own ego. Jesus said:

"For strait is the gate, and narrow is the way, which leadeth unto life and few there be that find it."

(MAT. 7:14)

"Not every one that saith unto me, Lord, Lord, shall enter into the kingdom of heaven; but he that **doeth** the will of my Father which is in heaven."

(MAT. 7:21)

"For if ye live after the flesh, ye shall die: but if ye through the Spirit do mortify the deeds of the by the body, ye shall live. For as many as are led by the Spirit of God, they are the sons of God."

(ROMANS 8:13-14)

The Way of Life or the Path of Initiation is similar in principle in most religions and Sacred Texts. The factors which need uplifting or raising up in man are the same all over. The gates which must be lifted up are the doors of the *chakras* and the mind. The Saints refer to them as cups placed upside down, and which must be placed rightside up before they can be filled with the Nectar of Nam and Shabd, the Holy Sound Current from above.

The everlasting doors are the soul energies. When raised up and joined to the Sound Current, the King of Glory enters into the consciousness of that devotee. The Holy Spirit is indeed the Lord of Hosts. (Psalms 24:7 to the end of chapter)

"For I know that my redeemer liveth, and that he shall stand at the latter day upon the earth: And though after my skin worms destroy this body, yet in my flesh shall I see God: Whom I shall see for myself, and mine eyes shall behold, and not another; though my reins be consumed within me."

(JOB 19:25, 26, 27)

"I know that my redeemer liveth" said Job with a firm conviction, in all his trials. This was **long before** the Christian era. This is the knowledge of the Logos or the Holy Word which is the One Living Energy Current by which all things were created and involuted. It is also the One Current and River which flows out of the Throne of God and back to God:

"And he shewed me a pure river of water of life, clear as crystal, proceeding out of the throne of God and of the Lamb." (REV. 22:1)

"So shall my word be that goeth forth out of my mouth: **it shall not return unto me void**, but it shall accomplish that which I please, and it shall prosper in the thing whereto I sent it. For ye shall go out with joy, and be led forth with peace: the mountains and the hills shall break forth before you into singing, and all the trees of the field shall clap their hands. Instead of the thorn shall come up the fir tree, and instead of the brier shall come up the myrtle tree: and it shall be to the LORD for a name, for an everlasting sign that shall not be cut off."

(ISAIAH 55:11, 12, 13)

This mystery was known to devotees of the Lord in many lands throughout the ages. Jehovah himself talked to these devout souls, as stated in many places in the Scriptures, such as Ex. 33:9; Deut. 5:24; Ezekiel 3:22-25, etc.

"Then the Lord answered Job out of the Whirl-wind, and said," (JOB. 38:1)

The Spirit of Jehovah is this Holy Shabd Current, the Voice of God or the Word. It is the Eternal Unfathomable Treasure. It is God's Decree and purpose of creation that It should be embodied by many souls as living temples and saints of the Lord. The soul longs for this Living Water and Nectar of God. The Saviors, Redeemers, Prophets and Messengers which the Lord sent into the world from time immemorial, were all embodiments of the Word or Logos, the Sound Current in various degrees of perfection, in different ages.

To limit God's creative energy current to one person only, is a mere mortal concept. Even Jesus said that he would send the Holy Ghost or Comforter which would teach the disciples all things.

"And I will pray the Father, and he shall give you another Comforter, that he may abide with you for ever."
(John 14:16)

"But the Comforter which is the Holy Ghost, whom the Father will send in my name, he shall teach you all things, and bring all things to your remembrance, whatever I have said unto you."
(JOHN 14:26 *similarly*, JOHN 15:26)

"He that believeth on me, the works that I do shall he do also; and greater works than these shall he do; because I go unto my Father."   (JOHN 14:12)

The gospel also teaches that we shall be like him when we see Him as He is:

"Beloved, now are we the sons of God, and it doth not yet appear what we shall be: but we know that, when he shall appear, we shall be like him; for we shall see him as he is."   (I JOHN. 3:2)

"And they shall see his face; and his name shall be in their foreheads."   (REV. 22:4)

So it is very evident that this Redeemer Energy Current is greater than any one person who embodies it. By it only can perfection be reached and salvation attained. Jesus said:

"Be ye therefore perfect, even as your Father which is in heaven is perfect."   (MAT. 5:45)

How else could this come about **but by the Lord's own Essence?**

Man can come to God through only this **One Son, the Logos, the Word** which is the Holy Shabd, the Holy Spirit, the Holy Ghost, the Comforter, the Gift of the Lord to creation. This is the greatest Treasure.

This Divine Energy Current of the Holy Word, the Holy Logos, **is** the Lamb of God slain from the very foundation of the world.

> "All things (and worlds) were made by him; and without him was not anything made that was made. In him was life; and the life was the light of men."
>
> (JOHN 1:3, 4)

> "This is the stone which was set at nought of you builders, which is become the head of the corner. Neither is there salvation in any other; for there is none other **Name** under heaven given among men, whereby we must be saved." (ACTS 4:11, 12)

There are so many references to this Holy Spirit of God as the Name, the Word, the Holy Ghost, etc. that it surely must have been a Reality to the inspired writers of the Holy Scriptures. (*See also Psalms* 20:1 & 5; 22:22; 72:17; 111:9; 138:2; *Isaiah* 63:12; *Zechariah* 14:9; *Micah* 4:5; *Hebrews* 2:12; etc., etc.)

The prophets in the Old Testament surely knew of this Well of Living Waters of their father, Abraham. It was also known in other lands and in other ages. Students of the Mysteries knew it as THE LOST WORD or THE LOST CHORD and symphony of life. Saints have always taught this Great Truth which was not limited to any one embodiment of this Holy Word or Shabd, the Eternal Sound Current also called the Logos. **He is the One in all**.

What we are trying to attain by striving to build temples, pyramids, churches, mosques, etc., as dwelling places for God, has already been fulfilled by embodying His living Word Current as the One Redeemer Energy in each human form or body. This is the real Temple of God designed by Him for that **one purpose only**.

> "What? Know ye not that your body is the temple of the Holly Ghost which is in you, which ye have of God, and ye are not your own?" (I COR. 6:19)

"Know ye not that ye are the temple of God, and that the spirit of God dwelleth in you?"

(I COR. 3:16)

"And what agreement hath the temple of God with idols? For ye are the temple of the living God; as God hath said, I will dwell in them, and walk in them; and I will be their God, and walk in them; and I will be their God, and they shall be my people."

(II COR. 6:16)

"Wherefore come out from among them, and be ye separate, saith the Lord, and touch not the unclean thing; and I will receive you. And will be a father unto you, and ye shall be my sons and daughters, saith the Lord Almighty." (II COR. 6:17, 18)

While the above quotations are from St. Paul in the New Testament, this deep mystic understanding was known to Job and other patriarchs in times of old. Truth is in the heart of things and beings. Pure like a mountain stream in the heights of devotion and Love, it loses that luster in the valley of the mind and sense consciousness. The mind's effort to purify itself and keep itself pure is a limitation to one person only, and even when achieved, the results cannot be lasting. But God's Love, Truth and all eternal verities cannot be limited by only one and, when realized, are everlasting. All God's children are in need of this Realization. It must be lived to be embodied and known consciously; even as a simple plant embodies the energy of the earth, the water, the air and the sunshine to grow to maturity and bring forth fruit, so souls embody this Eternal Essence which is God's and is God, and thus only can they become perfect as He is.

CHAPTER XII
SATAN AS THE ROOT OF EVIL

"Now there was a day when the sons of God came to present themselves before the Lord (Jehovah), and Satan came also among them. And the Lord (Jehovah) said unto Satan, Whence comest thou? Then Satan answered the Lord (Jehovah), and said, From going to and from in the earth, and from walking up and down in it."

(JOB 1:6-7)

This account about Satan puts him in an entirely different light and relationship than is usually believed and taught. If he is completely evil, how can he mingle with the sons of God and appear before Jehovah, like one of them? Also, if he is the devil, the incarnation of evil itself, how can he gain entrance into heaven? Is not hell supposed to be the abode of the devil?

Satan is Lucifer, the fallen angel who was the morning star of creation. **He is the personification of ego**, pride and lust for power, and as such he is the adversary of God. Ego is the beginning and root of all evil. It is a mind process which separates man's consciousness from God-consciousness. It acts as a wall between man and God. The greater the ego, the thinker the wall and the longer will it take that soul to reach God-Realization. Not that God is limited, for He sees and knows all, but the soul's consciousness cannot penetrate this thick wall without His help, which can only be obtained from a true Master who has Himself penetrated the wall and is in conscious union with the Supreme Being. It is the ego which is the root of all selfishness and its subsequent suffering and disintegrating forces, with endless lesser evils which result from forceful self-will and which only tend to make this wall of separation thicker.

Satan is not the evil which is called the devil, nor the disintegrating forces of evil in their lower aspects and details. The devils and obsessing evil entities, and countless isolated evils, have all been credited to Satan and laid at his door. But this is a total mistake, due to the lack of knowledge of what goes on in the higher energy realms or how temporal things came to be. Satan is still a son of God, although fallen; **but he cannot return** to the Father's House because of ego, self-interest and pride. However, he is still a powerful prince and the ruler of many a realm and worlds. This was plainly indicated when he tried to tempt Jesus by promising Him all the kingdoms of the world and the glory of them if He would fall down and worship him.

So also does Satan tempt sincere devotees on the Path, and even goes so far as to impersonate the devotee's *Guru* within; however, a sincere devotee who follows the instructions of his living Master cannot be deceived, as he has been told how to distinguish the real from the false within and without. But even the false within is so much more wonderful than what we have in this world, that unless a devotee is firmly established in His Love, he may be so engrossed that he may not wish to make the test, and so he is deceived. In the case of a disciple who has a genuine Master, the absorption in the false would only be temporary, if at all, as the Master sets him right as soon as the necessary lesson has been learned.

In Mat. 4:8-9 the same confusion exists; namely, translating the word as '*devil*' instead of '*Satan*'. But in verse 10, Jesus Himself addresses him properly and says:

"Get thee hence, Satan."   (MAT. 4:10)

It is quite obvious that a misinterpretation exists in referring to Satan as the devil in the previous verses. Jesus was a Prince who could not be tempted by small devils; neither could a devil offer Him the kingdoms of the world.

In the Christian world, the great Mystic, Jacob Boehme, came closest to telling the real story about Satan. He wrote that after creating the beautiful morning star called Lucifer, the Prince Lucifer came to pay homage to the Lord God, the Supreme Creator. He entered the magnificent royal palace of the Lord, where everything was serene and peaceful, and waited in a beautiful room that was not occupied by any one. Then he heard a sweet, childlike voice saying, "You are welcome, Lucifer." At this gentleness, Lucifer's ego began to expand in thoughts of what he could do to govern here by his might, etc. By that very thought, he himself set loose such forces that there were loud crashes of thunder and lightning which hurled Lucifer out into space, and he has been traveling there ever since.

In the Teachings of the Saints of the East, a much more complete account is given of all the events, sequences, stations and principalities and powers, administrators and rulers in the various realms, and an explanation is given for it all so it can be comprehended. Only saints like Swami Ji, Baba Ji, Maharaj Sawan Singh Ji and others who have traversed the highest regions of the Eternal Realm can give an account of the four topmost or Supreme Regions.

The Eternal Region of Sach Khand, also called Sat Lok, is the gateway to the Supreme Immortal Regions of Alakh, Agam and Anami Lok. While 'Anami' means 'Nameless', it is also referred to as Radha Swami. In Sach Khand, the Region below Alakh Lok, dwells the Lord Sat Purush, the Creator and Ruler of that Region and all other regions below it. While each region below has its own creator and ruler, yet each in turn is subordinate and draws its energy for creating and sustaining, from the one above it. So it goes on down from the Eternal Spiritual, to the Spiritual, to the Spiritual-Material which is also called the Mental or Causal Plane, then to the Astral and to the Physical Planes.

Saint say that in that immense and beautiful region of Sach Khand the intensity of the vibration and Light is so high that one hair of the Lord Sat Purush has more brilliance than the light of millions of suns and moons. This of course does not really refer to a hair as we know it, as no physical bodies or hair exist on that high plane, but to the emanations of Light radiating from the Lord Sat Purush. The Lord Sat Purush is the Supreme Creator of all that can be enumerated in all creations from Sach Khand on down.

According to the Saints, it is beyond the scope of words to even begin to describe the Eternal Regions of Sach Khand, Alakh, Agam and Anami. Mortal language can convey only hints here and there.

The great Saint Kabir who flourished in the fifteenth century wrote that the Lord Sat Purush had sixteen sons. They all dwelled in the Sat Lok Region of Bliss. But one son did not feel quite at home or satisfied there with all the Bliss and Love. He had a latent, inner desire to create regions and realms like his Father did, except that he wanted to create them for himself, so he could rule them and have power, was the 'adi' or original karma of that son. The first desire brings all the other subsequent karmas with it, as it brings all the other subsequent karmas with it, as it becomes involved and entangled in energy essences and substance of spirit, mind, emotions and matter.

The desire to be separate from God created an 'otherness' or an adverseness to the Unity of the Lord in the Eternal Regions. It broke the first commandment completely; however, that was before the commandments were handed down. This son of Sat Purush also upset for himself the perfect equilibrium by which things can be created and endured eternally in those Eternal Regions. "Absolute Unity" is the final and supreme reason for all things". (A Hermetic Axiom) When the perfect unity is destroyed, then the One Essence of that vortex of Love is mingled with other essences and less perfect reasons for their existence, which cannot endure. And so mortality enters the realm of creation.

In the two spiritual regions below Sach Khand the duration of the Manwantaras[1] or Yugas and Maha Pralayas is immense; but the Grand Dissolution reaches up to Sach. Khand just the same, because from below up to that region

---

[1] 'Manwantaras' are periods of manifestation or creations. 'Yuga' are ages. 'Pralaya' is dissolution and 'Maha Pralaya' is great dissolution or period of cessation of all existence below the Eternal Reality of Sach Khand.

there is impurity in the One Essence — or rather, covering that One Essence — which impurity must be resolved and removed before the Essence can be One with the One in Eternity. The lower the region, the greater the impurity or mixture with matter. Nothing except that which is of the Pure Spirit can reach and remain in Sach Khand.

The name of the one son of Sat Purush who had this desire of creating and ruling was '*Kal*' or Satan according to the teachings of the Saints. (Kal means '*time*', '*mind*' and outgoing energy bound by self-identification or ego. It also means '*death*'.) Since there were also myriads of other souls like him in their desire to create, who were left over from the previous grand cycles of creations and cessations, and who would benefit by this lower creation in which to work out their desires and ideas in realms of denser substances, the permission was granted Kal to go out into space and create. Thus he became a bright morning star or sun, more brilliant and potent than the others in his fiery trail of descent from great internal heights. There are four regions in the Eternal Realm from which creation originally proceeded and from which souls descended. They all brought a share of this energy with them for experience in the descent, called also involution.

So Kal left the Eternal Region of Sach Khand, as a proud creator and power in all the regions below it. The energy that came from the higher regions by the vast influx of souls, gave Kal more essence and energy to work with. However, Kal cannot create a soul. Sat Purush entrusted a vast but limited number of souls to Kal, for whom he may create all kinds of bodies, placing them first in one and then in another, according to each one's Karma. He can make all kinds of vehicles or bodies for the soul, as long as it is within his realm, but he cannot make a soul.

The first region created below the Eternal One of Sach Khand was Bhanwar Gupha, which means whirling caves of Energy Essence.

Below the region of Bhanwar Gupha there is a great void of space with most intense darkness, as an antithesis to the Great Light above.

Those who have come under the guidance of a true Master while in human form, and have come up to this or any other region, can continue to go up from there. But those who are in the involutionary stage, cannot go back to the Father's House without first incarnating as human beings and coming under the guidance and protection of a true Master. On the other hand, even if a soul should be able to go up to the height of Bhanwar Gupha either by himself or under the guidance of a teacher who had himself gone thus far and no further, before he could make further progress, he would again have to reincarnate as a human being and would have to find a True Master Who had Himself gone beyond this region or Who is the appointed successor of One Who has done so; unless the case is strongly recommended to a Perfect Master by the blessed souls whom the Master is taking through that region on the way to Sach Khand. The Merciful Master may accept their pleadings and give stranded souls a lift. This proves how fortunate are those who come under the guidance and protection of a Genuine Master during this lifetime.

Saints don't say much about these Sunna Regions because they are great voids of incomprehensible immensity. This is the largest of the Sunna Realms and is of the deepest darkness. It guards the approach to the Eternal Region, and none can pass through this region except a true Master who comes from the Eternal Region, and the souls who are under His protection.

Bhanwar Gupha and the region of Parbrahm, called Daswandwar by the Saints, are Spiritual Regions because there is but little matter or 'maya' in that Essence of Brilliant Light in those regions.

In the region of Trikuti, which is the mental or causal plane, the fine substance of the mind energy is the first real matter which forms the mold and design of all material things. It is the mind world and is ruled by the administrator called Brahm or Kal, which name also means '*time*' and '*death*'. Mind patterns rule the Universe. Mind energy expresses itself in creation, in time and space, as crystallized energy substance called matter.

The next region below Trikuti is called Sahasra Dal Kamal by the Saints and literally means '*thousand petalled lotus*'. It is in the astral or etheric realm, and in it lies the powerhouse of a thousand energy currents of light. It is like the heart or hub of the universe, which supplies and sustains all the energies which go into the physical world and its creation. It is the region of Prana as the life principle in the patterns and of the five Tattwas as the pattern substance of all matter and forms. It is the psychic realm of emotions. Kal Niranjan, the creator and ruler of this sphere is also the Lord God Jehovah of the Bible.

In each realm the Lord or Ruler of it is the custodian of the Supreme Father's Treasure of the Sound Current. It is the Sound Current or Holy Shabd which is the Essence and Life of every plane below the Source from whence it comes.

It may be well to state here that the Saints tell us that there are countless regions or realms called heaven. (JOHN 14:2)

Those which are mentioned by name, are merely to give us some idea of what lies beyond but can be fully comprehended only when we actually travel through them ourselves, under the guidance and protection of a true Master. This is done consciously and super-consciously in our finer bodies and higher consciousness, not in the physical one.

Throughout the Bible, as well as in the Kabbala, and especially in the older writings of the Zohar and the Talmud, are mentioned hosts of names of principalities, powers, rulers, archangels, angels, seraphim and cherubim, at the service of the Lord God of hosts, the Supreme Father and the Creator of all. This is but a glimpse of the hierarchies of heaven. All Sacred Texts have their own names for each one of these offices or principalities, rulers and powers.

The Eternal Supreme Father pervades all with His Essence at the core of all things, which sustains all motion, all beings and forms. In Him we live, move and have our being. Nothing happens without **His Will**.

Each principality has particular principles which are carried out at the law of the realm. Otherwise, the energies, currents and orbits of all motion and orbs would be confused and crash in their gyrations.

The higher the region, the greater is the Love and Spirituality, and there is no need for law justice. However, in this world of mind and matter, where there is only the tiniest spark of love and spirituality, law and justice rule supreme. Wherever there is lack of love and spirituality, then balance or justice is the law which keeps all things running in their orbits and in their appointed design. This was expressed beautifully by Guru Nanak in the couplets quoted later on in this chapter. The Great Master Sawan Singh Maharaj Ji always said, "Where there is Love, there is no law."

Only Love can reach beyond these conditions, into the Essence of Reality, to the Grace and Mercy of the Supreme Father of all. Faith, devotion and humility are also of that Essence beyond the harsh law of Moses and the Old Testament generally, an example of which is given in Exodus 21:12-36.

In the realm of Kal, justice rules supreme; but in the highest Spiritual realm of the Supreme Father, it is all Grace, Mercy, Love and Perfect Bliss. In the last two lines of the epilogue or shlok of 'Japji' or the Morning Prayer from the Granth Sahib, Guru Nanak summed up the effect of Grace, Mercy and Love in the lives of the devotees:

"The toils have ended for those that practiced NAM. O Nanak, their faces are lit with joyful radiance—many others they set free."

In stanza 34 of the Japji, a beautiful account is given of the creation by the Supreme Creator Who creates gods and administrators such as archangels, in every realm and plane, to carry out His Supreme Will, from the greatest to the least. Even the sparrows of the air and the lilies of the field are not beyond His infinite bounty and care.

The following quoted from the Japji:

34. "He Who made the night and day,
The days of the week and the seasons,
He Who made the breezes blow, the waters run,
The fires and the lower regions,
Made the earth — the temple of law.
He Who made creatures of diverse kinds
With a multitude of names,
Made this the law —
By thought and deed he judged forsooth,
For God is true and dispenseth Truth.
There the elect His court adorn,
And God Himself their actions honours;
There are sorted deeds that were done
and bore fruit
From those that to action could never ripen.
This, O Nanak, shall hereafter happen."

35. "In the realm of justice there is law;
In the realm of knowledge there is reason
Wherefore are the breezes, the waters and fire,
Gods that preserve and destroy, Krishnas and
Shivas?
Wherefore are created forms, colors, attire,
Gods that create, the many Brahmas?
Here one strives to comprehend,
The golden mount of knowledge ascend,
And learn as did the sage Dhruva.
Wherefore are the thunders and lightning,
The moons and suns,
The world and its regions?

Wherefore are the sages, seers, wise men,
"Goddesses, false prophets, demons and
demigods,
Wherefore are there jewels in the ocean?
How many forms of life there be,
How many tongues,
How many kings of proud ancestry.
"Of these things many strive to know,
Many the slaves of reason.
Many there are, O Nanak, their numbers
are legion."

37. "In the realm of action, effort is supreme,
Nothing else prevails.
There dwell doughty warriors brave and strong,
With hearts full of godliness.
In the realm of Truth is the Formless One
Who, having created, watches His creation
And graces us with the blessed vision.
There are the lands, the earths and the spheres
Of whose description there is no limit;
There by a myriad forms are a myriad
purposes fulfilled,
What He ordains is in them instilled.
What He beholds, thinks and contemplates,
O Nanak, is too hard to state."

38. "If thou must make a gold coin true
Let thy mint these rules pursue:
In the forge of **continence**
Let the goldsmith be a man of **patience**,
His tools be made of **knowledge**,
His anvil made of **reason**;
With the fear of God the bellows blow,
With **prayer** and **austerity** make the fire glow.
"Pour the liquid in the mould of **love**,
Print the Name (**Nam**) of the Lord thereon,

And cool it in the **holy waters**.
"For thus in the mint of **Truth the Word** is
coined,
Thus those who are graced are to work enjoined.
O Nanak, by His blessing have joy everlasting."

This is the real alchemy of Life by the Power of **His Word**, when found and used within as the Pearl of Truth.

In all the accounts given in Holy Scriptures, it is clearly indicated that the Original Sin was pride or egotism—a desire for self-love-separate and apart from the One Center and Welfare of **all beings** in that Love.

A desire for power equal to that of the Creator was the lurking impulse or motive of the ego. It wanted to be the center of all attraction in the orbits and realms it would create or could involute from the higher energy fields and substance.

Satan copied the creations above, and reproduced them as reflections of the Real, in lower regions of less vibratory intensity, all the way down into matter. He gave these regions or lower chakras the identical names as those which they represent in each region above, to cause confusion and lead soul away from the search for the Real True Home of Everlasting Bliss.

Once the soul has reached the region of Spirituality, Love and Bliss, he is out the reach and domain of Satan, and need not return again. Therefore, since Satan has only a given number of souls which he obtained as a boon after performing penance and austerities for many yugas—and he cannot create nor obtain new ones—one can readily understand why he makes such great effort at deception in order to retain the souls within his domain. His very existence as Satan was caused by the desire to rule, and he cannot continue to do so if his world should become depopulated, which it would if everyone were to become sufficiently disillusioned to seek the guidance and protection of a true living Master to show him or her the way out.

The true Masters never interfere with Satan, no more than did Jehovah in the cases of Job, etc. But when a true seeker has an earnest desire for God-Realization, and he is accepted by a true living Master and follows His instructions, he will be helped and protected. Sooner or later he will go to the True Spiritual Region, beyond the domain of Satan.

Following are a few quotations from the Bible, indicating how great is the dominion of Satan and the extent of his power. Jesus was accused, by the Pharisees, of casting out demons by the power of Beelzebub, the prince of demons.

"And Jesus knew their thoughts, and said unto them, Every kingdom divided against itself is brought to desolation; and every city or house divided against itself shall not stand:

And if Satan cast out Satan, he is divided against himself; how shall then his kingdom stand? And if I by Beelzebub cast out devils by whom do your children cast them out? therefore they shall be your judges. But if I cast out devils by the Spirit of God, then the kingdom of God is come unto you."

(MAT. 12:25-28)

At another time Jesus said to his devotees:

"Know ye not this parable? and how then will ye know all parables? The sower soweth the **Word**. And these are they by the wayside, where the Word is sown; but when they have heard, **Satan cometh immediately**, and taketh away the Word that was sown in their heart."

(MARK 4:13, 14, 15)

"And these are they likewise which are sown on stony ground; who, when they have heard the Word, immediately receive it with gladness; And have no root in themselves, and so endure but for a time: afterward, when affliction or persecution ariseth for the Word's sake, immediately they are offended. And these are they which are sown among thorns; such as hear the Word. And the cares of this world, and the deceitfulness of riches, and the lusts of other things entering in, choke the Word, and it becometh unfruitful. And these are they which are sown on good ground; such as hear the Word, and receive it, and bring forth fruit, some thirty-fold, some sixty, and some an hundred."

(MARK 4:16-20)

"And he said unto the, Is a candle brought to be put under a bushel, or under a bed and not to be set on a candlestick? For there is nothing hid, which shall not manifested: neither was any thing kept secret, but that it should come abroad. If any man have ears to hear, let him hear. And he said unto them, Take heed what ye hear: with what measure ye mete, it shall be measured to you: and unto you that hear shall more be given. For he that hath, to him shall be given: and he that hath not, from him shall be taken even that which he hath."

(MARK 4:21-25)

In the following statement Jesus referred to Satan as the prince of the world:

"Now is the judgment of this world: now shall the prince of this world be cast out." (JOHN 12:31)

In Acts 26:18, Jesus said:

"to open their eyes, and to turn them from darkness to light and from the power of Satan unto God."

According to Romans 16:20, Paul said:

"And the God of peace shall bruise Satan under your feet shortly."

In II Cor. 4:3-4, Paul referred to Satan or Kal as the god of this world:

"But if our gospel be hid, it is hid to them that are lost: In whom the god of this world hath blinded the minds of them which believe not."

"Humble yourselves therefore under the mighty hand of God, that He may exalt you in due time; casting all your care upon Him; for He careth for you. Be sober, be

vigilant; because your adversary the devil (an under-
ling of Satan), as a roaring lion, walketh about, seeking
whom he may devour:"

(I PETER 5:6-8)

Satan, also known as Kal, was given charge of hosts of
beings who involuted into the lower spheres with him. In
the Bible these souls are referred to as the Elohim. They
were allowed to create their own regions in which to live
and rule as they desired to do; for all desires must be fulfilled sometime; if not in one lifetime, then in another. It
is not only the desires themselves, but the resulting consequences of fulfilling same that must also be reaped eventually. That is why it has been truly said that we should
watch our thoughts and control our desires. Eventually we
will be put in the environment and position to enable us to
fulfill that desire. If the desires of the animal nature pre-
dominate in man, it may not be possible to fulfill them in
human form. As a result, he may have to be reincarnated
as an animal—insect, fish, fowl, or beast—depending on
the particular portion of his own accumulated conglomer-
ation of karma that is allotted to him in that life span.

Every incarnated soul and being brought about his or
her own condition and position in life by that individual's
own desires, thoughts, words and deeds. And as long as
he is reaping the fruits thereof, without seeking and obtaining the guidance and protection of a living true Master, he only succeeds in further entangling himself in the
domain of Kal. Jesus referred to such as "He that walketh
in the darkness and knoweth not whither he goeth" and
plainly indicated the need for those **who wished to be
saved through Him**, to **do so during His lifetime**; in the
statement made to the multitude shortly after His trium-
phal entry into Jerusalem, which we all know was less
than a week before His crucifixion:

"Then Jesus said unto them, Yet a little while is the
light with you. Walk while ye have the light, lest darkness come upon you: for he that walketh in darkness

knoweth not whither he goeth. While ye have light, believe in the light, that ye may be the children of light."

(JOHN 12:35, 36)

It, therefore, behoves us to follow the admonition of Jesus, to make the proper use of this God-given light in the human body and in the form of a True Master **during His lifetime on this earth!** And, during our lifetime as human beings, for there is no assurance that our next incarnation will be in the human form if we do not take advantage of the opportunity for which we were given a human body.

"That was the true light, which lighteth every man that cometh into the world." (JOHN 1:9)

"The light of the body is the eye: therefore when thine eye is single, thy whole body also is full of light; but when thine eye is evil, thy body also is full of darkness. Take heed therefore that the light which is in thee be not darkness. If thy whole body therefore be full of light, having no part dark, the whole shall be full of light, as when the bright shining of a candle doth give thee light."

(LUKE 11:34-36, and similarly in MAT. 6:22).

It is, therefore, plain to see that it was egotism, desire and abuse of God-given powers which got us into the mess in which we now find ourselves, and that it is necessary for us to travel up the same road by which we came down. But we have so covered up this light which is within ourselves, that we are full of darkness and need the guidance of one who is himself full of light, until we have again reached that stage of desirelessness and Perfect Bliss.

The desire which brought us down, has its latent force deep within the soul, which precipitates it into involution and experience. Only by testing our desires in the energy fields of resistance of mind, emotions and matter can we be convinced mentally; and through experience, emotionally; and through suffering, physically. That completes the gamut of our mental process and prowess in action and in life, as experience and proof of our own desire and folly in our cleverness.

Satan or Kal and Maya cannot create anything which endures for ever, because all their creations are in time and in the illusion of mind and matter. Their creations are not real in essence, because only that which is eternal and everlasting can be termed as Real and True. All else is but an imitation of the Real of the Eternal Father and His Holy Shabd Emanation.

The very name, Kal, literally means *'time'*; and that of Maya means *'illusion'*, like the solidity of matter itself. Hence all incarnated souls are working out their own creations and desires, in the realms of time and space, in the illusion of the mind substance as the essence of matter.

Whatever creation Kal precipitates in the essence or the positive pole of energy, Prakriti or Maya duplicates them in her own reflection as substance in a realm below that region of the positive essence, as forms and bodies. Maya, as Eve, is the mother of all living forms. She furnished the material substance and builds the house in which the Essence lives. The energy that inhabits the form is always the positive pole, which operates and moves the body and its levers. In this manner the vital body is the positive pole of the physical body, and they could well be spoken of as male and female in polarity. The positive pole gives the life principle and cause for action. The precipitation of this energy in a lower vibratory key becomes the feminine form principle called *'woman'* or *'Eve'* in the Bible. In Hebrew Scriptures, the Sacred Tetragramaton of the *'Yod-He'* forms the positive pole as the upper half of the circle, and the *'Vau-He'* the negative pole as the lower half, to complete the polarization of essence into substance for experience and experiment of souls. The Chinese call them the *'Yang'* and the *'Yin'*. Languages differ but the principles are the same.

The Kindergarten of Life is not only the physical plane of existence, but includes all the other planes of finer essences and substances, clear up through the spiritual regions, to the Eternal Region of Sach Khand. The reason for this is that the original desires of the soul go deep, far **into the soul essence**, and all these must have a chance to work themselves out in all realms of the same substance, as experience and proof to the soul that only the Eternal Creation of the Supreme Father and Creator of all is fault-less and endures for ever. Any existence outside of that Eternal Essence of Love and its One Center or Vortex is a folly and unreal, and only a proving ground for souls. It is the realm of pain, vanity and power of mental fame for the separated ego from God Who is Love Eternal and True. A beautiful quotation from stanza 31 of the Japji — the Morn-ing Prayer from the Granth Sahib, fits the description of the Almighty's Selfless Creation:

"The Maker having made doth His own creation view.
O Nanak, He made Truth itself, for He himself is True."

This is the keynote of understanding of the One Eter-nal Essence which is the Heart and Core and Support of all things, and selfless in its nature. Only the true mystic can find this, by becoming utterly selfless and surrendering his will and desire to the One Infinite Will of God Who sustains all beings.

In order to enter the Realm of Truth Itself, man must give up his ego and idea of separate existence outside of the Will of the Infinite One. Only by complete self-sur-render and love of the One Truth can the soul and mind escape its own illusion of self and selfishness in desire, thought and deed. It is here that Satan, as the desire and mind substance and essence, constantly tempts the soul away from the One Vortex of Love and Surrender to God, the Supreme Being. Since we have ourselves placed such a thick wall between ourselves and God, the only possible way we can surrender ourselves to Him is through a human being who is already One with Him in consciousness, and that is a true Master or Guru. It all leads back to first finding a living Master, and then following His instructions.

Promises of gifts and powers on any realm of mind and matter are but tests for souls, to prove to themselves their latent desires for possessions and power of ego expression. Even great ascetics fall by the very pride and success of their asceticism.

"Virtue itself turns to vice."   (SHAKESPEARE)

All that has been written plainly shows the true position of Satan as the creator and ruler of many worlds and the tempter of the Saviors, the virtuous, the Mystics, and the ascetics. **None** below the Eternal Region are beyond this reach. All things which the ego soul is and has are in Satan's power, as his temporal substance and essence, because he has been given rulership over it, not only in this world but also in the astral or psychic world, and in the mind and thought pattern world called Trikuti.

Trikuti, the causal region, is the origin or home of the mind, much the same as Sach Khand is the Home of the Soul. The soul cannot begin its homeward journey without the company of the mind, as the mind is no more at home in this world than is the soul. Therefore, in Mysticism, as one will find throughout all the Sacred Writings, the soul and mind are referred to as husband and wife, and the happy union is eulogized. This depicts the co-operation of the mind with the soul. Until the mind lovingly surrenders to the request of the soul, neither can make the homeward journey.

When the mind and the soul together reach the realm of Trikuti, the mind remains there in ecstatic bliss, and the soul may rest there before ascending to the next higher region of Daswandwar or Parbrahm.

All this clearly illustrates the root of evil and how deep it goes; how and why souls are hurled into the abyss of mortal existence in order to learn the lesson of Pure Love and Selflessness.

Kal or Satan is a hard taskmaster and rules by justice of the law. There is no mercy or eternal love in his being. His essence is mind and cunning itself. He is no weakling and has cleverness and ability beyond mortal ken. Severity and firmness are his virtues. He is the literal '*God of Wrath and Justice*', whose business it is to mete it out as each one deserves according to his desires, thoughts and deeds in life's testing lane.

Satan is interested in keeping his regions populated with souls under him, so he can rule, which is his desire and keynote. It is his business to administer justice in his realms, as **it is also his business** not to allow the impure or unfit to ascend beyond his realms. Naturally, he does not want things to get too bad, as evil destroys everything made; so when the world begins to get too wicked, he sends his angels down to destroy or wipe out wherever there is too much wickedness. In spite of the severity, his realms must still serve as an attraction for souls to dwell in and to be his citizens.

This should clarify much that is in the Christian Bible about the '*God of Wrath*' and the '*God of Love*'; between the Almighty Creator at the very center and essence of all energy and substance, and the god "who repented him that he had made man." It draws a complete line between God, the Father of all Mercy, Love, Truth and Bliss, and the god of wrath who punishes and hurls souls into hell, the Sheol of the Hebrews.

No amount of reading, reciting, learning or calculating, nor cleverness of quoting from Sacred Texts can raise a soul beyond the realm of mind and Kal, who is the **essence** of the mind's cunning. These things can help to purify the mind, but unless the mind surrenders its ego and accompanies the soul, it accomplishes nothing.

Only the power of the Eternal Shabd, the Sound Current, the Word of God the Inner Essence, can save the soul through the help of a living Master who can give this Word of Power to the disciple and also connect his soul energy inwardly to its Real Source in the Sound Current. That is the manifestation of the Grace of God to the soul, and is its only salvation. The soul's essence cannot rest until it blends with that One Essence from whence it came and which is its Real Home, its keynote, and the One and only Selfless Self of all Existence.

All this brings out the real problem of the soul, and the root cause of desire, which must be overcome by Love and Understanding, by the Grace of God, through a true Saint or Teacher of Love and Truth.

Denouncing and railing at evils are a waste of time and a cover-up for the real selfishness of desire in the soul itself. All that time would be well spent in Love and Devotion and real renunciation of all to the Will of the Supreme Father. **Only the ego can be judged and hurled into the pit of selfishness called hell. Love and selflessness are beyond judgment and desire, and hence out of the realm of Kal and mind**.

Only by cleansing the mind and the soul can they become perfect. And for this, the Grace of God and a Teacher are necessary. None can come unto the Father but through the help of Such an incarnation of Love and Grace Sublime.

Perfect Peace and permanent equilibrium can be established only in Unity. No lasting Unity is possible below the Eternal Realm and the "One Word" which created all there is. And to return to this Essence and Region is the **most important** task of the soul **at all times**. Only in this way can it transcend all the evils and the cunning tricks and diversions of the mind. According to the "Voice of the Silence", the mind itself is the slayer of the Real, and must be transcended. It is, therefore, imperative that the soul be lifted out of the clutches of Kal, the mind and the senses.

Salvation is a reality, **here and now**, in the body, and is made possible for earnest and devoted souls through the grace of a Master on earth. The task is a worthy one, and the only thing of real value in life. The soul's consciousness must rise and ultimately blend with the One Conscious Essence of Truth and Love Itself. There is no lasting safety or haven elsewhere.

It is the Eternal which draws forth the soul's love and beauty. And for this the complete and unconditional surrender of the mind and soul to the Guru, the Savior, and the Almighty is the only Way. As the ego or the self with its desires was the cause of the fall, then its surrender can free the soul from the bondage or energy block of desire which sent it into incarnation in this world.

If we would understand the cause of our being detained in the realms of Satan, let us examine our desires and attachments. This will give us a pretty good idea where the root of trouble lies. How much time or attention do we give to Devotion, to self-examination, and to concentration on the Eternal values of Life? Is our main objective temporal acquisitions, or is it in the search and thoughts of eternal verities? Where our treasure lies, there will our heart and our attention be also. Objective and purpose are the first requisites in Life or in traveling in any direction.

The One Word or Essence is the Way, the Truth and the Life, and so are the real Saints or Saviors who embody that Essence and are One with It. Truth is not a doctrine of many words nor is it a mere belief. Truth is the One Reality of Life itself. It is beyond creeds and religions. Truth, as the One Essence, is the Core and Substance of all things. It is sharper than a two-edged sword, cutting asunder the bones and marrow of illusions and crystallized limitations of the mind, the senses and the body. (HEB. 4:12)

All effort at reformation is done by the soul itself, in its own make-up and sphere. The great alchemical task of raising the soul out of the mire and limitations of the lower mind and senses lies within ourselves. Only when these are transformed into the pure gold qualities of love and surrender of them all to God's Will, can the soul rise on the Tree of Life.

When the Master Mason constructs the faultless temple of the Lord, made of pure cedar, and gold and silver inlays of soul qualities, only then is he constructing the eternal temple of Hiram Abiff, 'not made by hands of man'.

When Allah becomes **all** in the life of the devoted Sufi or the mystic Moslem, then he himself ceases to be and is lost in Allah, or becomes one with the Deity. In the Christian life, Jesus and His instructions can be a complete guide and an actual living doctrine, as many saintly followers have demonstrated. Jesus said:

"I am the vine, ye are the branches" etc.

(JOHN 15:5-6)

The Truth is One, the Life is One, the Way is One; but only true devotion, self-surrender and love can unlock the door to the One Life Eternal. The One Essence is in all. Let him who hath understanding, find the mystery of THE WORD!

CHAPTER XIII
THE MYSTIC APPLICATION OF THE LORD'S PRAYER

According to Matthew Chapter 6:5-21, in continuation of the Sermon on the Mount, Jesus said:

5. "And when thou prayest, thou shalt not be as the hypocrites are: for they love to pray standing in the synagogues and in the corners of the streets, that they may be seen of men. Verily I say unto you, they have their reward.

6. "But thou, when thou prayest, enter into thy closet, and when thou hast shut thy door, pray to thy Father which is in secret; and thy Father which seeth in secret shall reward thee openly.

7. "But when ye pray, use not vain repetitions, as the heathens do: for they think that they shall be heard for their much speaking.

8. "Be not ye therefore like unto them: for your Father knoweth what things ye have need of, before ye ask him.

9. "After this manner therefore pray ye: Our Father which art in heaven, Hallowed be thy name.

10. "Thy kingdom come. Thy will be done in earth, as it is in heaven.

11. "Give us this day our daily bread.

12. "And forgive us our debts, as we forgive our debtors.

13. "And lead us not into temptation, but deliver us from evil: For thine is the kingdom, and the power, and the glory, for ever. Amen.

14. "For if ye forgive men their trespasses, your heavenly Father will also forgive you:

15. "But if ye forgive not men their trespasses, neither will your Father forgive your trespasses.

16. "Moreover when ye fast, be not, as the hypocrites, of a sad countenance: for they disfigure their faces that they may appear unto men to fast. Verily, I say unto you, they have their reward.

17. "But thou, when thou fastest, anoint thine head, and wash thy face;

18. "That thou appear not unto men to fast, but unto thy Father, which is in secret: and thy Father, which seeth in secret, shall reward thee openly.

19. "Lay not up for yourselves treasures upon earth, where moth and rust doth corrupt, and where thieves break through and steal.

20. "But lay up for yourselves treasures in heaven, where neither moth nor rust doth corrupt, and where thieves do not break through nor steal:

21. "For where your treasure is, there will your heart be also."

The Lord's Prayer is the petition of the soul, incorporated in a human body, praying to the Lord, the Father of Creation and pleading that the mind, the wayward senses and the emotions be brought in line with God's Will and Decree. Reliable authority claims to have found a similar prayer in the old Talmud, in which the arrangement of the pleas was the same, for the fulfillment of the Lord God Jehovah's Will in all the centers or sephiras of the body, that they may be lifted up by His Spirit. The Psalmist of old expressed that idea clearly when he stated:

7. "Lift up your heads, O ye gates; and be ye lift up, ye everlasting doors; and the King of glory shall come in.

8. "Who **is** this King of glory? The LORD strong and mighty, the LORD mighty in battle.

9. "Lift up your heads, O ye gates; even lift **them** up ye everlasting doors; and the King of glory shall come in.

10. "Who is this King of glory? The LORD of hosts, he **is** the King of glory. Selah."

(PSALM 24)

No. 7 of course has reference to lifting up or setting right side up of the inner centers, within ourselves, so the King of glory may come in. in verse No. 10, the Psalmist calls the Holy Shabd the King of glory and the LORD of hosts. The Holy Shabd is the Sound which comes from the heaven above and is bestowed by the King of Glory when your attention and centers are facing in His direction to receive Him.

As the leaves of the trees hang down and shed rain, so do the unawakened centers on the individual tree of life, and waste the higher energies of the Lord God the Creator. But the awakened centers, doors or gates raise their petals upwards, like hands in petition, to receive and hold the bounty of the Lord's Nectar. Therefore, this is a prayer to the Holy Will and Spirit of Jehovah—called the Holy Ghost in the New Testament—to descend and fill the soul's cups or centers of life with His Spiritual Bounty, "until the cup runneth over" (Ps. 23:5). The censors containing the sweet fragrance of frankincense and myrrh, as used in the churches, are definitely symbolic of the awakened centers within the spiritual devotees. As long as our attention runs downward and outward in material pursuits and pleasures, it is not possible to hold and make proper use of the Divine Nectar from above. But when the centers are awakened through uplifting devotion, the Divine Energy is not wasted and we become filled with it.

"Our Father which art in Heaven" is the beginning of all beginnings, as the Creator and Giver of all. Saviors and prophets called the Lord who sent them into this world to do His work, their Father. Jesus stated:

> "The Son can do nothing of himself, but what he seeth the Father do: for what things soever he doeth, these also doeth the Son likewise." (JOHN 5:19)

The Hebrews word for heaven is *Shomaim* and literally means *lifted up*. In the cosmos, this would be the finer energy realm above the physical creation. In the individual man, it constitutes *Kether* the crown of creation, the uppermost portion of the brain called the cerebrum. Here all the spiritual faculties are located, like in a vault, or a well upside down. From this, the higher energies flow down into the body, the temple of God. The Tabernacle in the wilderness and the Kabbalistic Tree of Life were also arranged in this order.

The great and fearless Saint, Paltu Sahib, described this whole spiritual process most beautifully under the title: "An Inverted Well if There Above" (see page 305). The everlasting light or vigil light, used in some churches, symbolizes this inner eternal flame. The flame inside the human being is also the new name written in the forehead of the redeemed as mentioned in Revelations. Its reflection is in the human heart as the tables of the living law, written by the finger of God. This again establishes a closer unity between the writings of the Old Testament and the New, and the clear teaching of the modern Saints.

God's Essence is Truth and Love as One which flows through the central core to support and sustain all creation. Happy are His children who find this direct way of liberation, out from the heart of all things.

"Hallowed be thy Name": The sacred Name of God is His Word, His Holy Sound Current as Divine Energy and Music. It is His Holy Spirit which sustains all things. This is the true River of Life which flows from the eternal throne as God's breath of Life and emanation. It is the Holy Shabd or *Word*, according to all Saints. The Greeks called it the 'Logos', as the final reason for creation. The soul is trying to tune into that Eternal Sound Current by reverence and devotional attention inside, and can do so after the Saint or Savior has linked the soul to it.

"Thy kingdom come. Thy will be done in earth, as it is in heaven." The *kingdom* of the Lord is His Holy Sound Current as His Will in earth. The devotee prays this be in him also, in all the regions of this earthiness below his eyebrows, to direct him in every thought, word and deed.

"Give us this day our daily bread." This is really a prayer for Spiritual Nectar, the *Manna* from heaven, as symbolized by the showbreads in the temple. The Hebrew word *Bethlehem* means the *house of bread*. In the human body this is the region of the solar plexus. It is the fiery power of digestion, by which the body lives; so also the spirit or soul lives by His Nectar. The effort is to unify the inner and the outer life energies as spiritual and physical through the one current of His Holy Will or Shabd, the Word. Jesus was born in Bethlehem, the symbol of Manna or Nectar of Truth from heaven. The consciousness has now descended to the Manipura chakra, for which unity is pleaded in order to carry out His Will in all earthly deeds, made possible by Spiritual and earthy food.

"And forgive us our debts, as we forgive our debtors." Since all things flow out of the Eternal Sound Current, we should realize our indebtedness to God for all supplies and deal likewise with other souls in our daily conduct, in order to remain tuned into this current of Forgiveness and constant blessings of the Almighty as an ever-flowing stream of Reality.

Verse 12 as well as 14 and 15 bring out the very law of Forgiveness. As we forgive others through love, so are we forgiven **by Love alone**. If our hearts are hardened by our own self-righteousness, then we live in that mind pattern and are ensnared by it. The sinner may have repented many times and obtained forgiveness by doing better or even by sincerely trying to do better and continuing to do so. In other words, he becomes humble by realizing his weaknesses and endeavoring to overcome them through Love and the Grace of the Lord. While all this time the self-righteous person dwells on his merit on the one hand while remaining utterly unconscious of his weaknesses; so the energies are wasted first in pride and secondly in continuing with the faults which he fails to see in himself. Mat. 5:25, 26 as well as Mat. 6:14, 15 are good illustrations of this law which is stated very briefly in verse 12.

Attention or consciousness is the power by which the soul is bound, high or low, wherever its energy currents come to rest or dwell. It takes more understanding, faith and hope to hitch it to a star than to the mediocre, worthless things for which we have to suffer because of self-interest and ego.

"And lead us not into temptation, but deliver us from evil: For thine is the kingdom, and the power, and the glory, for ever. Amen." Here, the plea is for the physical creative energy of the Brahma Chakra to remain in tune with the Divine Purpose and plan of creation. The soul prays for strength to remain firm in the concentration of the inner Sound Current of Shabd, not to be led astray by the temptation of the senses and their plea for enjoyment. God tempts no one. He furnishes all things for man to choose from, so man can ultimately learn his own lessons through choice and suffering as paths of actions and reactions, called *Karma* in the language of the Saints. "For whatsoever a man soweth, that shall he also reap." (Gal. 6:7)

The soul now affirms that all is God's Essence as the Kingdom, the Power and the Glory for ever. In other words, it tries to convince the wayward mind and senses by a positive affirmation of Truth for Inner Realization and use. God is the Giver. God Himself is also the Gift. God too is the Receiver, by the gift of His Grace of understanding. **Only in that power of Unity can the mind be held firmly to humility, self-surrender and selflessness**.

This was the secret key to the alchemy of the ancients, which transformed the baser substances called metals, back to the selfless state of pure gold. The current from above, called the Holy Shabd or Word, has this power of transforming our earthy nature back into the Spiritual, by lifting the Essence up into its Source. This is the real Philosopher's Stone which the alchemists endeavored to find and reproduce.

As previously mentioned elsewhere in this book, the early patriarchs recorded their success in this process of internal concentration and prayer, as mystic progeny.

Positive results were recorded as sons given by God, and negative results were the daughters of men. The history of spiritual progress was all-important to the mystically devout patriarchs of old. Spiritual progress was the one aim and effort in their whole lifetime of wanderings on earth. The earth held little for them except the means of livelihood through their flocks. How could they be interested in writing a fixed physical history when their hearts were with God in all their trials and wanderings? The cry of the soul and its record is the same in all ages. Sacred writings, songs and prayers are the mystic recordings and roots of spiritual history.

The Mystic Application of
the Miracle of the Loaves and Fishes

As a physical reality the feeding of five thousand people with five loaves and two fishes, is all within the Power of the Master. But Jesus actually fed the people spiritual food of far more importance than the one meal of material food, recorded in this particular chapter, Luke 9:12-18.

Merely feeding the body is not the Father's work. Man has been given means and ways to support himself naturally, without the aid of miracles. God gives the physical increase to sustain mankind. But the spiritual food is the work of the Sons and Messengers of God, sent out from the higher regions to teach mankind in different ages and cycles of time. This is the real "*Manna from heaven*" or food for the soul, when given by a Saint of the Lord.

The miracle of the loaves and fishes is a symbol of the real food which Jesus gave to the souls and minds, for the mere physical food is never satisfying to a true devotee and besides the body soon becomes hungry again and has to seek a source of supply. But once the soul has contacted the Source of the spiritual food, the supply is eternal.

Feeding hungry souls is far more important than feeding hungry bodies. The Saviors' and Saints' mission is with souls, the lost sheep from the heavenly regions, to show them the way back home to the Father's house. The miracle of loaves and fishes is an external symbol of the real mission of Jesus on earth:

The five loaves represent the five chakras or centers in the physical body, the showbreads in the temple being located in the center of it.

The two fished are the two psychic currents of Pisces which go up and down in opposite directions, one on each side of the body, as sensory energy currents.

It was though this sensory energy in the form of the living Word given by Jesus that the cups or chakras or centers of the people were completely filled, so that all the twelve signs of the zodiac in the body were nourished, and twelve basketfuls were gathered afterwards as left-overs. This is typical of God's Grace and abundance of spiritual food which He is ever offering us; but we do not even as much as look up to receive it. First the centers in our body, instead of having the downward and outward dissipating tendencies, must be spiritually cleaned or set right-side up so to say, facing Him, in order to be filled with His Grace.

On this particular occasion, the cups of the multitude surely ran over with real spiritual blessings. (Psalm 23). Jesus was literally fulfilling the sayings of this Psalm by feeding the multitude such spiritual food. How much more important this is than mere physical food is readily understood by all devotees. The Word of God is the real spiritual food. It is the Manna from heaven in this wilderness of the desert of life, bereft of the spiritual waters of life. (Luke 4:4)

"Man shall not live by bread alone, but by every **Word** that proceeded out of the mouth of God."

(MAT. 4:4)

"For he that soweth to his flesh shall of the flesh reap corruption; but he that soweth to the Spirit shall of the Spirit reap life everlasting." (GAL. 6:8)

"And he humbled thee, and suffered thee to hunger, and fed thee with manna, which thou knewest not, neither did thy fathers know; that he might make thee know that man doth not live by bread only, but by every **word** that proceedeth out of the mount of the Lord doth man live."   (DEUTERONOMY 8:3)

Here scripture is spiritually fulfilled and beautifully illustrated.

The arranging of the multitude in companies of fifty was also significant, for it was according to the five sensory currents and groupings through which the appeal was made to them, with great success. It must have been a most remarkable stirring of the multitude in that desert, through inspiration given to Jesus by the Father.

CHAPTER XIV
THE HOLY GHOST AS SHABD, THE PRIMAL SOUND ENERGY

"And suddenly there came from heaven a sound as of the rushing of a mighty wind, and it filled all the house where they were sitting. And there appeared unto them cloven tongues like as of fire; and it sat upon each one of them. And they were all filled with the Holy Ghost, and began to speak with other tongues, as the Spirit gave them utterance.

"Now there were dwelling at Jerusalem Jews, devout men, from every nation under heaven. And when this sound was heard, the multitude came together, and were confounded, because that every man heard them speaking in his own language."

(ACTS. 2:2-7 — American Edition)

"Who, when they were come down, prayed for them, that they might receive the Holy Ghost: (For as yet he was fallen upon none of them: only they were baptized in the name of the Lord Jesus.) Then laid they their hands on them, and they received that Holy Ghost. And when Simon saw that through laying on of the apostles' hands the Holy Ghost was given, he offered them money, saying, Give me also this power, that on whomsoever I lay hands, he may receive the Holy Ghost. But Peter said unto him. Thy money perish with thee, because thou hast thought that the gift of God may be purchased with money."

(ACTS 8:15-20)

"While Peter yet speak these words, the Holy Ghost fell on all them which heard the Word."

(ACTS 10:44)

"By hearing the Word
One sounds the depths of virtue's sea.
By hearing the Word
One acquires learning, holiness and royalty.

By hearing the Word
The blind see and their paths are visible.
By hearing the Word
The fathomless becomes fordable.
O Nanak, the Word hath such magic for the worshippers,
Those that hear, death do not fear,
Their sorrows end and sins disappear."

(*Stanza No. 11, from*
'Japji' – The Morning Prayer from
the Granth Sahib)

This Eternal, Holy Shabd Energy was at the beginning of creation and is at the end of all creation as the One Object and Essence of attainment in Life, especially here on earth. In the middle also it is and was the Holy Spirit of the Logos, like an unseen Holy Ghost of the One Essence, which was working and molding all things by His Will or Mauj, so named by the Saints.

"In the beginning was the Word, and the Word was with God. The same was in the beginning with God. All things were made through him; and without Him was not anything made that was made.

In Him was life; and the life was the light of men. And the light shineth in darkness; and the darkness apprehended it not." (JOHN 1:1-5)

It was That Energy which Jesus called the Father who doeth all things. Even as Laotzu said:

"It is the Great Tao which doeth all things."

He is the Life of the creation. He is the Light which lighteth every man who cometh into the world. He is the Light and the Sound which human beings must find within themselves, and hold onto, to be lifted out of all darkness of Kal and Maya. The Holy Shabd is the one River of Life, Light, Love and Understanding which is the Bliss of the Holy Spirit.

He is the Essence of religion, the object of all devotion, and the Cause of all things. He is "the One Light which shineth into the darkness and the darkness comprehendeth it not" neither can it engulf it. He is the One Reality in all Life, which passeth all understanding. He is the Sound Energy — the Heavenly Sound — on every plane of existence, as the Core and Holy Center which supports all beings and things.

He is the Holy Ghost, the Comforter, the Illumination given to devoted disciples of the Masters, True Mystic or Saviors. He is all language and all speech, yet few there are who hear and understand. He is all Light and all Sound, and the Consciousness of Love's Essence, of Bliss. Attaining union with Him is the only salvation.

Prayers of devotion are steps to His altar within. Attention, with love, is the Way to His Abode. Only the words of Love at His Centers in all regions and realms are the powers against which nothing can prevail. The repetition of His Holy Names, as instructed by the living Guru, is the Way inward and upward, to His Holy Abode in the Sound Current of the One Essence. Jesus said:

"It is written, man shall not live by bread alone but by every WORD that proceedeth out of the mouth of God."

(MAT. 4:4)

There can be no true religion without Him, for He is the Cause of all religions. He is the object and aim of every devotion and creed. Without Him, naught can exist. He is the Essence in the teachings of all the Saints and True Masters, as the Holy Shabd or Sound Current or Holy Spirit mentioned in all Sacred Scriptures. None can limit or possess Him; but all are invited to come to His Feast, prepared for the children of men.

He is the Supreme Gift of the True Guru or Teacher to His devoted disciples. Without **that** Pearl of Great Price, nothing has value. When the soul findeth it, it *sells all it has;* namely, gives up all other attachment, and buys that pearl. Not with physical wealth, of course. Only by such undivided attention to devotion in concentration, can **He** be attained.

"Be not deceived; God is not mocked; for whatsoever a man soweth that shall he also reap."

(GALATIAN 6:7)

Only the Essence within us can meet that Essence. Nothing else can enter the Kingdom of that Heaven of the Supreme Being. Purity of heart is essential as the One-ness in Aim and devotion. No mere talk and words of the mind can reach His Abode, only the sincere devotion of Love and Attention in adoration, by listening to His Holy Sound. External music and hymns are but symbols of the Real and reach not His Gate. The Hem of His Garment drips with the power of the One Essence and is adorned with the Jewels of Love. His Garment is woven of One Piece, and men cast lots for it, because it cannot be di-vided. Who is worthy to possess such a *'Wedding Garment'* of the Spirit? Only Love can choose wisely here.

Oneness, singleness of purpose—"let thine eye be sin-gle"—with sincerity, is the Way of the Single Eye in the center of the forehead. It is the Jewel of jewels in *'Revela-tion'*. (REVELATION—CHAPTERS 14 AND 21)

Nothing is Real except He. All other things and Kar-mas are in delusion. Beholding Him, the ecstasy of the soul knows no bounds. He is as deep and deeper than all the seas, and mightier than the ocean's roar. He is the One True One, for He Himself **is** Truth. Whosoever abideth in Him, need not fear. There is no power in all the heavens and earths which can compare. There is rest and safety under His Wings.

In the shadow of the Almighty, there is Peace beyond understanding. Nothing reaches beyond Him or His Abode. The Soul's highest reach is in Him alone. Unity is His Essence and Love is His Code. Might is but a mean-ingless word without His Reality. How can we adore such a One? Only silence and devotion can absorb His Bounty. Only attention **with our whole being** can sing His Praise.

"He alone can His own greatness measure.
O Nanak, what He gives we must treasure."

(Last two lines of stanza 24 of 'JAPJI'
The Morning Prayer from the Granth Sahib)

Where shall we look for our Beloved? Shall we seek Him in the garden of the body, or in the mountain of spices in the fragrance of the pure soul essence? He is everywhere; but in heart of hearts is His Core, and His Abode is there. WITHIN OUR HOLY SHRINE OF SILENCE IS THE SOUND OF THE SOUNDLESS ONE.

Who shall say on which Way we shall meet Him? He Himself **is** the Way, the Truth and the Light of Life. How can we adore Him Whom none is before?

If we go within,
We merge the self in Him.
Our Beloved is most fair.
If we were but one heir,
His Holy Bliss to share!

Love needs no convincing, but the intellect is blind in spiritual things. Reading these Truths before retiring at night lifts up the mind to a higher level of consciousness during sleep, and the repetition of what was read goes on automatically in the mind. It helps to purify the subconscious and straighten out its energy lines in the direction of the True Goal.

CHAPTER XV
SHABD QUALITIES

After reading about the arrangement in creation — that agents and subsidiary powers from the Greatest down to the least, rule the lower activities of life with which we are acquainted — one naturally wonders WHERE and HOW can one contact the Supreme Father, the Creator of all? Where can He be found?

Since man is a microfilm of everything there is, created and uncreated, then all these powers and principalities are also **within** him. We have within ourselves the faculties of mind powers, emotional energies and physical forces, which are **our** administrative representatives for the expression of the soul in creation through our bodies — fine and gross. The same qualities as are in the universe are also in us.

Which do we want to use and why? Which energy or principal quality do we tune into daily? And how can we learn to do this consciously and intelligently in the first place? Where are our main interests? Where is our heart's desire? When we take time to ascertain those things which we wish for, and desire most, and long to obtain and possess, or to fulfill our longings, then our primary motive in life stands out clearly before us as the root of thoughts, wishes and deeds, and indicates to us the direction in which we are going.

Each soul could and should ask himself daily, "Whither goest thou, O soul, O mind, O desire and action?" From whence do the energy breezes blow, on whose currents we are sailing? Is it from self, for selfish gain and pleasure? or is it from the heights of Love, Devotion and Service which lead to God-Realization? Then and then only is it apparent in whose dominion we like to dwell, where we enjoy ourselves most, and where we actually abide — consciously or unconsciously — day and night.

What soul longs for conscious union with God, the Essence of Love, Kindness, Truth and Humility, night and day; and sheds silent tears in this longing throughout the night and in the early morning hours? Only Saints and True Mystics constantly dwell on God and in God, through love and devotion to Him at all and in times, in **every** thought, word and deed. Even one breath, without the consciousness of the Beloved God, is truly non-existence and unconscious darkness in matter. Material wealth is of no comfort or solace to the True Mystics. To the Mystic, **God is all** in all. **He sees Him everywhere** as the heart and goodness in all things and beings. The True Mystic performs his daily duties with his hands and feet, but His consciousness always dwells in the Reality and He sees with the One eye of Love and deep understanding.

In that Inner Region of True Devotion, True Humility and Selflessness, only God resides; for those who have reached that stage are One with Him. Goodwill and kindness, in fact, Infinite Mercy and Grace, flow out of such a fountain of Reality more easily and naturally than from a bubbling spring. These are the Real Waters of Life and the Stream is referred to in the Mystic Writings as the Holy Shabd, the Holy Spirit, the Holy Ghost (REV. 22:1), the Comforter, the Never-failing Spring (ISA. 58:11), Oil of Joy and Comfort (ISA. 61:3), Breath (or Wind) Reviving (EZEK. 37:5, 9, 10), Well of Living Waters, The Water of the Holy Spirit (JOHN 4:5-27), Rivers of Living Water (Ps. 1:3, 16:4, ISA. 41:18; JOHN 7:38, 39), etc.

When Living the True Mystic Way, no effort whatsoever is required in order to be good or righteous, as that happens automatically when one is devoted to Him to the extent of being ONE with Him in spirit. However, the ego or the self, like a child, needs to be praised and encouraged until it can be properly tuned in to the wavelength of that Reality where the ego is not.

For souls who wish to tune in on this wavelength, the Hold Shabd, the Supreme Father provides the True Mystics or True Masters in human form. These Great Masters deign to incarnate in a human body for the very purpose of connecting the souls of those who wish to return Home, to this very Sound Current which will lead them and carry them; the Master Himself being an Incarnation of God and the Current which leads the soul back to Him.

In the Mystic's life, God does everything. The Mystic stands by and listens to the heavenly music within, and keeps tuned in, much the same as we listen to a radio playing in the background while carrying on our work; but with all our attention when not otherwise occupied. So also with the Hold Shabd. The Saints say, "the better the tuning, the better the reception."

Once we have been properly connected by a True Master, it is up to our **attention** to do the tuning. And when the attention is properly tuned in, then the static of the mind and senses is automatically eliminated. Also, as with the radio, if there is some defect, it must be repaired before the reception is satisfactory, no matter how loud and clear the broadcast may be at the source. These defects symbolize the karmic conditions with which we have covered the soul through our own thoughts, words and deeds, and which must be cleared before we can hear the Holy Shabd within. When the radio is beyond repair, or we wish to have one of better quality for still better reception until one actually feels as though one is at the very source of the broadcast, we obtain a new one of the quality desired. The human body is the top quality equipment, and we have it right here and now, with which to get perfect reception and on which to travel Home, if we but find a True Master to connect us, and then, through devotion, tune in accordingly.

The Saint lives as simply as a child. He is utterly unconscious of His virtues. While He actually toils day and night in God's Vineyard, He claims that He of Himself does nothing, but that His Beloved does everything for Him. So completely is He One with God in His consciousness! (JOHN 5:19-20; JOHN 8:16; JOHN 10:30; JOHN 14:10-11, JOHN 17:21, 22, etc.)

Such simplicity of faith, love and humility is the very keystone of righteousness referred to in the Bible, in the life of the Patriarch Abraham. That is how he walked and talked with God. Only such selfless deeds of utter surrender and devotion are acceptable to our Heavenly Father, and they all accredited to the devotee as Righteousness. Whether with or without creed or religion; circumcision or uncircumcision; with or without temples or forms of ceremonies; this TRUTH remains the same in all creation.

The Commandments are good, the Sermon on the Mount is excellent, all religions are good. They are all rules of conduct and teach us to lead and honest and upright life, which is not essential before one can even begin to think of ascending beyond the realms of Kal or Satan. Yet, without the guidance and protection of a True **living** Master, we cannot even succeed in permanently living an honest and upright life in this world, much less accomplish anything spiritually.

He that **lives** the Life, shall know the Truth and dwell under the Protective Wings of the Almighty. Why should the Mystic be bound according to the dictates of men of flesh and mind, or any set forms, when the Living God shows the Way?

Who can declare the Way to the Lord, but a True Mystic? Who can play good music, but one who loves that art and is an artist in that field? The same is true of all endeavors. Genuine interest, to the extent of undivided attention, absorbs and dissolves all ideas of work, of labor and of time. **Attention** to the keynote of any art furnishes the necessary energy to carry on. There is no drag nor lag in real creativeness in any art where the **interest and attention come naturally**. Then the accomplishment is without effort. It is an expression of that which the heart and mind are full of.

All this is well-known and understood on the surface in the arts, crafts, professions, executive ability through intensive interest, etc. But the Mystic Way is rare, unknown and unique. That is why the Mystic is not understood.

The true artist—in any field, whether it be in painting, sculpturing, music, any profession or trade—has no selfish motive. **He works for the Love of it**, and the good Lord gives all and more than he needs. His real food and gift consist in a greater ability and absorption in his beloved art. Many times, prosperity and Physical abundance are withheld so he can better fulfill his devotion to art and selfless creativeness, without interruption. A true artist would rather starve in an attic with his beloved art than sell even one of his creations. It has happened many times and cannot be termed a mere physical attachment because the love of the art itself was greater than all physical wealth. That is why great souls are seldom heard of or appreciated during their lifetime, but often become famous after death.

Great souls do not want nor need fame. They want only peace and quiet for their art, their concentration and Inner Work, close to the Source. All outer things distract the mind, scatter the attention and interrupt the true devotion to the Beloved God, the art, or the point of absorbing interest where the heart is consciously attached. In the light of art, perhaps the ways of the Real Mystic can be understood. Also, by analogy, perhaps the Truth Religious, Mystic Life and Way can be understood or pointed out when compared with true art or creativeness in any field requiring undivided attention to the extent of full absorbing interest.

Here we find the key of Creation repeated over and over again: The primary starting point, the pivot of all, **is our attention and interest, in a totally selfless way**. It is the first commandment, applied practically:

"Thou shalt love the Lord thy God with all thy heart and with all thy soul and with all thy mind."

(MAT. 22:37)

Whenever the combination of mind and ego replaces that of soul and mind, and enters into any such concentrating and absorbing interest in arts, beliefs or creeds, it becomes fanaticism by declaring and insisting on limitations of interpretations, set observations, special beliefs and formalities, etc. These then spring up like weeds and want to overrun the world in reform, each forming a separate sect. Each group wants numbers and followers to rule over, as it happened in the fall of Satan in the beginning. The creative mind,

"turned from true birth, stumbleth on abuse"

(SHAKESPEARE)

If mere physical endeavor and skill call forth such devotion and concentration for its successful accomplishment, cannot the devotion to God do likewise? Is the most important endeavor in life less worthy than the other? Does any one need to ask how to become a good artist, a good doctor or lawyer, or a good tradesman?

Is it not simply a matter of love for work, seeking and finding the right teacher, and then practicing with attention, attention and more attention and practice? The ways, the means, the principles involved and all other things reveal themselves as the attention is applied, and often excel all accepted beliefs and traditions. Only in such a manner are new ideas and concepts born, which are a boon to humanity. Souls perish for lack of vision. (PROVERBS 29:18)

Naturally, the resistance of the old or obsolete is great. This is true in public life and within each one of us as the small world in which we rule and govern. We form set ideas and habits, and how we fight to hang on to them even after superior ways and means have been offered. It is the same. We suffer in the without as a cosmic reaction, and within ourselves as our own individual reaction to the powers that are of our own making and doing.

Thought-forms, habits, beliefs, emotional qualities and stability are all molds and patterns of energy for us to overcome and train into new concepts and fields by a greater vision and devotion to that which is the most desired accomplishment in our life.

The very Truth which we wonder about and the questions we would ask about it in a religious and devotional life, are similar to our daily life and pursuits. Truth is **in** life itself, as it is in art or any worthwhile Objective. The main point is our sincerity in our first choice or that which we deem most important, and the attention we give to it.

God is Life, as Life is God-given. Then how do we except to find Him in mere mental concepts and beliefs, without the vitality of Life and a sincere devotion to Him? Where does God dwell, if not in the hearts of His Mystic devotees? So our search is really a sincere effort toward deeper tuning in ourselves, to attract from within and without, that which we need for our next step forward on the Way of Truth.

God is the Word of Life and, as the Holy Ghost, or the Holy Shabd, dwells within the very core of our being. We can tune into this Eternal Energy by sincere and deep devotion, through the aid of a living Mystic Master who is one with **that** Energy.

We tune into our mind energy by thinking; into our emotional energy by feeling; and into our physical energy by action. In the mind's tendencies are downward, it keeps the soul in bondage along with it, and both are miserable. Whereas, if the mind *tunes in* and co-operates with the soul, everything else falls in line and both are happy in their upward or Homeward journey.

Is there any question as to where we would like to be? Do we tune into the programs we want, or listen to those we don't want when we know that something better is on the air? **The difference** between serving God or Mammon **can be as simple as all that**. It all depends on whether we wish to continue to labor and suffer in the world of Kal, or prefer to be devoted to the Eternal One within us by tuning into the Holy Shabd which is calling each and every one of us Home, if we will but listen to His Word within this temple.

"What? Know ye not that your body is the temple of the Holy Ghost **which is in you**, which ye have of God, and ye are not your own. (I COR. 6:19)

"Behold, I stand at the door, and knock: if any man hear my voice, and open the door, I will come in to him, and will sup with him, and he with me. To him that over-cometh will I grant to sit with me in my throne, even as I also overcame, and am set down with my Father in his throne." (REV. 3:20, 21)

"Let your loins be girded about, your lights burning; and ye yourselves like unto men that wait for their lord. When he will return from the wedding; that when he cometh and knocketh, they may open unto him im-mediately. Blessed are those servants, whom the lord when he cometh shall find watching:"
(LUKE 12:35, 36, 37)

"If any man defile the temple of God, him shall God destroy; for the temple of God is holy, which **temple** ye are." (I COR. 3:17)

Love and Love alone is the key to Life's 'Open sesame'. If we would dive deep, we must put on the garment of Love and Humility, which alone can sustain us in that depth of inner pressure and intense Light. How can we escape forever from the dominion of Kal and his world? By practicing the virtues and powers of the soul, which are natural and inherent in the Eternal Realm. Devotion with attention gradually leads to true Love. The ego has no place in the Eternal Abode, and when one has True Love, the ego no longer exists. The Supreme Being can be approached only through His qualities and Essence.

"Who shall ascend into the hill of (JEHOVAH) the Lord? or who shall stand in His Holy Place? He that hath clean hands and a pure heart."

(PSALM 24:3-4)

In other words, sincere devotion is the approach; Love is the Way; and Humility is the non-ego or the selflessness which is the essence of purity before God. **This is the Way**

of the Bible, and this is the Way of the Living Saints. Are we ready to choose that way and walk it?

Saints say that this is not only possible, but can best be done while living an ordinary, everyday life, because it does not depend on external observation of forms but on internal effort and devotion, while at the same time fulfilling our duties and obligations in this world. Thus while we are working in the world for temporal things, we are **in** Kal's or Satan's world **but not of it**, because the heart, mind and soul—as a result—are **set upon God** and **depend on His Love and Grace** leaving all results in His Hands.

Whose tools are we working with? When we work in the realms of thoughts and deeds of the mind and the senses, the emotions and physical accomplishment, we are working with Kal's tools because all this equipment belongs to his domain. It is necessary for our livelihood and education in this material world. Even the obstacles, thorns and sufferings are necessary goads to overcome the self and get out of Kal's realm. Therefore, trials and tribulations often descend on the devoted who are about to be freed, to enable them to pass the final test. (JOB).

The Spiritual Life is not a trouble-free life on this earth, but the earth life is a test in our overcoming those lower tendencies by the strength of the Inner Grace and Love. How can we grow strong in spiritual muscles, without tests and trials? Does one gain physical strength without exercise? Sant Sat Guru, Baba Sawan Singh Maharaj Ji, used to say that the idea is not to remove the thorns, for they may grow again, but to put on strong boots so that we can walk over the thorns without being harmed or hindered. The greater the devotion and love in our efforts on the Path, the greater is our protection. This protection is referred to as the *'strong boots'* that enable us to proceed under all circumstances.

It was not intended that the Path be smooth and easy, until we have been sufficiently purified. That which is Eternal and True is absolutely Pure, and nothing with the slightest taint of impurity (ego) can enter that Realm. As gold is refined by fire, so is the soul by trials and tribulations. Even Jesus and His disciples went through constant tribulations and sufferings. Spiritual grace can be earned by **effort** on our part. The Great Master Sawan Singh used to say that the more effort we make, the more Grace we receive to make more effort; that effort and Grace go hand in hand, until we reach the Goal.

Merely to remove all difficulties is not the answer. Our vehicles of mind and emotions would not get the training in strength and fortitude gained through resistance by trials. Neither would the soul have an opportunity to remain steadfast in faith and devotion throughout all vicissitudes. If this earth and our experiences in it were not necessary, they would not exist.

Only that which has usefulness or serves a purpose survives in Nature. All else perishes the moment it has outlived its usefulness. The same is true of the experiences which the soul has in its descent and ascent, until it reaches its final Goal. This Kindergarten of Life is a testing ground for souls, and is very necessary for progress to the Eternal Regions. Experience and more experience, **with a sincere effort at improvement**, is the way of understanding through learning with objective tools. Such a life—learning though suffering.

To sum it all up in a few words, it could be said that Spiritual qualities, when used, produce Spiritual results; mind, when used, produces mental effects; emotions, emotional effects; and physical effort produces physical effects. Only the quality of the essence can produce reactions in that Essence of Substance. The mind is the link which, when co-operating with soul qualities, travels via the True Spiritual qualities of Holy Shabd—the higher the region, the purer and clearer the Sound and the swifter the travel—until the Highest Heaven or Supreme Abode is reached.

So the choice is not a mystery, but a preference in our own selection and consequent action or inaction. God is nearer than breathing and closer than hands and feet. But the mind, in the cleverness of Kal, puts God far off in an external heaven or attempts to confine Him in a temple or other structures made by the hands of man; when, in reality, **God Himself built the temple of the human body and dwells therein**, waiting for us to consciously contact Him so that we need not again be born in the flesh. Until that time it will be necessary for us to assume coverings of flesh in one birth after another, seeking without for that which is within us.

Most of us have been wandering in the lower realms for so many countless ages that we have forgotten not only from whence we originally came and want to return, but we have also forgotten God's Omni presence as well as His Love which sustains the soul with every breath.

While God dwells within every living being, He is also beyond the comprehension of mind and reason, as these do not go deep enough. Those who would worship Him, can do so in Love and in Truth. So the questions as to where God is and how to find Him have been answered. It is merely a matter of whether we are ready for the mystic life or not.

There are souls in all stages of development of involution and evolution. Some have labored long in the Vineyard of the Lord, and they take to the Mystic Way **at once** in this life; others may have been in but a short time; still others may be entering for the first time; and most have yet to enter.

All *karma* is individual; and it is the individual's own previous thoughts, words and deeds which determine not only the nation but also the race, the family, the environment and circumstances into which he is to be born; also whether he is to be tall or short, lean or fat, healthy or sickly, rich or poor, etc. So it is with Spiritual progress. It is dependent on the individual awakening of each soul and its inner longing for the Lord. Thus the soul can attract the Lord's Grace and benefit by its abundance.

Saints can only shower Grace on those who are ready to receive it and benefit by it; otherwise it would be squandered in useless pursuits. A wise father does not give his son the physical heritage until he is able to properly manage and use it. Even physical wealth, not used or improperly used, is of no benefit to anyone. The true aspirant or devotee is the one who recognizes the Word of the real Mystic at once and applies himself accordingly.

"Blessed are they that hear the Word of God and keep it."

(Luke 11:28)

CHAPTER XVI
THE FIVE RIVERS OF SHABD

Out of the Eternal Region of Sach Khand flows One River of Sound Energy, in its perfect purity and essence. The Sound is so sweet that it cannot be compared with anything in this world, but for the sake of some kind of a hint that we may comprehend, it can be compared with that of the stringed instrument called the Bina or Vina, and the Light is said to be indescribable.

This River is the Real Essence of energy and the prototype of the river which flows out of Paradise; however, the one out of Paradise flows out of the lowest region of the Sound Current and Energy Plane. It is a step-down of five planes or octaves in the Essence of vibratory intensity of the Real River of Life which comes from the Eternal Region. At the lowest rung of the Eternal Essence the substance of the river from Eden begins and flows into the lower regions of the material creation, out of paradise, and splits into four rivers of a lower potential of polarized energy currents which animate the human body.

The saints are concerned only with the Five Rivers of Shabd and the regions produced by that Essence. From the Eternal Spiritual Region the One River of Energy Essence divides into two, and so on down into and through the regions below. But the Saints deal only with the Five Principal Ones, the Five Holy Shabds, which lead the wandering soul back to its Source. The True Master gives to His disciples the secret key Word for each Region through which he is to travel. This conveys the idea and energy rhythm before the conscious mind in its effort of ascent through concentration. These Five Holy Names are given at the time of Initiation, appropriately called 'NAM'. They are of value only when received either from the living Master direct or through some one designated by Him to impart these instructions. They have their Source in the True Guru as the link to the Eternal Reality.

The physical region is called 'Pind' by the Saints, and is not given much attention. It is an effect of the other regions, as a final crystallization into matter. The energies involved in it are of a lower key and are not used by the Saints for spiritual progress, since They do not use the lower five chakras of the River of Paradise as the conveyor of consciousness upward. Saints deal Only with the True Sound Essence as a current in the five spiritual regions which are above the physical and psychic regions. But the physical and psychic regions are all sustained and set going by the consciousness or *atmic* (soul) energy which permeates the whole body, though it is centered behind the eyes. It has to be gradually detached and drawn up to its center before one can start on his or her spiritual journey. In the process of Spiritual Growth and concentration, the consciousness and energy are drawn from the lower centers in the body up to the higher ones, in the brain and in the Inner Essence.

Through Shabd and its Five Rivers, the soul involuted into the lower regions, unto Eden as the last stop-over before merging into matter itself, called the physical plane. It is also by the direct route of the Five Holy Shabds that the living Master enables the soul to return to its Source. The rivers or roads within are more numerous and confusing than any we can imagine in this world, many of them leading to blind alleys and even deceiving us by cunningly diverting into the opposite direction. Hence the need of a true and competent guide. However, when one has a True Guide, He points out the Way of the Five Holy Rivers or Sounds which the soul may confidently, lovingly and joyfully follow direct to the Source, without the least fear of deception.

It may be well to point out at this time the need for unconditional surrender to, faith in and love for the living Master, Whose astral, spiritual and Shabd Forms we contact at the progressive stages within, and Who guides us within the same as we depend on physical guidance in this world, whether it is a person or only a road map. We all know how conflicting and confusing directions can be even in this world, especially when given by more than one person and each with a different opinion and perhaps also a different motive. But if you **know** that you can go or turn to one person on whom you can depend, and whose directions and instructions you can follow implicitly, without wavering, even though the directions may not seem right to you at the time, you are certainly not going to listen to anyone else nor are you going to waste more time in getting further entangled, mired and lost in seeking your own way. Of ourselves we can do nothing, and we cannot even determine right from wrong, especially when we follow instructions from those who are themselves lost on the way, but are not even aware of it. Therefore, it is imperative that we decide what we wish to do, then look for a True Guide. And when He has undertaken to guide and protect us, we should wholly and completely submit to Him by following His instructions to the best of our ability, for He alone has the best interests of the soul at heart. In fact, a True Master is more eager for the welfare of our own soul than we ever can be, until we too have reached the Eternal Region. Without His help, we are too apt to be satisfied with less and then we would still find ourselves in the region of Kal.

As previously stated, the region above this physical one is more beautiful, the days and nights are longer, and each region above that is more beautiful and grander than the one below it, until one minute is equal to years on this earth. Until one reaches up to the Eternal Region of Sach Khand, one is still subject to time and so eventually, at either a 'Pralaya' — dissolution — which reaches up to Trikuti — or a 'Maha Pralaya' — grand dissolution — which reaches up to the top of Bhanwar Gupha, depending on the heights reached, the soul is still liable to be reborn into the physical plane. But, when one has a True

Guide and has no desires which necessitate his re-incarnating into the lower regions, even though he may still be in one of the lower regions at the time of a dissolution or a grand dissolution, the Master, in His Infinite Mercy, places the soul in some safe place during that process, and he can continue going up from there without again reverting to the lower. This proves how deceptive our contentment would be if we could manage to get to one of the higher regions below the Eternal, without the guidance of One Who has Himself gone up to the Supreme Region, or who has been appointed by such a One to guide the true seekers.

The Shabd or River of Life which is the **Spirit** of Jehovah in the Old Testament, becomes the Holy Ghost in the New Testament, as the fulfillment of the law through Love, Faith and Devotion. The Old Testament portrayed its message in symbolic forms and definite stages on the Tree of Life, which the New Testament embraces in the form of Bhakti Yoga or Devotion and **living** the Life.

According to the New Testament, Jesus promised to send the Comforter to His disciples, which He did.

"But the Comforter, which is the Holy Ghost whom the Father will send in my name, he shall teach you all things," (JOHN 14:26)

"Receive ye the Holy Ghost:" (JOHN 20:22)

This blessing was the Sound Current Energy of the Edenic Realm, or Paradise; and was a part of early Christian teachings, and the heritage of the devoted followers. But the mystery and the Inner Value of even this has been lost, and no longer exists in the religions of the world. Only the True Saints continue to initiate and acquaint Their devotees with the Five Holy Sounds of the Spirit, from the Eternal Source.

The student is given a method of concentration and devotion which he is to practice daily in order to raise his consciousness to that Essence, to see the Light and hear that wonderful Sound within. This is the True Mystic Way to the Living Truth Within the soul itself, to unlock its doors of limitation and blend its essence with the One Essence on every plane, and bathe in every one of the Five Spiritual Inner River of Life.

The effort and the time spent in this Way of thought and practice is indeed working in the Father's House or laboring in the Lord's Vineyard. (LUKE 2:49) This *'wine'* is the Spiritual Essence or Nectar of Life, and is not the fermented juice of the physical grape, which inebriates the mind and the senses. The uplift of the Real Nectar within has a beneficial effect on the mind and the senses, which is deeper and far more real and lasting than any physical wine or strong drink.

The vineyard which Noah planted was not physical; neither was his inebriation. The *'wine'* of Omar Khayyam had a similar meaning to the Mystics of the Middle East. The Sacramental Wine and Bread instituted by Jesus at the Last Supper, also had this Inner Spiritual meaning.

Mysticism applies the same ideas throughout the ages. It utilizes that which man can understand as a symbol of the Real. It bears all the earmarks of the One Essence mentioned in all Sacred Texts. It is not a creed or a religion, but a **Life** in the Essence and in the Truth of the One Who made all these things for mankind. It pertains to the Central Energy Current of Life itself. Therefore, it does not contradict nor conflict with any or all the Rives which split off from the One Essence. They all bear a measure of the Water or Nectar from this One Life Stream of Creation.

The Mystic does not argue, for His life and Inner Gifts are His proof. His mind has been subdued by the Holy Shabd Itself, and has found the Peace for which it had longed. The Mystic's will is One with the Father's Will.

Arguments and mere mental concepts are not the Life nor the Truth. The mind is clever and evasive; it is a tool of Kal. Whoever listens to it, is lost in its embrace and will not be able to extricate himself from that power of Kal and Maya.

Only Love and Inner Devotion can transcend the mind and reason, and bring Peace to the soul. The mind itself longs for redemption and peace, but it is a slave to the senses which in turn have ruled it for so long that it has forgotten even how to seek everlasting peace and contentment. Appetites and habits are giants.

We are creatures of habit. Habits are not changed easily, and character is not built in a day nor in a year. All things must have their season of planting, of attention, of growth and of final maturity. The seed of the One Eternal Essence is in the fruit, to perpetuate its perennial youth. Only in the Essence of the Life itself lies the Mystery of the Word which is All in all.

CHAPTER XVII
SIN AND REPENTANCE

These two factors form a prominent part of the Bible in both the Old and New Testaments. Whenever the people of a nation repented of their sins, Jehovah did not destroy them, even though His prophets had been instructed to proclaim and prophesy the destruction of the nation. The New Testament holds out a similar view, under the Grace of the Savior, through Love and Mercy.

Both conditions can be better understood when the process of the original cause and its sequences are known and are transcended through steadfast devotion to the Eternal Sound Essence, symbolized as the *'Spirit'* of Jehovah in the Old Testament, and the *'Holy Ghost'* or *'Holy Spirit'* or *'The Comforter'* etc. in the New Testament.

The outstanding features of the New Testament and the Teachings of the Living Saints are Love and Humility, through the Grace of the Savior, the Master or the True Guru, to save the soul from damnation.

"For the wages of sin is death; but the gift of God is eternal life" (ROMANS 6:23)

"Now the works of the flesh are manifest," (GAL. 6:19)

"But the fruit of the Spirit is love, joy, peace, long suffering, gentleness, goodness, faith, meekness, temperance: against such there is no law."

(GAL. 6:22, 23)

Spiritually speaking, we **die** when we are born into this world of mind and matter; and we are **born** again into the Spiritual Realms, when we can die unto the self **while living in the body**. The true birth and salvation of the soul is brought about through a true living Master or Teacher who embodies the Holy Spirit and connects us with the Eternal Sound Current.

"Marvel not that I said unto thee, Ye must be born again. The wind bloweth where it listeth and thou hearest the sound thereof, but canst not tell whence it cometh, and whither it goeth: so is every one that is born of the Spirit." (JOHN 3:7, 8)

"No man hath ascended up to heaven, but he that came down from heaven, even the Son of man which is in heaven." (JOHN 3:13)

"Blessed is the man to whom the Lord will not impute sin." (ROM. 4:8)

"For sin shall not have dominion over you: for ye are not under the law, but under grace." (ROM. 6:14)

"For the law of the Spirit of life in Christ Jesus hath made me free from the law of sin and death." (ROMANS 8:2)

Man has not the power to extricate himself from the clever meshes of Kal nor from the Maya of illusion of his own mind and senses. All self-righteousness has so much vanity in it of the ego, that it defeats its own purpose of salvation.

One often wonders why so much mention is made about one sinner who repenteth, being better than many self-righteous men? (LUKE 15:7) The reason is obvious. There is no love, no humility in self-righteousness. There may be some devotion to the Lord, but it never forgets to proclaim its own righteousness and effort. The ego and its vanity are there still as the primary desire and the one original sin. Wherever there is ego, there is self-will and separation from the Sound Current, the Supreme Father's design of salvation for all creation and all creatures.

Since God's Will and Way were not man's choice in the beginning of his involuntionary cycle, he is living in condemnation, without grace, by his own willful separation from the Infinite Bounty in the Eternal Will of the Sound Essence, until he is again connected with It (reborn) by a living Saint, the Conscious embodiment of God on earth. No creation could exist without the support of this Word Eternal as the Energy Principle and Life and Light Essence of all which lives, breathes and moves.

The Eternal Father furnishes all and allows His children to do as they please, so they may learn their lesson of independent will, ego and desire as their choice of sensory experiences in life.

By examining the nature of sin, we find the same manner of enticing in our own mind as was presented to the souls in Paradise, and as recorded for our benefit in the accounts of the temptations of Jesus, Abraham, Job, etc.

'Nafs' is the serpent or lower mind principle in Paradise, and is duly present in our own mind, through Kal's agency of mind substance and desire. The serpent power of mind climbs down the Tree of Life, from the brain or its crown, and seeks satisfaction in the lower regions of sense desire and matter (GEN. 3:1-5). By so doing, it draws on the original energy in the brain and squanders it on sensory indulgences of every kind.

The illusion of satisfaction is perfect, because the soul experiences energy release in sensation. And this main illusion of **something for nothing** carries all through life, like a Nemesis to the soul. It wants to expend that which is not rightfully its own, and also seeks pleasure in doing so. (GEN. 3:6)

Even today, the voice of the serpent as suggestions, temptations and imaginations, is not wanting. It is the same process now as it was in the beginning, only we recognize it not and always seek to place the blame on others in order to justify our own actions. The very tempter looks like a bright angel of cleverness and promise of so much gain, satisfaction and self-glory. However, when we finally wake up and stop to examine this trick of our own mind, we find sadness in experience and delusion. The very same tempter and temptation within ourselves become the accuser. The bitter remorse sets in.

None is more cruel than the accuser which is our own mind, when led by the senses instead of the soul. The lower tendencies of the mind promise so much light, life and extra enjoyment and gain to the self, through the mind and senses. This same mind also becomes the judge as well as the accuser, after having succeeded in tempting and ensnaring the unwary soul into its net. Self-condemnation is a natural sequence of this process.

Such is the gamut of this clever inspiration of the lower mind and Kal, which promise so much to the ego through sensation and pleasure or the glory of self-expression in its own childish way. A host of evils and sufferings follow in its train, as the result of the original desire and the first action which results in all the other complications. This primary path of the Original Sin is repeated over and over again, daily, and we are not aware of it but continue to place the blame on Adam and Eve instead of our own ego and its own desires.

We suffer for the sins of our past thoughts, words and actions, as well as for the present indiscretions. Energy must be balances or repaired in kind, in the economy of the universe, to maintain the equilibrium in matter and in motion of energy potential.

Having analyzed the process of involution, of sin and desire, let us examine the evolution **out of** this mire of pain and suffering to which all creation is subjected. This whole creation groans under the load of oppression and drive of the involved *karmic* energy. (ROMANS 8:22-23).

We are not aware of causes, only of the resulting effects and suffering. The soul knows, but it is helplessly trapped like a bird in a cage of energy bars, from which it cannot escape until the mind also wishes to do so and accompanies it. The union of God and soul within the body is the marriage referred to in Mystic Writings and oral teachings. Until this union has taken place, all that the soul can do is to suffer and endure the results of the self-inflicted causes and attachments. The mind, too, is miserable because of its having squandered the soul's energy, and is equally as helplessly bound by the senses, so that it is not possible for it to accompany the soul until a living Master comes to the rescue. (II SAM. 22:2, 3; Is. 19:20)

The Hell, Sheol and Purgatory mentioned in the Bible, have their origin in this state of exhausted energy fields, where light is absent and darkness abounds. Without energy or power, there is no light. When the fuel is burned, the light and warmth disappear. This fact we know in our own material experience of heating and lighting our homes. As below, so it is above in the true energy fields. Re-action is the result of previous action, and expenditure of energy is a given direction. This re-action, from both good and bad actions, is termed 'Karma'. Some is good, some is bad, some is pleasant and some unpleasant. Some is apportioned to one lifetime and some to another, and all the while the mind and soul continue to accumulate more for the future. Still we each have an incomprehensible amount of accumulated *karma* from past lives, which is yet to be accounted for, and only by God's Infinite Mercy and Grace, through the help of a living Master, can we ever get out of this mess. It is only with the help of the living Master we can learn how to keep ourselves free from new *karma* while we are paying off the old, under His guidance and protection.

Life is simple in its Essence and at the Core and Center. But it becomes complicated when multiplied in expression and action, whether in thought, word or deed. It is like a wheel which has but one axle and one hub, but how many spokes are necessary to carry the load to the rim of the wheel! In turn, the rim or shell must be strong and thick enough to carry the load, or it breaks down. This simple analysis gives us a picture of the soul's energy in motion of balance or imbalance, for every wheel must run true to its center or it breaks.

Now we come to the point, why repentance is Praised so much in the Bible. The soul, in suffering, cries out to God, like Jonah did in the belly of the Whale or in the depths of hell (Jonah 2:2). The **Spirit** of Jehovah, the Omnipresent Grace in the Sound Current Energy, hears the cry of its beloved child, the soul, and comes to its rescue with its abundance of Grace and new Energy, and lifts the soul out of Sheol or hell of its exhaustion and suffering. It is like rescuing a child who calls for help while it is being swept away in a torrent of water.

"O Lord (Jehovah), thou hast brought up my soul from the grace (Sheol, hell); Thou hast kept me alive, that I should not go down to the pit."

(PSALMS 30:3)

"For great is thy mercy toward me; And thou hast delivered my soul from the lowest hell (Sheol)."

(PSAMLS 86:13)

Suffering is due to poverty of substance necessary to do with or to eat thereof, or a poverty of energy ensues. To sense truly, and to be happy, is normal. But to dwell on grief, fear, self-pity and despair, or any negative state of mind, and to indulge in them, leads to a pitiful state of exhaustion and a feeling of dull woe. This is in no way repentance, but is in itself a great sin. Despair itself is a willful negation of God's Grace which is always waiting to help any soul who turns to Him in all sincerity.

"For godly sorrow worketh repentance to salvation not to be repented of: but the sorrow of the world worketh death." (II COR. 7:10)

The only possible salvation is the exact opposite of the original sin of separation from the Eternal Father and His abundance of Energy of Love and Mercy and Grace. When the self or ego has come to the end of its rope of free travel and choice in experience, then can the mind, like Pharaoh, be convinced by its suffering. Then it realizes that the path it chose and the dwelling on its little self, which locks up the mind and soul, is nothing but an illusion.

The soul longs to return to the Father's House, like a tired child which ran away to have a good time. But it soon finds out that the experience encountered and in which it allowed itself to become involved by forgetting its Source, is more than it bargained for. Now, in suffering and humility, it is ready to return Home to the Father, bruised but much wiser and with greater appreciation so that it cannot again, under any circumstances, be coaxed to make the mistake of leaving the Home of Perfect Bliss.

The beautiful parable of the Prodigal Son, related by Jesus (LUKE 15:11 to end chapter), gives the entire setting of the picture, with a wonderful background of the Father's Love and Grace in receiving the lost son back home.

The experience of suffering is not easily wiped out nor forgotten. A greater humility and compassion is possible for the soul who has himself undergone such an experience. Through deeper understanding, a deeper humility is possible in all realms of energy fields through which the soul has passed in the negative pole of suffering and want. The vacuum thus created allows room for God's Grace, abundance of Love and True Bliss. This is the ultimate knowledge or Gyan of all things and Essences. The True Knowledge or Eternal Gyan in its pure Essence is the beholding of and being One with the Supreme Father. Such is the path of the soul in its glorious return journey which could well be called, "The Prodigal Son Comes Home."

According to the Teachings of the Saints, the connection of the soul with the Essence or the Eternal Sound Current is the only true way to Eternal Happiness. This method, through the humility and effort of the mind and soul, and the Love and Grace of the Eternal Father, is very much like the Way given in the Bible:

"For by grace are ye saved through faith; and that not of yourselves; it is the gift of God: Not of works, lest any man should boast." (EPHESIANS 2:8, 9)

(Similar statements are made in I Peter 1:9; I JOHN 3:1; etc.)

The illusions of the mind and senses are hard to overcome, and so there are many falls on the way of experience. But the Love of the Eternal Father conquers in the end. Finally, the soul sees Lover everywhere, **Lives** it and becomes One with it through the central current of the Eternal Essence in his own being and consciousness.

Repentance, praised so highly in the Bible, is really an inner process of re-penning or returning the Energies into their natural sphere and proportion of balance, in perfect relation to the Central Axis of the Eternal Essence within the soul. Then, the influx of Grace and Divine Help is possible, and these are much greater than the powers of the individual soul. Therefore, it is praised so highly in the Scriptures.

"But the meek shall inherit the earth,"

(PSALMS 37:11)

(Similar statements in PSALMS 69:32, MAT.5:5-10; MAT. 11:29, 30; I PETER 3:4; etc.)

Mistakes in life, which lead the soul to this state of Inner Awareness **of the need of help and Grace** from the Eternal Father, bring about the humility which is genuine, and by which the soul can be **tuned into the reception** of the Eternal Radiant Broadcast of the Constant and sweet music of the Holy Shabd, the very essence of Sound within all creation. It is the Primal River of Energy, Life and Bliss.

The Sacred Scriptures of the East and the West, and the Teachings of the Modern Saints are not so far apart in Essence as it seems at first glance. In fact, the Essence in all is the same. This is easily understood when the One Reality and Essence of the Eternal Sound Current, the World, the Cause of all beginnings, of the middle and of the end, becomes the cornerstone of understanding and Unity at the Core of all being and things. This is the Alpha and Omega of all creation. This Essence is the stone which the builders rejected, and which must again become the head of the corner. (PSALMS 118:22; MAT. 21:42; PETER 2:4, 2:7)

Only at the Center can Unity be perfect in a world of creation of endless multiplicity. To look for Truth or Unity in the mind patterns of multiplicity and varieties, is nothing but foolishness and a lack of discrimination in the proper use of the mind. Why should all doctrines agree?

How could we then have multiplicity? Are climates and seasons the same everywhere on earth? Do we have a right to condemn People who live in other climates? Oneness, sameness and Truth are possible only in the Essence of the One Who is Changeless and Truth Himself. Material facts are proven in the material world. Truth is proved by the inner life in the Spirit Essence and in Truth itself on the Spiritual planes.

CHAPTER XVIII
THE SONG OF SOLOMON

The symbolism in the Song of Solomon is about as difficult to put into writing as that of Genesis or Revelations because it pertains to Mysticism beyond the experience of everyday consciousness, and yet it is portrayed through the medium of that which usually ensnares the mind. As we know from historical accounts, it is called "The Song of Songs" or "The Holy of Holies" and was assigned to the eight day of the Passover. Its special holiness and authorship made it survive much opposition. It was only because of that unknown Mystical consideration that it was accepted among the Canons, even before the Christian Era.

The firm defense by Mystics among the Rabbis enabled it to survive. At the Council of Jamnia, in 90 A.D., Rabbi Akiba spoke in its defense in high veneration:

"The whole world is not worth the day on which the Song of Songs was given."

It is matchless panegyric upon True Love, bases upon a higher unknown Love, which atones for any coarseness in its symbolic portrayal.

A theory was suggested and formulated by Budde, that is was a Folk Song. He mentions twenty-three varieties which are sung after weddings in Syria. In 1873, J.G. Wetzstein, the Prussian Consul at Damascus, published some of them.

In 1544 Castillo declared the Song was an expression of Solomon's love for the maiden, Shulammith, and this declaration was unanimously accepted. According to that version, Solomon found her in her own country and brought her to his place; but she was in love with a shepherd and remained true to that love.

In Syrian weddings, the bridegroom and the bride are honored by their guests during their eight days of celebration, as King Solomon and Queen Shulammith, and the Songs of the Festival are supposed to portray a higher love, symbolized by the Marriage and its feast.

Some authors tried to interpret it as a Greek drama. But as a drama there are none of the usual indications concerning dramatic personae, scenes, etc. Even as a song, it has vacancies which have to be filled in as sequences.

Back in the sixteenth century, in the Preface to his book entitled 'CONSIDERATIONS ON THE SONG OF SONGS', the Spanish Mystic, Juan De Los Angeles wrote:

"If any book needed the spirit of prophecy it would be this one; and not that alone, but also a knowledge of an infinitude of natural things and their properties, because at every step these are introduced as the symbols of things spiritual. In the **first chapter** alone, **which has occupied me more than two years**, I have met so many difficulties that I have wished to turn back from the task, and much weariness and discouragement has assailed me because I have become entangled in so vast a maze."

Interpretation and definite application are in a realm beyond the ordinary experiences of man, or it would not be venerated as "The Holy of Holies."

Songs are usually written by an exuberant spirit to express that with which the heart is filled and runneth over. For poetic speech, the Psalms have a considerable amount in them (PSALMS 120-5, etc.) But the Song of Solomon is outstanding and unique in its exotic expression of an Inner Uplift of the Spirit by an experience beyond the power of sensory perception. It clearly belongs to the veiled Mystic Writings of the East, in an early period. Solomon ascended the throne in 971 B.C., when he was not yet twenty years of age.

To interpret 'The Song of Songs' as the love of Christ for His church, or that of the church for Christ, amounts to rather vague prophecy, about one thousand years ahead of its time. That explanation is not apt, as it does not pertain to the personal inner experience of the author of the 'Song' at the time he wrote it.

Spiritually speaking, it is possible that Solomon was a Mystic who transcended the mere physical pleasures which his position and harem could provide in abundance, and found a greater Reality in Love itself, which made him the Wise King of Ages. He prayed to God for wisdom, and his prayer was answered (I KINGS 3:9-12). For, whoever wrote that account and that was supposed to have been Solomon—clearly describes a transcendental uplift in a higher realm of energy fields than that of the physical world.

The language and terms of comparison used in the 'Song' were acceptable comparative symbolism used in the East at that time. Mystics and Great Teachers still use this type of symbolism in describing the delight of the soul when it ascends upward, on its Inner Journey and touches the Sound Current, the Essence of Life, Light and Bliss. Some Teachers have used the simile of the delight of the young mother at the touch of her new born babe, to give a hint of the joy of the soul at the contact with the Holy Shabd. The Holy Shabd is the life-saving line onto which the soul can hold and be safely towed and lifted onto the Ship of that current which will take it safely across the ocean of existence into that Oneness of the Beloved Father.

Such emotions overwhelm the soul on the realization of its own new birth in the Sound Essence. But it is more than that, for it fulfills all longing and need or desires of the soul. It is also symbolized by the Feast which the father gave to the Prodigal Son who had left home, squandered his inheritance, became lost, and found his way home again.

In the Holy Scriptures everywhere, all feasts and songs and gifts are but symbolic of an Inner Reality which is beyond the power of mortal language to describe. So the Mystic uses the similes and metaphors most acceptable to the minds of his audience and his readers, in an effort to give a hint of this sublime experience of the mind and soul.

The union of the mind with the soul is referred to as a marriage but the REAL MARRIAGE IS THE UNION OF THE SOUL WITH THE SOUND CURRENT. The greatest delight on earth is as nothing compared to THAT experienced within. That is the Wedding Feast of the Soul.

Even Jesus said:

"If I have told you earthly things and ye believe not, how shall ye believe if I tell you of heavenly things?"

(JOHN 3:12)

Matter-of-fact material things are far removed from the scope of Spiritual Experiences of Mystics Who, in Their Ecstasy, give hints of Their supreme delight in terms which we can understand. Neither is this psychic eroticism, but a reward of faith and sincere effort in devotion and concentration of the consciousness of the mind and soul to a high pitch of efficiency and vibratory intensity in conscious awareness in higher realms.

In the physical world, a trained and steady mind determines the value of a person in any line of business endeavor, or in professions and in trades. Concentration is efficiency. In Spiritual training this is even more true; for no progress can be made at all until the mind is held still in concentration, so the Inner can be perceived, seen, felt, heard, etc. similarly as we see, hear, feel, etc. in the physical world.

The Spiritual training and concentration of the mind challenges the efforts of otherwise strong and upright characters, for it is impossible to proceed on the Way until every weakness has been conquered. Those who did so were called the Heroes of old, like the Patriarch Abraham and the leaders of Israel (Moses and Joshua) etc., in the Bible; also, Hercules, Theseus and other Greek heroes; Arjuna in the Bhagavad Gita, etc.

The songs, folklore and operas of other nations, such as the Nibelungen Ring of the Wagnerian Operas and the heroes therein, also Parsifal and the Holy Grail, Tristan and Isolde, etc. are all accounts of mystic accomplishments. The accompanying songs and music were **symbols of the Sound Energy Current**.

There are and always have been Mystics in the East because the very atmosphere is mystical in its many religious aspects. There are always a few first fruits among the fruits of any tree (ROMANS 8:23; I COR. 15:20; 15:23;

JEREMIAH 2:3, etc.) These, toil harder and longer and are more in tune with their efforts, because of the previous labor in the Vineyard of the Lord. The individual is always apt in that which he loves.

The Song of Solomon
1

The Bride speaks with the Daughters of Jerusalem who symbolize souls or swans in the Inner Mystic Realm.

"**1.** The Song of Songs, which is Solomon's.

"**2.** Let him kiss me with the kisses of his mouth;
  For thy love is better than wine."

The first part is that of the usual greetings of lovers. Physically, wine is considered a stimulant, and it symbolizes the same in Spiritual substance. The love and attraction of the Holy Shabd, the Sound Essence, is termed even better than the wine. It is a spiritual nectar. Received on entering that stage of Inner Awareness or Soul Life.

"**3.** Because of the savour of thy good ointments."

Spiritual fragrance is a well-known fact among Mystic of attainment, and with it goes a great happiness. The Great Master, Sawan Singh Maharaj Ji, related that in the early days while He was an engineer in Government Service, one day as He was travelling in the mountains on horseback, He suddenly began to feel very happy and that as he rode on, this happiness greatly increased. He was also aware of a sweet fragrance, the like of which is not known on this earth. When both, the fragrance and the feeling of happiness were sublime beyond description, He noticed a holy man sitting near the road; whereupon He dismounted and paid His respects to the Saint before proceeding further on His journey. Such is the Unity of Inner Understanding and Love between Mystics of attainment. Only one who has mystic qualities within himself can recognize them in another.

Oil was used as a symbol of peace and balance of the Spirit. It quiets disturbed waters. It was used for anointing the heads of Kings and High Priests at their coronation or consecration. Holy oils are still used in the sacraments of Holy Orders and Extreme Unction, and many religious rites and ceremonies.

"They name is as ointment poured forth."

The 'name' signifies 'NAM', the One Word or Essence, as the Sound Current which soothes all wounds of the soul or spirit. It is referred to as the "Oil of Joy and Comfort" in Isaiah 58:11. The expression of "Joy and Comfort" in the Old Testament has the same meaning as "The Comforter" in the New Testament.

"Therefore do the virgins love thee."

Pure spirits are called virgins, hansas or swans in higher regions. The Essence or Shabd is always positive and is addressed as The Beloved. At this stage souls, either male or female, are termed as female because they are negative to the Eternal Current and are attracted and elevated by it. They are drawn to it as iron is drawn to a magnet, or as the sun of this universe draws forth the essence in vegetation and the planets.

"4. Draw me, we will run after thee;
    The king bath brought me into his chambers:
    We will be glad and rejoice in thee,
    We will remember thy love more than wine:
    The upright love thee."

The King is the Beloved. The soul has attained admittance into the Sound Current. Those who rightly love are the pure souls who ascend unto this mountain or Holy Hill or Will of God, and are included in the term 'we'.

"5. I am black, but comely,
    O ye daughters of Jerusalem,
    As the tents of Kedar,
    As the curtains of Solomon."

Here a new aspect is brought out by the ascending soul's humility. It proclaims to be black, unworthy, like the black sheep of the family. Kedar was one of the sons of Ishmael, and the soul feels as unworthy of this great heritage of Spirituality as did Ishmael because he was not entitled to share equally with Isaac. Kedar and his tribe lived in tents made of black goats' hair. The black curtains of Solomon, which covered the Tabernacle, were also made of black goats' hair. There were eleven curtains. This number is also symbolic of the five *chakras* in the body, the sixth being the door or curtain between the five centers below and the five above; or between the unconscious centers below the eyes and the conscious centers above, in the brain.

The Bible plainly describes the size and placement of the eleven curtains and states that one was placed over the door. The door or gate in Mystic Writings refers to the *'third eye'* or *'Tisra Til'*, through which the soul must pass before it can begin the journey to higher regions. The mind or ego must become small before it can accompany the soul through this narrow gate. By becoming small, it becomes humble and realize its unworthiness and feels that it is only a cover over the tent which holds the Holy of Holies and the Mercy Seat in the inner consciousness.

"**6.** Look not upon me, because I am black,
Because the sun hath looked upon me:
My mother's children were angry with me;
They made me the keeper of the vineyards;
But mine own vineyard have I not kept".

The mind begs not to be excluded and that its unworthiness be not noticed; for in its earthly heritage of birth it also feels as a misfit. Her mother's sons or children made her the keeper of the vineyard—the house or garden — and they were angry with her because of the time spent in day-dreaming or Mystic contemplation. The last line is typical of the lament of the souls who have longed for and have been given the Path, but who realize that they have spent so much time on everything else except the one purpose for which they were given a human body. What honest soul ever feels satisfied with the Spiritual effort put forth or time applied in concentration and devotion to the Beloved Lord of all?

"**7.** Tell me, O thou whom my soul loveth,
   Where thou feedest, where thou makest
   Thy flock to rest at noon:
   For why should I be as one that turneth aside
   By the flocks of thy companions?"

The soul wants to know the place of Nectar, the high noon hour when the rays of it feed all there, for why should it be veiled or turned away from that delight?

"**8.** If thou know not, O thou fairest among women."

The daughters of Jerusalem and the fairest among women symbolize the souls in the Sound Current Vibration. Then the soul delights in telling that it knows the Way.

"Go thy way forth by the footsteps of the flock,"

Follow the rays of the Sound Current and feast on the Nectar.

"And feed thy kids beside the shepherds' tents."

And feed thy kids, the young sprouts of love, beside the Shepherds' tents, the Beloved Saints which are the Centers of Nectar.

"**9.** I have compared thee, O my love
   To a company of horses in Pharaoh's chariots."

The word *'Pharaoh'* means *'great house'*, undisputed monarch or king. The swift steeds were the outstanding means of travel and communication at that time. In order to reach the Great House of the King, such swift steeds were needed (Also in Esther 8:4). These are the energy currents upon which the souls travel. The Alborak of Mohammed, which carried him to the moon, is a similar symbol of the attention currents of the mind and soul.

"**10.** Thy cheeks are comely with rows of jewels,
   Thy neck with chains of gold.

"**11.** We will make thee borders of gold
   With studs of silver."

Ornaments and jewelry were symbolic of Inner Currents or Virtue in the etheric essence and in Spiritual Realms. Besides the symbolic portrayal of the Inner values, jewelry and precious stones were worn to attract those currents out of the atmospheric energy fields and to concentrate them on the person of the wearer for health, vitality, good luck, etc. This was the origin of charms and amulets, as points of concentration for universal energy attraction. It was an ancient method of tuning into the Universal Energies. The Urim and Thummim, attached to the breast plates of the high priest, as mentioned in Exodus 28:15-30, had similar application. All the jewels used in them represented Cosmic Energy, and were used for tuning into the psychic realm and etheric essence, in order to receive answers to problems (Ex. 39:2-22; LEV. 8:7-10; I SAM. 23:9-14; I SAM. 28:6; EPH. 6:14; THES. 5:8).

"**12.** While the king sitteth at his table,
My spikenard sendeth forth the smell thereof."

The tables used in the Orient were usually round and of various materials, and of a height for squatting around them on cushions. The table was a symbol of a common center of Wisdom which nourished the mind as well as the body (PROVERBS 9:1-7). The table of Showbreads had a similar meaning, for Inner Nourishment of Spiritual value, like the wafers in the Christian Sacrament. (Nu. 4:7; LEV. 24:5-9)

The Inner Spiritual Qualities of devotion and love without any taint of ego or self, produced the aroma as a substance, which was symbolized by perfumes, spices, spikenard, etc. and their uses. The fragrance sent forth was that from within, by the precipitation of the Real Chemistry in the higher realms. Spikenard was a special ointment, made from the pure oil of Nard, which was extracted from a bearded grass grown in India. It was very costly. (MARK 14:3; JOHN 12:3)

"**13.** A bundle of myrrh is my well beloved unto me:
He shall lie all night betwixt my breast."

Myrrh was often worn on the chest by the ladies. It is symbolic of the finer virtues and **inner devotion**, expressed by the delightful fragrance. Spices were called

'Bsamin' in Hebrew. The Holy Ointment was forbidden to the people. Even the symbol of the essence or holy oil was forbidden to the outsiders, not of the priesthood or who were not sanctified servants of the Lord in the Holy of Holies.

Exodus 26:6-8 shows the deeper, sacred meaning of all these external applications. "And let them make me a sanctuary that I may dwell among them" (Ex. 25:8), explains the real object and purpose of all these Preparations and symbols. The real ingredients were LOVE AND DEVOTION, and nothing else. The form or symbolism only expresses the Life, **it cannot provide it**.

"**14.** My beloved is unto me as a cluster of camphire
     In the vineyards of En-gedi."

The word *'En-gedi'* literally means *'a spring of the kid'*, and possibly it is the origin of the *'fountain of youth?'* For what is younger, more spry and full of life than a kid?

Henna or camphire was used among the ointments and also as a dye. (S.S. 4:13). To literally become born again by being dyed in that color and rejuvenated, is similar to the expression: "Behold, I make all things new" (Rev. 21:5; Rev. 21:1; Rev 3:12) Could it be possible that some Mystics had already penetrated this sphere which was seen by John, the Revelator, and described by him almost a thousand years later? Is there really anything new in this world? Or does it merely await our discovery and claim to it by a deeper penetration of understanding and the ability to enter that realm?

"**15.** Behold, thou art fair, my love;
     Behold, thou art fair
     Thou hast dove's eyes."

The eyes are the windows of the soul and express finer currents of Love. "Drink to me only with thine eyes, and I will pledge with mine" is a typical version of this exquisite uplift of Inner Reality in the fullness of Love.

When a true Master wishes to bestow a special favor on a disciple, He gazes at him intently. In an instant, some Great

Essence has overflowed and the devotee is the recipient of it. The uplift is beyond the range of words to describe. In fact, outside of the gift of Nam Itself, this is the greatest blessing that can be bestowed upon a human being. Even the hem of the Saint's garment has virtue and power in it, from the radiance of the Saint Who wears it (LUKE 5:13; MARK 5:28-31).

Again, we marvel that Solomon knew of this Grace and managed to hide it most cleverly under this exotic symbolism of Love. Who can read these words, but a lover or a devotee of "His Love"? And for such these jewels written and effectively hidden in mere were words.

The dove is a symbol of The Holy Spirit, or Love, of Innocence and Harmlessness (MAT. 10:16; Ps. 68:13; 74:10) The appearance of the dove at the Baptism of Jesus symbolized the Holy Spirit or Holy Shabd over the head of Jesus. The symbol of the dove is used to denote pure love and peace, even in this physical world. "The love of turtle-doves" has been a common expression. In ancient times, the dove was also used for certain sacrifices.

"**16.** Behold, thou art fair, my beloved, yea,
　　pleasant:
　　Also our bed is green.
"**17.** The beams of our house are cedar,
　　And our rafters of fir."

Solomon speaks of having attained Reality, in exotic terms of union and oneness. *'In the king's great house'*, *'at his table'* and *'our couch'* are very expressive terms of an Inner Experience of a Higher Love. A couch is a support and resting place. Green is the color of growing things. Fertile and refreshing are His valleys in Nature; but even more beautiful and restful are those which we find within.

'The Cedars of Lebanon' have become a byword for trees of quality, whose wood endures long and withstands much moisture (Ps. 80:10). The beams of a house are its support. Solomon mentions that they are cedars, which refers to quality and endurance, even as the cedar which was used in the building of the temple of the Lord and overlaid with

gold and silver. This symbolizes the realization of the living temple within, of which the outer is but a crude copy.

The fir tree is ever fresh and green (HOSEA 14:8; ISA-IAH 41:19; 44:14; 55:13). "Of such our rafters are made". The above, as well as the below, is green and alive, pulsating life itself, because all is Love. Love is the *'Song of Songs'*.

There are many other exotic and ecstatic comparisons of inner attraction, which need not be explained. With the key given thus far, it should not be difficult to read the mystic meaning in all Sacred Writings, and in the songs, poems and dramas of a mystic nature.

Deep feeling and Life itself cannot be interpreted into mortal language. Only Inner Experience and the Lord's Grace can convey the True Understanding of His Way with devoted souls on the Homeward Journey, in the River of the Essence of Holy Shabd. Saints refer to it as *'The Unwritten law'* and *'The Unspoken language'* which is Real Love.

Mystic Inner Travel is on the Current of the Sound Energy, much the same as we travel in this world on a river of water, or as light travels in beams. It is said that Mohammed traveled on the Alborak up to the moon and entered its sphere. This is also symbolic of the travel on the attention Current up to the inner Moon Region, situated below the City of the Thousand-Petalled Lotus, also called Sahasra Dal Kamal, where the Real Sound Current starts upward to the higher regions.

Since all true Mystics, Saviors, Saints and Prophets have traveled that Royal Road, and all speak the same Truth, it should not be so difficult to figure out what they are talking about when they try to tell us some of their experiences on the Way, in the manner mostly easily understood by those who are sincere seekers.

Walking in the Way of Devotion and Love has its own compensations in blissful experiences of which the *'Song of Songs'* is but **one** narrative. Great Beauty, as well as the uplift of the spirit and the fullest expression of the soul as LOVE itself, lies in the Higher Energy Realms and Regions.

In interpreting any text, many uses and ideas and versions are possible. It all depends on what we have in mind and what we are looking for. The Spiritual or the Mystic value is supreme. It is the Jewel in any Lotus or setting. And this has been the one objective in interpreting the first chapter of the '*Song of Songs*'. Mental, emotional and physical meanings and applications are all possible and plausible; but our concern, in this interpretation, is with the Heart of the matter, for which the text intended when written by the Mystics.

Love is the theme and Song of Life itself.
But where are the ears to hear It,
And the hearts to receive It?
Whose bosom rises and responds
To Love beyond all mortal bonds?

Attraction **from** the central core back **to** the central core is the play of Love, after the separation which occurred in Creation.

Absolute Unity in the light of the highest consciousness of Bliss and Essence of Understanding (Spiritual Gyan) is the final purpose of all things.

Function and equilibrium are established by uniting centers and separating the poles. The energy of attraction is always fixed at the center of bodies; that of repulsion is on the surface, or on the outside.

The motion is an unrolling from above downward, and from below upward, from the conscious above the eyes, to the unconscious below the eye level; from Kether, the Crown, to the soles of the feet. Heaven meets the earth and draws forth its verdure and essence. The movement is like the sun's attraction and repulsion of all its planets.

The movements are successive, simultaneous and perpetual, in spirals or ovals of opposite directions.

Physical function depends on metaphysical action and energy impulses. So does Life and Love work from within outward and from above downward, its wonders to perform; riding on a breath of Life, as God rides in a storm.

CHAPTER XIX
BREEZING THROUGH THE
HEXATEUCH

After covering the salient points of spiritual value in the Bible, the writer realized that there are many incidents of Mystic revelations and happenings, especially In the Old Testament, which puzzle and confuse the Bible students.

Most of these high points in the Mysticism of old cannot be interpreted historically and make sense. No available explanation satisfies both mind and soul. Yet these very stumbling blocks in the Holy Scriptures are the most valuable lessons which the Great Teacher left behind for those who can read and understand the cryptic text. With the groundwork laid down thus far in this book, it may be possible to point out a way to disentangle the literal meanings of some of these verses, into lessons of Mystic Value for the soul rather than for mere intellectual comprehension, or as history.

True Mysticism deals with Eternal Essences of the Sound Current on all five strata of intensity, regions or realms. These are the Five Real Rivers of Life, which flow through all creation and water it, sustain it and refresh it, as the original life impulse. The ruler of each realm is the deity appointed by the Supreme Father to guard His Treasure, the Eternal Sound Essence of Shabd, in that particular realm. Each one of the lower regions derives its energy from the region directly above it, until the very Source is reached, from whence All proceeds and must eventually return in conscious absorption, as fruitful servants of the Great Lord; or, unconsciously, as unwise servants absorbed in the Pralaya of that cycle. The parables of the Five Wise and the Five Foolish Virgins and of the Wise and Foolish Servants, given by Jesus in Matthew 25:1-30 perfectly illustrates this principle.

Why are we here, and whose business are we attending to? The *'Father's Business'*, which is that of working toward the liberation of our own soul? or the worldly acquisitions and pleasures of the mind and senses? It is obvious that only the lamp which is clean and in good working order is filled with the OIL OF THE SPIRIT, and the wick of Consciousness is **constantly trimmed**, cleaned and adjusted, can furnish a bright light unto our feet, on the Way to our Eternal Home. With this background in mind, an attempt is made to clarify some of the more difficult chapters of symbolic narratives in the Old Testament.

The knowledge of Good and Evil
(GEN. 3:22-23)

The lower mind was the serpent and the evil, even in Paradise, because it is separate from God, the Center of all Good, All Balance, All Love and Selflessness. One naturally wonders why it was created at all, and put there for a snare unto man and woman in Paradise.

When we question this, we overlook the fact that the entire mind is nothing else but a stepped-down expression of the soul's lower energies, desires and free will; the craving for its own separate experience called the life of **self**, and its experience in space and in matter. The soul's own ego is the cause, the tempter, and also the cruel taskmaster of Kal. The latter is through the mind's own process of function as sensory or motor, in temptation or in action of attempted satisfaction of its desires.

The serpent is the mind energy itself. No new beast or reptile was introduced here to spoil the happiness in Paradise. The mind is the outer shell and negative pole of the soul. It is situated below the soul where it accumulates the dregs of the soul's desires. These dregs of 'Adi Karma' must be gotten rid of so the soul can survive and rise in consciousness.

This proves of purification and free expression of self will and desire was the purpose and object of creation. This has been explained in the chapter on 'Satan', pointing out the Original Sin as the EGO, which is the ROOT OF ALL EVIL, for personal sensory (feeling) or motor satisfaction of action.

In the involuting process, the mind expresses the soul's desire through sense energies. By this very action AND DESIRE FOR FURTHER ACTION AND SENSATION, THE MIND ITSELF BECOMES CONDITIONED AND BOUND BY THE REACTIONS OF EACH ACTION. Then it no longer acts according to the desires of the soul but becomes a blind slave of the senses. Thus the soul is enveloped with stored karma which has been accumulated throughout the past ages and which is called '*Sinchit*'; also with the karma which has been allotted to it as a portion of the stored karma, for this particular lifetime, and which is called '*Pralabdh*'; on top of that, the soul is every day accumulating the results of good and bad actions as well as thoughts, to be paid off at some future date, and that is called '*Kriyaman*'. The latter may be either added to the reserve store of Sinchit, or may be included in that which is to be paid off as Pralabdh on this lifetime.

This was clearly understood by the Greek Psychologist who wrote the great drama of '*Prometheus Bound*'. The god Prometheus brought the fire of Life down to the consciousness of men, and for this he was punished by being bound on Mount Caucasus, with the vultures devouring his liver. The water for which he thirsted so much, would tantalizingly reach up to his chin, and then recede. That is the story in brief. It seems so unjust and arouses the sympathy of men for such a benefactor.

This representation is so much like the suffering of Jesus on the way to Calvary, when He comforted the women of Jerusalem by saying to them:

"Daughters of Jerusalem, weep not for me, but weep for yourselves, and for your children."

(LUKE 23:28)

Jesus understood the problem of the soul, its descent and its necessary liberation, and He suffered for it without blaming or condemning anyone.

Like Hercules and the Greek Heroes who conquered the twelve labors of the Zodiac, then ascended unto

Mount Olympus and their father, the God Zeus or Jupiter; Jesus also passed through the twelve stations of the Cross in His suffering. The drama is similar, but the import may differ for each soul. Each story or incident explains the other, in the problem of Good and Evil and our struggle here on earth.

Prometheus symbolizes the soul. The fire of Life which he brought down to the race of men called Adams, refers to the very energy of the soul itself, the Holy Shabd, borrowed from higher regions. The mind and senses, by improper use, consume this soul energy that is apportioned to them, in an effort to enjoy the fruits of this Tree of Life. If this were allowed to continue, the soul and the higher regions themselves would be dragged down to the level of sensory pleasures. Therefore, it is quite plain that man as well as woman, Adam as well as Eve, originally fell because of the desire for knowledge and sensation. But when the desire **for** sensation and the crystallization for this energy for psychic and sensory enjoyment appeared on the scene, it has to be cast out of Paradise. (GEN. 3:24)

The gods, called Elohim, were the souls from higher regions. They had gone through this experience in previous cycles of creation and knew the evil which was let loose here for souls on the path of involution. They had a great responsibility and a problem on their hands. And they acted justly, as had been provided for in the plan of involution.

The Prometheus myth or drama tells a similar Story. The god, Prometheus, symbolizes the soul. The desire of the soul to enjoy sensory life forever it, after it became so entangled that it forgot the Source of Eternal Happiness, was also curtailed by punishment. Mount Caucasus represents the head and the brain, as the seat of the mind. Here all the return messages of sensation and action are received by the conscious mind and the soul. Complete satisfaction is **never** reached by the mind and the soul in the lower spheres, because these are not their Source or

Home. Just as Prometheus could not drink of the water that came only up to his chin, so also the mind and soul cannot bend down to drink of the Water of Life for the sake of pleasure, as desired, or they would wreck and drown themselves by the evil of **their** very desires.

The vultures which eat the liver of Prometheus, represent the consuming desires and frustrations, and the fires of anger and remorse.

Cain and Abel
(GEN. 4:1-18)

In the light of the preceding chapter on Good and Evil, this will be somewhat easier to follow and may make sense, even though it is the reverse of all the accepted theories of this story. In this narrative, a few very pertinent questions arise:

1. Why did Cain slay Abel, over so small a cause?
2. Why did Jehovah God protect Cain after the slaying, with a mark on his forehead?
3. Where did Cain go, from the presence of Jehovah?
4. Where was the Land of Nod, where Cain took a wife, and who was she, when only a few souls existed on earth?

"And Adam knew Eve his wife; and she conceived, and bare Cain, and said, I have gotten a man from the Lord (with **the help of** Jehovah.)" (GEN. 4:1)

All the dramas are usually symbolic of corrective measures for balance. No matter how unjust they may seem to our sense consciousness, there is a deeper purpose behind it than we can comprehend. The need for correction arises from a deeper cause, in the depth of the soul itself. The administrative power in each region must attend to justice and equilibrium.

1. Cain was the eldest son, "gotten with the help of Jehovah". He is a symbol of the true mind in the Causal realm of Trikuti. Abel was the younger son and symbolize the mind substance which deal with the flocks of the

animal world—desires and sensations. He tended the flocks, and represents the lower mind and the craving for fulfillment of desires of the senses. Flocks symbolize the thoughts and desires of the lower mind.

In ancient times, and even to-day in some foreign countries, the elder son rules the younger.

The burnt offering which was brought by each before Jehovah is symbolic of their activity.

"and unto thee shall be his desire; and thou shalt rule over him." (GEN. 4:7)

Thus spoke Jehovah to Cain.

The god of this world accepts and approves of sense action, symbolized by the sacrifice of animals; but not of the hard toil of concentration and attention within, represented by the fruits of the earth as offered by Cain. Nevertheless, the above quotation is a partial admittance of Cain's position and desire to slay his lower mind and "rule over it", which he did.

2. Jehovah protects Cain with a sign or a mark on his forehead, at the seat of consciousness, as a stamp of approval and for protection from the lower forces.

This symbolizes an internal sign in Tisra Til. The center between the eyes, where the consciousness dwells when one is in the state of wakefulness. It is spoke of in REV. 7:2-9 as "the seal of the living God", "we have sealed the servants of our God in their foreheads". In PSALM 37:37 is mentioned:

"Mark the perfect man, and behold the upright: for the end of that man is peace."

When people come to a Saint for Initiation on the Path to God-Realization, He merely looks at the condition and trend of their consciousness, the accumulation of past actions and reactions in thought, word and deed (KARMA), including the present attitude and degree of sincerity and devotion. There is a sign on the forehead of those who are ready to tread the Spiritual Path, and this the Master can see in an instant, whether the applicant is in His physical presence or far away. Those who have it, are accepted; not others. They are told to come back some other time.

"And they shall see His face; and His NAME shall be in their foreheads."   (REV. 22:4)

In the drama of 'Romeo and Juliet' a similar situation arises under an entirely different setting. The bantering, playful Mercutio, the friend of Romeo, was slain. Romeo, however, was not yet ready to give up his bantering mind and its enjoyment, so Tibalt slew Mercutio with the help of Romeo, by his intervention in the fight. Mercutio exclaimed: "I was hurt under your arm", when Romeo deflected Mercutio's weapon.

Romeo, as a seeker of pure Love beyond the senses as symbolized by his ideal, Juliet, presents a picture from the European Continent which is similar to the Oriental story of Majnun and Laila—the soul and its play. Love is an absorbing interest. The idea is the same, but all settings differ. However, from a spiritual standpoint, these incidents do not refer to personal, physical experiences. It must always be remembered that they are all Mystic stories of the **soul** and its quest to overcome the mind and senses, and find absorption in the true Love of the Essence. These are all inner conditions and experiences of the individual soul and mind, incarnated in the same body.

The moment we lose the Mystic viewpoint of Inner Accomplishment and soul progress, we miss the real purpose of the Sacred Text, the song, the poem, the myth of the story. As Shakespeare truly said, life is but a dream, and all the world's a stage. When we accept the personae of a story as real, then we have but a drama or a play for enjoyment or weeping. Such entertainment was never the object of Mystics in reducing these things to writing. Only the edification of the soul and the higher mind was of consequence to the Mystics, as the One Objective in Life. All else was but dross and "vanity of vanities", said Solomon.

In all dramas the personae is but a mask of a character portrayed by the actor and is not really accepted as a person, even in ordinary plays. The why should myths, parables and stories in Sacred Texts be taken as real, separate persons in history?

Cain had to dispose of Abel, even as all souls must eventually give up the desires and their pampering of the animal passions, before the soul can make any progress on the pathway of the Inner Life. That is the Mystic implication of Cain and Abel, as characters portraying the mind and the soul in the human body.

Jehovah God approved of the actions of both, Cain and Abel. Even as God does not interfere with our choice of doing right or wrong, but nevertheless punishes or rewards us accordingly, without favoritism. The higher mind must go on in its function, if the soul is to survive in a higher consciousness. Jehovah God had to protect it, for man's own sake. The mark on Cain's forehead denotes confirmation in a higher consciousness, after having liberated his mind from sensory dross. In REV. 4:1; 14:9; 21:7, the writing in the center of the forehead, and the new NAME given there, have an uplifting meaning and effect, as a reward of accomplishment.

3. When Cain left the presence of Jehovah, he had to go either up or down in consciousness on the Tree of Life, even as Jonah did when he fled before Jehovah.

4. "Cain went out from the presence of the Lord (Jehovah) and dwelt in the Land of Nod, on the east of Eden." (GEN. 4:16)

This quotation verifies the correctness of this Mystic interpretation, because Cain went upward on his Tree of Life, back into the Garden of Eden, and eastward of it, in the fine sensory perception of the Sound Current out of which Eden and the Garden of Paradise were precipitated. The Land of Nod is the Sound Current of this region, and it is called 'Nada' in the Vedas. Cain blended with this Current as his 'Nada' in the Vedas. Cain blended with this

Current as his Leela, the heart center of this Nod, symbolized by the wife he took unto himself. And his further meditation bore fruit in the spiritual accomplishments, because of the mention of a son born unto him out of this union. This means that he went higher than before in his inner progress of consciousness.

That makes sense in Mystic parlance, and the text corroborates it. Other dramas and stories reveal similar results, which perpetuate the Mystic quest of the soul like the quest of the Holy Grail. When dramas and stories became mere shows of entertainment, their Mystic value for soul education, called the higher education at one time, was lost sight of entirely.

Noah's Ark
(GEN. 6TH, 7TH, 8TH AND 9TH Chapters)

The story of Noah is a real problem, if taken literally. How could a structure three hundred cubits long, fifty cubits in breath and thirty cubits high (a cubit being about eighteen inches long) contain **all** the species of animals, male and female, one pair of the unclean and up to seven pairs of the clean animals, plus Noah and his family? Food and provisions are not even mentioned here for the one hundred and fifty days during which the water prevailed and Noah was in the Ark.

It is clear that some Mystical meaning was intended to be conveyed in this account rather than any literal acceptance of the personae mentioned. Noah found favor with God because he was a devoted and righteous character. Only to such qualities of Faith and Devotion did the **Spirit** of Jehovah, the Sound Current Energy appear and save them from the downward current of destruction. Thus the reward of Jehovah to the faithful ones was upward progress instead of further accumulation of downward evil tendencies of the mind and the senses.

The waters of the flood mentioned in the text, are not only physical but also psychic and emotional energy floods of the watery powers of the creative energy in Nature and in man. And creation emerged out of this water. The root of life's energies was bestowed in the power of generation of all vegetation, beasts and humans. This observation gave rise to the Fallic Worship of old, because all their wealth of flocks, grains, and offspring depended on this gift to mankind. This external evidence of pleasure and possessions became a snare and led man to deterioration. The higher qualities were subordinated to this drive and impulse of sense satisfaction to its limits. This was the evil and the destruction of soul qualities in man.

There are records of 'The Flood' in various Sacred Texts. Colonel James Churchward, the noted archeologist, spent many years in tracing such records from very old tablets found in India. His archeological research was profound and thorough. He records TWO such floods, based upon this research. One was the sinking of the Continent of Mu in the Pacific Ocean, and the other was the sinking of Atlantis in the Atlantic Ocean, at a much later date.

"all the fountains of the great deep broken up and the windows of heaven were opened"   (GEN. 7:11)

From a physical and historical standpoint, Col. Churchward explains this in his records by the statement: "The island of Mu went down in flames and water."

The flames were caused by the breaking through of the gas pressure from its deeper strata of three layers. When it reached the top layer, it literally blew the crust of the earth off by violent explosions and flames, which shot up. Into this vacuum of space of the gaseous caverns, rushed the sea, when the volcanic action had subsided. The gaseous layers and caverns were literally "fountain of the deep".

External history and internal events are combined here, as records, and it is hard to say where one begins and the other ends. That Noah, his family, and a few of his livestock could have been carried over for one hundred and fifty days in a structure like the Ark, is possible. But that this structure could hold all the species of animals in creation, is not plausible. Then it is quite plain that this record has an inner Mystic meaning.

The Great Floods in this physical world were vast but it is not yet established as to exactly how much of the earth was inundated at one time. Animals to inhabit the earth, could have been created after the flood, the same as before.

The fact is that the Ark itself is a symbol of the human body, which floats upon the waters of energy in space, and contains a pair of **every** animal quality in creation. Of the clean and more peaceful ones, up to seven pairs are in the constitution of man's make-up as the microcosm. Even our Zodiac is made up of animal pictures, and energy whirls in the etheric substance of the body are also symbolized by animals in nearly all the Vedic writing and illustrations of old.

The event described in the Bible depicts a definite epoch in the life of human beings on earth in their involutionary experience, when survival was at stake. It is always the good, the true, the gentle and the beautiful that survives, because it is balanced and close to the equilibrium of the Eternal Source of Energy Distribution. This principle was well known to Mystic of old. It always takes at least one human being who is touch with the Light and life of the Radiant, Sustaining Sound Current, to maintain the balance on earth.

The Gracious Eternal Father always sends down His messengers, as Saints, Saviors, Sadhus or Prophets, to save mankind from complete crystallization into matter and its forces, where he would lose all consciousness and choice. Not all of them teach or point out the way; some of them lead an obscure life on this earth while keeping in touch with the Eternal Balance of the Holy Shabd, and thus maintain the link for mankind in that Wave of Grace. Survival, not redemption, is the keynote of that particular dispensation.

The great Persian Saint, Shams-i-Tabriz, was once asked if it were true that often there are obscure contemporary Saints in this world, who do not teach; or mankind in this way. The Saint pointed to a coolie who was laboring on the docks. So Much Mystic value can be hidden in a simple event, if we can but see or understand.

The story of Noah is such a story of great import in the survival of the human race. The three stories in the Ark symbolize the superior, middle and inferior parts of the body of man:

1. The head and neck.
2. The chest.
3. The abdomen, with the pelvis as one cavity.

The door on the side refers to the psychic door from where souls involute and are connected with the finer energy regions. The navel, as the umbilical cord, is such a tie in front, in the sensory area. In the motor area, in the spinal nerve centers, it is the etheric *prana* center with more cerebrospinal fluid at the second lumber vertebra, where the spinal cord proper ends. When these two, the sensory and motor areas, are linked, it can become a real door for finer sensory and motor impulses in and out of the body through the neuter organ of the spleen, which is the etheric exchange center for the function in and through the blood stream. The three 'doshas' or energies in the circulation have their sway here in their ebb and flow as energy waves.

Noah first lets out a raven, which denotes the darker or lower qualities which fly over the earth until the waters abate, then settle there. This sheds some light on some strange old stories of a similar nature, such as that of the great warrior, Fredrick Barbarossa, who died in one of the Crusades because he plunged into the river with horse and armor in his impatience to get into battle. It is said that he sits in a cave in a mountain in his homeland and occasionally asks his servant to go and see if the ravens still circle around the mountain. It was predicted that his liberation would be at hand when the ravens disappeared. This is true of all souls. When the dark and lower impulse — symbolized as ravens, vultures or crows — are gone, the soul may rise from its dungeon of slavery to impulses and sensation. The story of the bondage of Israel in Egypt has a similar meaning.

Later, Noah sends out three doves. Two return; one with an olive branch of peace. The dove and the swan are both symbols of pure souls and pure spirit. Even the Holy Ghost is often symbolized as a dove. The good sent out, returns with peace and also spreads it on the land, as symbolized by the dove which did not return.

"Cast thy bread upon the waters: for thou shalt find it after many days." (ECC. 11:1)

Every soul who has faith, love and devotion is **a Noah**, on earth, **floating in the ark of his own body**, over the great Sea of Life and its experiences. All qualities are within ourselves. Which will we let out, and which will we generate?

"And the ark rested in the seventh month, on the seventeenth day of the month, upon the mountain of Ararat." (GEN. 8:4)

Geographically, Ararat is a volcanic mountain with two peaks in Eastern Turkey, near the boundary with Iran and the Soviet Union. But in the Mystic interpretation it would be in a region or center above the water's highest level within, which is the Manipura Chakra, and is situated above the Brahma Chakra.

This valley is very fertile, and Noah planted a vineyard there. He drank of the wine, and lay intoxicated in his tent (GEN. 9:20-25). Here another incident is recorded that seems unreasonable. Especially in a hot country, what sin or shame could there be worth mentioning if a man took off his clothes in this own tent or house, even if one of his sons did come in?

The vineyard which Noah planted was not it this material world, but was symbolic of the Lord's Vineyard, often mentioned in the parables of Jesus. What Noah performed was spiritual labor and inner devotion. Mystically speaking, we all stand naked before God, for He sees and knows all. The wine which Noah drank was really Spiritual Nectar within. The intoxication referred to was Spiritual Ecstasy, the Mystic's reward in the Vineyard of the Lord.

The sin of Ham was the irreverence and disrespect shown toward his father's spiritual efforts and absorption in Spirituality. The three sons of Noah could symbolize the three *gunas* or qualities. The negative or Tamas quality always sees evil, by its own tendency. But the neuter or Sat, and the positive or Rajas energies go into the tent backward—from the front to the back and upward and inward—and they disturb not the Sacred Center. This describes their secret method of concentration for withdrawing the energies from the body, upward and inward, without disturbing the Prana or motor currents. This veiled Truth is told by the garments on their shoulders, used in meditation for going in backwards, from below upward, to draw up the sensory currents preparatory to Spiritual Transport.

The Story of Lot, his wife and two daughters
(GEN. 19TH CHAPTER)

This symbolic story of Lot is the most touchy subject of all, due to the way was the symbolism is expressed. And because of that, it has been a thorn in many minds. Why should it be in the Bible at all? Again, it is because of that unknow, hidden import in a gross symbolic form that made it survive. Like the *'Song of Solomon'* and other similar exotic Oriental expressions of symbolism which were current in those days, probably the deeper, hidden meaning behind the personae was sensed and thus these narratives were allowed to remain in the text.

The story of Brahma and his own daughter, variously named Vach or Saraswati, and mentioned in the Satapatha Brahmana, has a similar history and Inner Mystic meaning. Brahma creates speech (Vach), then expresses himself through speech or Saraswati.

In the Bible the story starts out with a righteous man called Lot, who lived in the wicked city of Sodom. Here also the original evil is portrayed as two cities or centers which misused the creative energy, and only the fire from above could purify them. Lot, in his simple devotion, lived untouched in those centers or cities. But when the two angels of the Lord entered, the wickedness of Sodom and Gomorrah, and Jehovah's intention to destroy the cities by fire, were made known to Lot.

Lot was willing to surrender his two virgin daughters to the mob in order to save the two strangers who were the angels of God. His two daughters represent two unsuccessful spiritual efforts of long duration. But, in order to keep the Grace of the Spirit of Jehovah which had come into his house, he was willing to give up any claims of reward for his efforts. His devotion to Jehovah made his sacrifice easy. But the sacrifice was not needed (similar is the occasion in I SAM. 15:22 and in GEN. 22:1-12). The Spirit of Jehovah saved him by drawing him into the house and upward, into greater and higher Spiritual Realization. He and his wife and two daughters were ushered out of those two centers while these *chakras* of consciousness were being destroyed and purified by fire. His negative aspect of desire for a home in matter, symbolized by his wife, looked back and froze or crystallized into a pillar of salt, the essence of the Sea of Generation and earthiness.

After Lot left the plains and the little city of Zoar, he dwelt in a cave in the mountains with his two daughters. The mountains signify a higher state of consciousness, and the cave refers to a center of consciousness within. Here, his sacrifice and all his efforts in Spiritual Growth were rewarded by Jehovah. Having surrendered all to Jehovah, he made his progress bear fruit now. All the years of Lot's Spiritual Efforts are represented by his two daughters as unsuccessful spiritual endeavor. The wine which intoxicated him was this very devotion which he thought was unfruitful, and he had reconciled himself to the uselessness of his efforts at concentration and devotion. In all humility, he continued his efforts without being conscious of his inner success, and was lifted up in real absorption, like Noah. His seemingly unsuccessful efforts now bore fruit, symbolized by the birth of a son to each daughter. And each became a nation or a completion of growth of their own kind.

Such is the symbolism of old, which is like a nut with a hard shell that breaks many a tooth.

The Cryptic Cipher of Israel's Flight out of Egypt (EXODUS)

This epic of the soul is so cleverly buried under history factors that its extraction becomes a process of inner tracing and sublimation, to find the jewel in this obscure mystic setting. The story has its equivalent in the Mahabharata and the Ramayana of India. All these are jewels of the soul rather than mere historic recordings. This fact makes them Sacred Texts and it is the reason for their survival as a vital message to man's immortal life rather than the mere physical one.

If one tried to understand all these things **literally**, one would have to set reason and intelligence aside and believe in a forceful demonstration of miracles, out of all proportion to the usual events in Nature up to this time.

Why is all this Sacred Text written in that style and manner? This is a very logical point. **Why**? The logical answer is that this is all Mystic Text, dealing with man's soul travel, his mind action, his lower mind as the emotional reaction, and their sequences. **It is a hidden message**, written for those only **who walk the Inner Way of Life** and can benefit by the patient study of the Text until the Light breaks through by *'His Grace'*. Only such a one will see the **obvious** and **deliberate** mistakes and the **intentional** illogical presentations which make the seeker **stop, ponder and seek** some more. Here also, "he who seeks shall find." A wise and true student of Life will know at once that there lies a secret message for the soul, to be deciphered and enjoyed as a lesson. It was never intended for the everyday mind of man, as it deals with the Spiritual Qualities of Truth only. Metaphors are but for the sake of illustration.

This clever device of Mystic writing, with an inner key for understanding and interpreting the Texts in the entire Old Testament as well as the New, was for the same purpose; that is, for the benefit of the student in the **mental field**. This is similar to the Ideal seen inside by the Seers of old who made a statue to symbolize what they saw, in order to **arouse** the **devotion** of the simple-minded devotees and draw their attention upwards, toward this ideal. It was not the symbol which was to be worshiped, but for the devotee to endeavor to reach that which the image represented. **Both serve** as a means of **concentration** of the mind **through study** and **devotion**.

Without such attention to these Jewels, the passages in the Bible would remain in their shell of words, as cryptic external symbolism. What sincere seeker after Truth Eternal is so eager for quick results and immediate proof, that he takes no time to ponder over these Sacred Texts and gets into the true rhythm of their revelation so that the understanding may become enlightened? **The text itself is the test** which separates the true seeker who will continue to **ponder** upon God's Word night and day, from those who read and walk away. No one judges, no one excludes anyone from the wedding Feast of the Soul, prepared by the Almighty King and Merciful Father. All are invited!

Are we prepared to bring our sacrifice to the alter of the Beloved? And what animal is that? Not one animal. But all the animals of our *'Ark of Noah'*, the soul incarnated in a body which floats over the waters of space, like a boat. This contains all the selfish natures and lower impulses of our mind and emotions which we feel we have no time to give up in order to find this Pearl of Great Prize. According to our present state of consciousness, this is too difficult, it is too severe and takes too long. The enjoyment of selfish pleasures and acquisitions seems so much easier, more real and satisfactory. However, this illusion exists only as long as the mind and senses are attached in the material world. Once the mind has become ruler of the senses, and a true companion of the soul, there is no difficulty in rising above or *'sacrificing'* the lower tendencies, no matter by what name or symbolism they are portrayed as a needed sacrifice.

Where is the soul's Wedding Garment of devotion and purity, free from all the dross of self? When we expect *'quick results'* without first purifying the mind and heart, is this the proper respect for such a Miracle of Bliss and Liberation? Such is the state of the soul which comes to its own Wedding and Union with the Lord, but without a Wedding Garment. This is the principle illustrated by Jesus in His beautiful parable of the Wedding Feast (MAT. 22:1-15). The modern Saints give a beautiful discourse along these lines, entitled "My Shawl has become dirty, Who is going to wash my Shawl?" A true Master is really a *'washerman'* of souls, for it is only through His help that the filthy covering of the lower mind can be washed away from the soul.

Jesus always taught in parables, which is the Mystic way of illustrating deeper things.

"He who hath ears to hear let him hear" etc.

(MAT. 13:9-43)

The reason for parables is also given in MAT. 13:10-11: To the true seeker who hath patience to seek and to the devotee who hath sincere devotion, all things are given. To those who have none of these, or who have not, from them is taken even what they have (MAT. 13:12-19). Why this apparent injustice in the New Testament? Because they do not make it proper use of what they have, neither do they cultivate in with proper time and attention. Does anything in Nature grow this way? Does it not also perish if abused or neglected?

Another time we find that True Mystic interpretation of the Old Testament is fulfilled and further explained by Jesus in the New Testament, in MAT. 13:44-45, 46. The sacred Mystic Thread runs through like a shuttle weaving the same fabric of Truth as the Wedding Garment of the soul. It should really stimulate the search for the One Truth mentioned in the Bible and in all Sacred Texts. Books and words can but give hints.

"God is not the God of the dead, but of the living."

(MAT. 22:32)

EGYPT, the symbolic land of the fleshpots of sense enjoyment! Once more the reader's attention is called to the obvious mystic trend of this parable of the soul in the Old Testament. No land nor people on earth could withstand all the vicissitudes which were inflicted upon the Egyptians at one time and still survive, unless that also was a miracle. Other factors are, the crossing time of the Red Sea, the mystery of not only feeding and clothing all the people but also all the livestock which they had with them in the wilderness for forty years, etc. etc. etc.

Why is there such an intense persistence that all miracles must be performed physically, in this sense world? Is worldly history and are worldly events of such importance? Is the miracle of the soul not more essential to us, to our own welfare and awakening than the mere history of physical events? We can do nothing about history, but we certainly can learn the mystic lesson and decide whether or not we are interested in liberating our own souls out of this Egypt state of sense indulgence and servitude. The miracles performed on the inside, in our consciousness, are far more important to the soul's redemption than any miracle that could be done outside.

Is not this Mystic Text vitally important to all souls? Has it not a similar value as when the Saviors, Saints and Prophets explained it to the devotees in other parables? Does it not fulfill every jot and tittle? The symbolic story of the Exodus is beautifully laid out, like an expert dramatic portrayal of the soul consciousness of Israel in the grip of the senses and its pleasures of indulgence in Egypt, the lowest *chakra* and state of consciousness possible to the soul after its descent into Egypt or sense consciousness.

Our own mind and its attachment to the sense world is the Pharaoh within who is so hard to convince to let the soul go free and to go with it into the sense desert to worship the Lord. The stubborn mind tries every trick and deception in its power to keep the soul in bondage an in servitude to the rulership of the mind. This struggle is well known to all disciples on the Path. It goes on daily. The aspirant must be ever watchful and keep in Love and Devotion all the way up on the Jacobs's ladder of ascending souls. (MARK. 13:38; LUKE 21:36; MAT. 24:42; II TIM. 4:5.) Timothy calls the disciple an evangelist, and his watchfulness full proof of his ministry in the service of the Lord.

The dramatic setting of the personae of this particular epic in the Bible is as follows:

1. The Lord God Jehovah, the creator of this world and the mentor and supporter of the soul while in it, through the power of the Eternal Sound Current Energy is the Astral Region. This is called the **Spirit** of Jehovah and emanates from the center of the seventh *chakra* which is situated above the eyes and is the seat of lotus of one thousand energy currents of power, called the Sahasra Dal Kamal.

2. Israel, the involuted souls into the state of physical consciousness and existence. Israel, the chosen race of souls, did not mean a certain race, group or sect, but is a composite name indicating: 'IS'—pertaining to the goddess Isis; 'RA'—the sun god, Ra; 'EL'—the Elohim, who were most helpful in creating man and still had a responsibility to fulfill in order to rear and raise the souls in mortal forms.

3. Moses represents the higher and true mind of man, as a faithful servant of Jehovah, who is drawn out of this River of Nile and indulgence, to faithfully serve his people, the souls of Israel, throughout all trials and tribulations.

4. Aaron, the brother of Moses, who becomes '*Buddhi*' the intellectual and eloquent speaker for the mind before his people and before Pharaoh, the lower mind.

5. Pharaoh, as the King and Monarch of all Egypt, the land of material culture and of indulgence in all the senses and sense pleasures. Pharaoh portrays the lower, selfish mind, which feeds the emotions and is the essence of the animal instinct of the mind for material gain and indulgences in power and external show with pomp and ceremonies.

Pharaoh's magicians, priests and soothsayers are the personifications of power as thoughts and actions, to thwart Moses and Aaron, the higher mind.

6. Pharaoh's daughter typifies the motherly instinct in this sphere, and saves Moses.

7. The parents of Moses represent the soul of Israel. They remain submerged and absorbed in interest with Israel's cause.

Setting of the scenes:

1. The land of Egypt
2. The Red Sea of passions and instinct for possession and power which must be crossed.
3. The desert, the way between stages of consciousness; the suffering by privation of the pleasures left behind in Egypt; and the arduous struggle of training the soul impulses of Israel through this ordeal of transition for purification of the lower dross of Egypt, by the power and guidance of the Lord God Jehovah and His faithful servants Moses and Aaron to lead Israel through all the vicissitudes of the soul's travel. It is a story of Initiation, with far more details and specific trial over a longer period of time than that of Job or of Jonah. It is probably the most detailed account given anywhere, and covers the books of Exodus, Leviticus, Numbers and Deuteronomy. It is similar to the visions of Daniel, and to the seven plagues written of in Revelation.

8. With Joshua begins the conquest of the Promised Land. The word *'Joshua'* means Salvation. He is the hero of soul realization, who enters the Promised Land consciously.

The story begins with the soul in Egypt, under the pressure of the taskmasters who are the cruel lower mind and sense cravings, the drive for more and ever more.

EXODUS, chapters 1 and 2: the command of Pharaoh to drown all the male children in Israel, really means that the soul had no chance to express any spiritual idea, thought or devotion in that setting of consciousness which was called Egypt. All male children signify positive spiritual success or birth in the Mystic way of inner ascendance into higher realms of consciousness. Therefore, the soul must escape or flee from Egypt, to worship God in the wilderness, a free state of consciousness where nothing is, and the soul can spend time in concentration and observation of Jehovah's laws and its sacrifices to the Sound Current, through devotional surrender. This principle is summed up by Jehovah in Deuteronomy 10:12-16:

> "And now, Israel, what doth the Lord (Jehovah) thy God require of thee, but to fear the Lord (Jehovah) thy God, to walk in all his ways, and to love him, and to serve the Lord (Jehovah) thy God with all thy heart and with all thy soul, To keep the commandments of the Lord (Jehovah), and his statutes, which I command thee this day for thy good? Behold, the heaven and the heaven of heavens is the Lord's (Jehovah's) thy God, the earth also with all that therein is. Only the Lord (Jehovah) had a delight in thy fathers to love them, and he chose their seed after them, even you above all people, as it is this day. Circumcise therefore the **foreskin of you heart**, and be no more stiffnecked."

Jesus gave similar advice on several occasions.

Moses was brought up and trained as an Egyptian by Pharaoh's daughter. But his heart was with Israel and he, as the higher mind, was devoted to the soul; so he slew the Egyptian **in him** and fled to the land of Midian (Ex. 2:11-16). This is similar to Cain's experience in the story of 'Cain and Abel'.

The Priest Jethro of Midian becomes the Initiator and Preceptor of Moses, and gives him his daughter Zipporah to wife, because Moses had helped them draw water (of Life) for their flocks (thoughts). In Mystic parlance, the priest instructed Moses to concentrate on a *chakra*, and Moses had fine results, symbolized as the birth of a son. Because of this accomplishment in the Mystic Practice, Moses.

"came to the mountain of God, even to Horeb. And the angel of the Lord (Jehovah) appeared unto him in a flame of fire out of the midst of a bush: and he looked, and, behold, the bush burned with fire, and the bush was not consumed. And Moses said, I will now turn aside and see this great sight, why the bush is not burnt. And when the Lord (Jehovah) saw that he turned aside to see, God called unto him out of the midst of the bush, and said, Moses, Moses. And he said, Here am I. And he said, Draw not nigh hither: Put off thy shoes from off they feet, for the place whereon thou standest is holy ground. Moreover he said, I am the God of thy father, the God of Abraham, the God of Isaac, and the God of Jacob. And Moses hid his face; for he was afraid to look upon God. And the Lord (Jehovah) said, I have surely seen the affliction of my people which are in Egypt and have heard their cry by reason of their taskmasters; for I know their sorrows; and I am come down to deliver them out of the hand of the Egyptians, and to bring them up out of that land unto a good land and a large, unto a land flowing with milk and honey; unto the place of the Canaanites, and the Hittites, and the Amorites, and the Perizzites, and the Hivites, and the Jebusites. Now, therefore behold, the cry of the children of Israel is come unto me: and I have also seen the oppression wherewith the Egyptians oppress them. Come now therefore, and I will send thee unto Pharaoh, that thou mayest bring forth my people the children of Israel out of Egypt."

(EXODUS 3:1-10)

It was on Mount Horeb that the initiation of Moses was completed. The same is true in the observance of the real Mystic Practice today; that is, the living Master gives the instructions to the applicant and internally connects him with the Holy Shabd, and the soul is conscious of the Real Initiation Within when the mind and soul together have reached that point of concentration where the Astral Form of the Living Master is met within, from whence He can be consciously contacted and conversed with **any time** by the devotee. As the soul's love increases and the consciousness is raised higher and higher, the Radiant Form of the Master inside becomes even more beautiful (it always is so, but until this state, the vision of the soul is clouded by the ego), the devotee's happiness increases, and ultimately ALL IS SHABD, ALL IS LOVE, ALL IS BLISS!

Jehovah appeared to Moses in the mystery of the Burning Bush. This indicated that Moses had entered into the higher region in his consciousness and beheld the fire of the Jod (Hebrew), also called Jot or Jyoti (Sanskrit), the flame which comes out of the Light, and is a well-known Mystic accomplishment. Madam Blavatsky writes of it also in 'The Voice of the Silence': "You will enter the Light, but never touch the flame."

Moses, the Mystic, had this experience, and by strength of this Inner Communion with Jehovah, he could go back into Egypt and free Israel by the power of Jehovah's command, the Sound Energy Current of Sahasra Dal Kamal. The entire plan had been given to Moses; that is, what to do and how to do it, and the results were also foretold by Jehovah.

Exodus 4:2, 3, 4, concerns the mystery of the staff of Moses. Similar is the following quotation from the Psalms:

"Yea, though I walk through the valley of the shadow of death, I will fear no evil; for thou art with me; Thy rod and thy staff, they comfort me."

(PSALMS 23:4)

The shepherd's staff was for guiding the sheep and the crook could be hooked around the neck of the sheep, of lift them out of crevices where they may have fallen. To the higher mind, such a staff is Reason. The Staff of Moses and Aaron has the same symbolism as the Staff of Hermes or the Wand of Mercury, or the Caduceus of Egypt and India. Its place in human body has been clearly illustrated in books for doctors, because this Staff of the Caduceus was also the sign and insignia of the physicians of old. It symbolizes the sun and moon energies which entwine the spinal column. The brain is pictured on the top of the Staff as the wings of the mind. When the Staff is thrown on the ground, it becomes a serpent, the tempter, as sensory currents. In Paradise it deceived Eve by presenting such clever reasons for disobeying that it looked like a bright angel of promise (GEN. 3:4, 5, 6). The shepherd's staff with its crook is also a representation of the finer energy currents in the spinal cord, which flow from the center of consciousness anteriorly in the cerebrum (the Tisra Til, between the two eyes), upward, backward and down the spiral cord, over all the five *chakras* in it, to give them energy and life. As indicated by Friar Lawrence in Shakespeare's *'Romeo and Juliet'*, when mind and reason are prevented from fair use, they revert from true birth and stumble on abuse. The process is ever the same; only the incident is new.

Moses had been given the Power of the Word, so he could handle the serpent by picking it up by its tail. By reasoning on the end result, the serpent's cleverness and poison is seen and it becomes harmless. In other words, Moses was given that Power so that he could go back to Egypt and conquer the cunning minds there. When the

Egyptian magicians were able to do the same, the snake of Moses swallowed all the other snakes. His Reason subdued all of the others.

Another sign given to Moses was that his hand became leprous after he put it into his bosom, at Jehovah's command (Ex. 4:6-7). Jehovah thus demonstrated to Moses that all external works by the hand of man, when taken inside of the Bosom of the Mystic Life, are as leprosy, and reek of self. But when done under the command of the Lord, **with the proper mental attitude** and as a devotional service to Him in Love, **without self**, behold the hand comes out clean! These reasons must be presented to the soul of Israel for its belief, and also to Pharaoh, the indulgent mind and senses. Of course, they will not listen. Israel is afraid, and Pharaoh is too proud and powerful with the success of exploitation.

Still another sign was given to Moses by Jehovah (Ex. 4:9). The water of the River of Life is the vital force which sustains Life. "Pour it upon dry land, and it will become blood." When the vital force is turned out of its natural course and poured upon the earth, the lower form or body, it turns to the red blood of passion. "Show this to then, tell them," etc. "They will not believe you."

In Ex. 4:10 to 18 Moses makes it plain that this is **not** a mere matter of performing tricks of magic, but of speech and intellect, and he remonstrates with Jehovah, insisting that he is no orator, and persists in it until he angers Jehovah. Thereupon Aaron, the symbol of the Intellectual faculty (the Buddhi) of the mind, represented in the story as the brother of Moses, is given the assignment of speech. Then begins the real test with Pharaoh, and to carry the Children of Israel along also was the task assigned to Moses and Aaron, the sign of Aaron's Rod and the serpents (already explained), and the turning of the water into blood, all appear before Pharaoh.

The Plague of Frogs (Ex. 8:1-8). It is the nature of frogs to croak, especially at night. Endless empty talk has been likened to the croaking of frogs. Frogs are also said to proceed out of the mouths of those with vicious minds. Idle tongues become oppressive like frogs, or toads, and cause much mischief. A Turkish proverb states that the tongue is sharper than the sword. The Plague of Frogs symbolizes a pestiferous state of mind due to lack of devotion and higher attention.

The Plague of Lice (Ex. 8:16-20). The sedimentation of the air is dust. Out of the dust of the earth, lice were produced. The air is the sign of the mind. Its sedimentation and dregs of impurity become as lice to all. This signifies the annoyance and misery of the uncleanliness of mind and body. They did not believe.

The Plague of Flies (Ex. 8:24). Flies breed in filth and decay. Physical and moral qualities are implied here, and the meaning is similar to that of the lice, in annoyance and disease.

The Plague of Death to the Cattle of the Egyptians (Ex. 9:1-8). Cattle, etc. are all part of the animal nature of man. When that gets the upper hand, and is an adversary to Jehovah and His Energy Current, there is murrain among the cattle, and loss in the household of the soul.

The Plague of Boils produced by Moses from the ashes of the furnace (Ex. 9:8-13). The furnace in the body is the digestive system. The end products of this digestion form its ashes and dust; the impurity of which is due to indulgence in rich foods. Again, it is an example of Cause and Effect—Karma.

The Plague of Destruction by Hail (Ex. 9:22-27). Hail is due to coldness in the air, to the extent of freezing the moisture in its descent. Even so, the mental air acts like hail when it becomes cold, hard and selfish. Then the fire of anger mixes with it, and the poor soul is really in trouble. This was demonstrated before Pharaoh who symbolizes that type of mind power. He would not believe it.

The Plague of Locusts (Ex. 10:12-16). Locusts devour all crops. They are the epitome of greed and represent the voracious mind. This was shown to the lower power of the mind, but still it did not let go of the soul for its journey upward!

The Plague of Darkness over Egypt (Ex. 10:22-23). Ignorance, Pride, Greed, and Selfishness form a thick coating of darkness which can be felt as well as seen, where man cannot see man as a brother. This was the sequence also shown to the little mind of selfishness, but it believed not. Similar are the lessons of all the other Plagues.

The Last Plague, The Slaying of the First-Born of Every House in Egypt (Ex. 12:29-30). This really strikes at the root of everything. The Egyptians could not stand it any more than could the Children of Israel withstand Pharaoh's order. When the stubborn, selfish mind is finally presented with the proven facts that all his first and best ideas and impulses — all first-born of man and beastly impulses — must be slain or surrendered as a personal possession and presented to the Lord in genuine self-sacrifice, then and then only will it let go of its grip, when it has no further power to prevent it. This Moses did by the might of Jehovah's Spirit as the Sound Current Energy, which was with him as a Gift and Promise from Jehovah.

How, then, did Israel escape? (Ex. 12:17-21).

1. The Feast of the Unleavened Bread. 'Ye Shall eat nothing leavened". It is said that a little leaven, leavens the whole lump; anything left over, sours. This signifies that no dross can be with Israel at the time of the Exodus out from the lower indulgences. In other words, when the currents of the lower mind are to be sublimated, there dare not be any thoughts, ideas or feelings of craving for that which must be left behind. So the fermenting or fermented type of mental and emotional food is forbidden to those who wish to be free; and pure substance, **without ferment or desire** is ordered for Israel, as an external symbol of an internal process.

2. The Slaying of the Lamb of the Passover (Ex. 12:21-29). This is the basis and has the same meaning as the

Easter Ceremony in the New Testament. The lamb, which was killed, symbolized the sublimation of all animal qualities. With a bunch of hyssop, the lintels (the top, the head) and the side posts (the hands and feet) of the door of each house (body) in which this rite was performed, were doused **with the blood of this lamb**. This is like the sign on the forehead and on the hands, as mentioned in Revelation. When the avenging angel saw the blood on the upper and lower door posts (mind and action), he spared the occupants of that house. In all Mystic writings and discourses, the house usually signifies the human body. **Now**, after having been released from the oppressive ego and the dregs of self, Israel is free to go and worship God.

The account of these trials is a bit lengthy, but is given in the order of appearance in the Old Testament. All these details can now be used in shedding light on the beautiful aphorism in "LIGHT ON THE PATH" by Mabel Collins. The quotation is a brief description of what purification man must go through before he can see The Light of the Spirit:

"Before the eyes can see, they must be incapable of tears.
Before the ear can hear, it must have lost its sensitiveness.
Before the voice can speak in the presence of the Masters, it must have lost the power to wound.
Before the soul can stand in the presence of the Masters, its feet must be washed in the blood of the heart."

The blood of the lamb, referred to in the paragraph above, has the same significance. That is the idea and Mystic meaning behind all sacrifice. It is really, an **inner** principle and **surrender of all beastly qualities and self**, rather than an external sacrifice of animals. About twelve centuries after the historical event of the Exodus, St. Paul referred to a similar sacrifice in Heb. 9:21-23.

The Flight through the Red Sea (Ex. 14th Chapter). "Israel encamped before Pihahirot, between Migdol (a tower) and the sea." This could be the origin of the old statement: "Between the devil and the sea," indicating internal mind pressure. In this extremity of Israel before such a formidable obstacle, Pharaoh, the clever and scheming mind, again summons all his forces for one more assault on the poor soul. But the Eternal Sound Current Energy of Jehovah protects the soul and parts the waters of the sea of passion and salt, or substance of crystallization as hardness or power of matter. So Israel goes through on dry foot, but the pursuing Egyptians are drowned. When all the powers of the soul are geared to merely physical pursuits of personal domination and gain, then the soul is ruled by the lower mind, the Pharaoh of the Egypt **in us**. When the soul escapes, like the children of Israel, the lower mind in pursuit of the passions of life dies in its own watery grave by being overwhelmed by the cosmic waters against which the individual interests are fighting. The souls who depend on and co-operate with the Spirit of God are led through safely, like the children of Israel. These are the children of the **living faith** of Abraham, and not the children of the flesh of Abraham. All true mystic messages are of the Spirit and not of the flesh (John 3:6)

"flesh and blood cannot inherit the kingdom of God; neither doth corruption inherit incorruption."

(I COR. 15:50)

There is an end to all the powers of force, cunning and evil, at that gate or stage of progress. But the battle must be fought again and again at each gate. When the evil becomes immersed in its own substance, it dies. Even the smallest germ cannot live in its own excreta. That is how evil destroys itself. It is up to us to be on guard and rise above it with the help of the Sound Current. That is the only way we can truly heed the admonition of Jesus, when He said: "Resist not evil". **Then we** literally **stand still** in concentration **within** and witness the salvation of the soul.

Chapter 15 begins with the jubilant song of Moses and the Children of Israel over the deliverance from Egypt. Now begins the treck "between the desert and the *'sawn'*," as the Sufi Mystics would say.

Ex. 15:22-27 gives a record of the Bitter Waters of Marah. This symbolizes the first experience of bitterness after the renunciation of all the pleasures of Egypt. The water of Life, or living at this stage, seems bitter. The tree which Jehovah showed Moses and commanded him to cast into the water to make it sweet, signifies the Tree of Life and proper discrimination, which lifts the mind up over any bitterness toward Life and Progress. This quality of detachment from all things transitory is called "Vairag" (Renunciation) by the Saints and in the Vedas.

Then came the cry for food, and Jehovah sent Manna from Heaven (Ex. 16:14). On the Inner Journey, the soul feeds on Nectar from the Essence above, which gives it strength to go on. This is the Bread of Life and is a reality, symbolized by the Showbread in the Temple and in the Sacraments. It is an external symbol of an inner Sustenance for the soul. Saints give it to their disciples when they come to that stage of development within. It is mentioned in all Sacred Texts. Jesus also said:

"I have meat to eat that ye know not of."   (John 4:32)

The occasion was when His disciples begged him to eat material food (John 4:31-35). Incidentally, the word *'meat'* **does not mean flesh** food, but food of any kind. Even candy is called a *'sweet meat'* in foreign countries.

The cry for flesh or more solid material substance for food was answered when Jehovah sent flocks or quail to the Israelites (Ex. 16:12-18). By grosser food here is implied the teaching and training of the mind. Quails are birds of the air and symbolize mind substance.

Even in Shakespeare's *'Hamlet'*, mind is illustrated as a "biting and an eager air", while **waiting** for the ghost to appear.

Ex. 16:26 records the first Sabbath celebration in freedom. Sabbath signifies a period of rest for the soul, where it may dwell in Inner Concentration and Absorption, as Jehovah did on the seventh day or period of creation. The **mind** and desires **must first** come to **rest** or it is not a

Sabbath of the Lord God Jehovah in His Spirit and Sound Current Energy, which raises the soul to heights of Bliss and Understanding.

The next incident in the soul's journey, signified by Israel, is recorded in Ex. 17:5-8. "Water out of the Rock." A similar incident, where water gushes forth out of a rock at Meribah, is recorded in Nu. 20:11. Here Moses doubted the Word of Jehovah for only an instant when he smote the rock twice before Israel. Because of this doubt, he lost contact with the Sound Current, the Spirit of Jehovah. Instead of having faith, he depended upon physical effort at that instant rather than utter reliance **upon the Power of Jehovah** within. His concentration and devotion were incomplete, and for that reason he could not enter the Promises Land. He could not make his mind stand still like Joshua did, to behold the Inner Sky and the Sun and the Moon, as the real Promised Land of the soul of Israel.

The mind itself is weak, and **can be controlled only by the Sound Current Energy.** This is the **"Rock of the Ages," cleft for all**. This is the REAL WATER OF LIFE FOR THE FAMISHED SOUL. Nothing else can sustain it.

Ex. 17:8 to the end, gives an account of King Amalek who fought Israel. Amalek was Esau's grandson. Note the end of the chapter, where Jehovah declares war on Amalek from generation to generation. This is because Esau sold his birthright to Jacob for a mess of pottage when he was hungry. This indicates that he really sold his spiritual birthright for material comfort. Such are not Jehovah's devotees.

According to Ex. Chapter 18, Moses is reunited with his wife, Zipporah, and her two sons. The mind reminisces and goes over the ground of spiritual values gained before Mount Horeb in Midian.

Ex. 19:16-21. Mount Sinai is the high point in the travel of Israel, the soul, in the wilderness of the unconscious, which signified that portion of the body and all *chakras* below the eyes. The Ten Commandments were given at Sinai and written by the finger of Jehovah on the tablets of the soul and in their hearts. These tablets were broken through human weakness, but a duplicate was made of stone and placed in the Ark of the Covenant. Over it was built the Mercy Seat, guarded by two Cherubim whose wings covered it. It was the Holy of Holies as the symbol of God in man, in his innermost being, the soul, and the body as its outer temple.

Mount Sinai represents the seat of consciousness called Tisra Til. It is the center between the eyes in the human being, where God in the form of the Sound Current meets the concentrated mind and soul, when it reaches this state of consciousness. According to the Teachings of the Saints, this center or *chakra* is the starting point of the soul's real upward progress.

The Fall of Jericho
(JOSHUA 6-10)

The next step is the Inner Sight of the Inner Sun and Moon, of which the outer are but replicas. This Joshua accomplished in his struggle of concentration in the Valleys of Gibeon (the Sun) and Aijalon (the Moon) (JOSHUA 10:12-15).

Joshua fought against the five kings who symbolize the five passions of *'kam'* — lust, *'krodh'* — anger, *'lobh'* — greed, *'moh'* — attachment, and *'ahankara'* — ego and vanity (Joshua 10:16-28). These five kings he had cornered — by concentrated effort of mind energy — in the cave of Makeda, a *chakra* or center, and slew them there. These were the enemies of Israel, and he needed more time and light in order to conquer them. This was given by the light of the Inner Sun and Moon, and he went from conquest to conquest, on to the **Promised Land**, the **Higher Regions of Consciousness**.

The Cloud over the Tabernacle of Jehovah represents the Grace of the Lord's Sound Current over the seat of soul consciousness in man. (Nu. 9:15-18).

In Nu. 12:3 it is clearly stated that Moses was **a very meek man**. That explains the greatness of the true mind

238 | Mystic Bible

of man. For it is only when the mind becomes meek and humble that it can accompany the soul and be of great help on the way to the Liberation of both. But the Sound Current, as the **Spirit** of Jehovah, always leadeth the Way, protects, helps and guides until the Goal is reached. According to the Teachings of the Saints, it is the Inner Form of the living Master who showers all this Grace by means of his Astral, Causal and Shabd Forms in the Higher Regions. He thus performs all the inner miracles for the benefit of His devoted disciples. This is the mystery of Grace and Mercy. However, the disciple can fully realize this only after he himself becomes sufficiently purified to reach this state of consciousness.

Another very interesting account is given in Joshua, Chapter 6, in the unusual way in which the walls fell in the destruction of the City of Jericho. This city was a powerful center, across the Jordan, at the gate of the Promised Land. Jericho symbolizes the city of the giant ego, the self. Two spies, the symbol of two energy currents of consciousness, had been sent out, and they were saved by the Harlot Rahob who dwelt on the wall of that city. The Israelites had been instructed to march around the walls while blowing trumpets and shouting in unison on the seventh day, which caused the walls of Jericho to fall. All is but an external symbol of the Sound Currents, by which the walls of the ego fall by means of the repetition of the Five Holy Names and Inner Concentration.

If this were not a symbolic account, there would have been little use for Joshua to send his two spies into the city after the walls fell, to rescue Rahob, who lived upon these walls and was bound by oath to stay in her house until the two spies came for her. It seems strange that the faith of the harlot was greater than that of all the people of the city. As a result, she was brought forth and saved, and dwelled with Israel.

Rahob represents the generative energy. It is situated on the wall, the rim of the pelvis. When the city fell and the ego of Jericho was killed, the generative impulse was relieved of ego oppression and did not need to play the harlot any longer. She and her house, her function, were saved as a natural process, necessary for the continuation of the race.

Balaam The Mystic
(NUMBERS, CHAPTERS 22, 23 AND 24)

By studying this cryptic incident in the Bible, was found an even more unsuspected statement that is usually overlooked. That appears in the twenty-second chapter of Numbers.

Balaam was a prophet of Bel, the god of Light of the Babylonian Triad of Anu-Bel and Ea, in the land of the Midians. He was consulted by princes and great men of his day. King Balak of Moab sent messengers unto Balaam, with gifts, and asked him to come and curse the Israelites who were about to invade Moab. Balaam did not give an immediate reply, but first sought guidance from God. **And God talked to Balaam**.

"Thou shalt not go with them; thou shalt not curse the people." (NU. 22:12)

Whereupon Balaam refused to go with them. After more messengers and more princes bearing gifts and promising great honors were sent to Balaam, he gave them a straightforward answer:

"If Balak would give me his house full of silver and gold, I cannot go beyond the **Word** of the Lord (Jehovah) my God to do less or more." (NU. 22:18)

Jehovah God **was** as **real** to the Seer Balaam, as was Bel Marduk of Babylon!

Again, this unusual incident points out that TRUTH IS ONE IN THE ESSENCE WITHIN, NO MATTER HOW DIVERSE AND OPPOSITE THE EXTERNAL APPEARANCES MAY BE. Israel was making war on the followers of Bel Marduk, the Moabites, but the Seer Balaam listened to the Word of Jehovah God. As far as the author knows, this account has not been brought to light anywhere. It is there, buried with many other gems in the Sacred Mystic Text.

After many entreaties from King Balak, and upon receiving permission from God to do so, Balaam finally goes with the men of Balak in order to please the king and to show his loyalty to him. Balaam's ass is the hero of this account. Balaam must have been a very devout and upright man who spent a lifetime in conquering his mind, as did and do many Saints and Seers in the East. His lower mind, the subconscious, is represented by his ass, upon which he rode on all occasions because it served him faithfully. Only trained and purified impulses can do that. This purity saved Balaam's life, as he was the higher mind in action.

It was merely to be patriotic and out of loyalty to his king and country that Balaam went when Jehovah gave him permission. While en route, the angel of the Lord blocked his way because he had put the lesser cause ahead of the greater. Balaam did not see the angel because the sense of duty obstructed his inner vision. But his highly trained and purified lower mind, symbolized by the ass, saw the angel of the Lord. The ass tried to turn back three times, and Balaam smote it in anger. Finally, the Power of Jehovah, as the Energy Essence made contact with Balaam's lower mind direct, and it spoke to Balaam within. Then he too saw the angel of the Lord (NU. 22:23-36).

This is **a most unusual incident** in that a pure lower mind saves the higher mind from destruction through stupidity. It is the reverse of all natural processes, and can only be explained by the purest life and the most severe training over a long period of time. That is much more important as an outstanding incident than that Balaam's ass talketh.

And now comes the Inspiration of Balaam, with the impact of the Current of the **Spirit** of Jehovah upon him (NU. 23:1-9).

"From the top of the rocks I see Him; and from the hills I behold Him." (NU. 23:9)

It is like the vision of Arjuna, when his eyes were opened by Krishna, as recorded in the Bhagavad Gita, and he saw the Vision of the Lord of many Hosts.

The next two lines describe the Mystics as a people who conquer the animal qualities, symbolized by idolatry, **in themselves**, and **do not serve them**.

"Lo, the people shall dwell alone,
And shall not be reckoned among the nations."

(NU. 23:9)

This also refers to the individual's inner progress, and to Mystics who stand alone. As we know, the external Israel became a great nation.

Even as far back as the time of Balaam, *'Parable'* was used; Jehovah taught in parables and the Mystics spoke in parables:

"And the Spirit of God came upon him. And he took up his parable, and said, Balaam the son of Beor saith, And the man **whose eye was closed** saith:"

(NU. 24:2, 3) (*quoted from American Std. Edition*)

This refers to the single eye of the Spirit, situated in the center of the forehead and also called the *'third eye'* or *'Tisra Til'* in other Sacred Writings and discourses. Spiritually, he was blind, like St. Paul in the New Testament, then his **inner eye** was opened by the Holy Spirit. What a miracle, by the Grace of God!

"He saith, who **heareth** the **Words** of God,
Who seeth the vision of the Almighty,
Falling down, and having his eyes open."

(NU. 24:4) (*quoted from American Std. Edition*)

Here is an incident similar to that recorded by St. Paul many centuries later. Whether the Name applied is the *'Spirit of Jehovah'*, the *'Holy Ghost'*, the *'Holy Shabd'*, or the *'Sound Current '*, it is all the same Truth which works the same throughout the ages and is the keystone and Essence of all Sacred Texts.

Again, the same is repeated in NU. 24:15, 16:

"And he took up his parable, and said,

Balaam the son of Beor saith,
And the man whose **eye was closed** saith:
He saith, who heareth the Words of God,
And knoweth the knowledge of the Most High
Who seeth the vision of the Almighty,
Falling down, and **having his eyes open**."

(quoted from American Std. Edition)

This is the way of all Truth, and is even now the Way, according to the teachings of the Old Testament as well as the Masters and Saints of modern times. To recapitulate, according to NU. 22:31:

"Then Jehovah **opened the eyes** of Balaam, **and he saw** the angel of Jehovah standing in the way, with his sword drawn in his hand; and he bowed his head, and fell on his face,"

(per American Std. Edition)

This was the first stage of Enlightenment. It happened that way throughout the ages and is happening even now to the sincere followers of the true, living Master. Even the very stages of spiritual progress are revealed in these three instances; namely, first came **Inner Sight**; the second time, **Inner Hearing**; and the third time, **Inner Knowledge** was added. These three repetitions indicate three degrees of Enlightenment and Grace upon the Prophet Balaam, because he was devoted to God and sincere in his actions.

NU. 24:5 to 10 reads much like Jehovah's address to Job, in parables. Such are the Wonders of the Holy Spirit of Shabd, whether called the Spirit of Jehovah or any other Name, with men of true devotion and sincerity, in any land or at any time.

The Tower of Babel
(GEN. 11:1-10)

This was a huge ziggurat, called Etemenaki, which literally means *'house of the foundation of heaven and earth'*. It was called the Temple of the God Beland at Babylon, named *'Babel'* in Hebrew. It was begun by an unknown, prehistoric Sumerian king; but was left unfinished, probably on account of much opposition from within as well as invasions from without.

For thousands of years its ruins were one of wonders of the world. King Sennacherib tried to obliterate it when he destroyed Babylon, but its massive foundations resisted his efforts. King Esarhaddon, and two other kings after him, endeavored to finish this temple, but did not succeed. Nebuchadnezzar was the first king of Babylon to bring the tower to completion. In his inscription, he gave an accurate account of its appearance. The bottom stage was three hundred feet in length and breadth, and about one hundred and twenty feet in height; and above this, there were six other stages that diminished consecutively in size. Since the decline of Babylon, its ruins have served the surrounding country as a brick quarry, for many centuries. Now, all that is left of the tower is a hole three hundred feet square, where the foundation once stood.

The historical facts concerning the Tower of Babel are given here in order to clarify the idea for which it stood. Mounds and Pyramids, all over the globe, had a similar principle in their portrayal of the seven strata or levels in the creation of the finer energy realms which linked the heavens above with the physical world below. That was symbolized by the statement in the Bible, in Gen. 11:1-9, when the men of Shinar proposed to build a tower whose top might reach unto heaven. The seven days of Creation, as recorded in the Bible, have a similar meaning.

The seven planets in Occult Philosophy occupy a similar position as the *chakras* in the body, which are but reflections of reflections of reflections of the One Sun in the Center, and swing and vibrate around Its orbit, expressing the One Energy from the Central Core.

The historical Tower of Babel, being an earthly structure, naturally the foundation had to be put on the ground in order to support the weight of the building. This structure, like man himself, is an inverted picture of the Real One above it, and is being demonstrated or imitated according to the pattern above. Man's roots are in his brain, from which all his energy flows to support him. So the foundation is the first cause in the Etheric Energy Field of the Central City of Sahasra Dal Kamal, the thousand rays of energy and light which support all the visible creation. The connecting link between man and the first Great Region above, also called the Thousand Petalled Lotus, is within man's own head. This is beautifully illustrated in the following poem by the Great Saint, Paltu Sahib, and translated into English by Professors Jagmohan Lal and Janak Raj Puri:

"An inverted well is there above,
and therein burneth a lamp;
The lamp burneth therein without the oil and without the wick. It burneth night and day;
for the six seasons and the twelve months, 'tis lit.
He alone seeth it who hath the Satguru with him. For, without the Satguru it ever remaineth unseen. From within the lamp's flame cometh a melody.
He alone listeneth to it who sits in *'Gyan Samadhi'*. Whosoever listeneth to it, O Paltu, is the one with perfect fate.
In the inverted well above burneth the lamp that never pales."

(This is a very unusual form of poetry and is called a *'Kundli'*. Paltu Sahib was a Master of this particular kind of poetry. An attempt to retain the original form has been made in rendering this translation.)

In the Bible this **light within man** is referred to in Revelation 22:5 as follows:

"And there shall be no night there; and they need no candle, neither light of the sun; for the Lord God giveth them light: and they shall reign for ever and ever."

The Great Pyramid of Gizeh was built on the center of the earth, as a temple of God on earth, to commemorate His Creation and to give hints of its Inner Mystery to posterity. It has symbolic passageways and chambers inside to further explain the mystery of man to himself.

The Atlanteans had built a similar huge tower like that of Babel and which resembled the Pyramid. The ancient Indians of North and South America also built their mounds, pyramids and temples for a similar reason, besides the intention to worship either in them or at the base.

The original intention was to bring to man's over and over again, in various ways and symbols, that all these are but replicas of the real place of **worship within himself**. But, alas, man has forgotten the symbolism and origin of the external temples, churches, mosques, tabernacles, etc. in which he externally worships God. These outer forms are venerated as sacred places while **man's real shrine, the soul** within his own body, is neglected or forgotten. "Mine own vineyard I have not kept" (Song of Solomon).

Behind it all there was an urge for man to build a structure of some kind in which to worship God, and to leave it to posterity as a sign and symbol of what had been experienced internally. This very impulse explains all the idols, statues, religious objects, rites and ceremonies ever built or instituted by man. It was not foolishness, nor was it due to gross ignorance that images and idols were created by minds of men in many lands and throughout the ages.

The building of the first Tabernacle in the wilderness (Exodus 20:24, 25) was to create a house of God among men; a house which they could see and in which they could worship. The pattern of this tabernacle was shown to Moses by Jehovah on Mount Sinai (Exodus 25:8, 9). And the tabernacle was built as an exact duplicate of that vision.

The leaders of the races, such as the Rishis who saw and heard the finer energy currents and their structures in the universe, tried to convey this to the people by means of the embodiment of their vision into some figure or image which would demonstrate its powers and abilities of action. It is impossible to do justice in endeavoring to convey that which is beyond the mind, to the mind. So images of deities were designed with three heads, many hands, etc. because that particular energy did so many things in the field of energy which the man does not see. Similarly, the Rishis heard the four great Truths, called the "Mahavaks", upon which the four Vedas were founded. The Essence is simple and Real but the effects and the writings and symbols of its portrayal are many.

What Saints and Mystics have done in the ecstasy of an internal experience, others try to imitate in an endeavor to reach the Source of that ecstasy. But, unfortunately, throughout the years even that very objective is forgotten and only the empty form of expression is carried on. The Light goes out. Only the forms are left behind.

It became the specific duty of the Sages, the Patriarchs, the Prophets and the Judges of Israel in the Bible, the same as the Manus or Law-givers in Vedic history, to instruct their people and posterity in that which they had seen and believed to be true in their lifetime. In some lands this became idol worship, or pilgrimages, or worship in temples or at the foot of mounds or other structures symbolizing the base of the Throne of God Who created this world.

Worship and Devotion was the keynote; no matter how, where or why it was done. **Devotion alone expresses the urge of the soul.** And since the people in general could not withdraw their attention from the outside and go within their own being, the real temple of the soul — made by God Himself and in which God always dwells in Essence and in Reality — the outside temples and images filled a need to picture to their minds the ideas which would incite their devotion to God.

All means have an end or an objective, and it, in turn, has means or paths which lead to it. If a picture of a Saint or a statue of the Savior or the Virgin Mary brings out the devotional qualities of the soul and permeates the mind, then it has an uplifting effect in its purpose. In essence, it is helpful to the worshiper.

Of course it is all symbolism, since the Reality resides **within** all beings; only man's consciousness cannot be aware of it without the necessary connecting Link. Anything which engenders the feeling of devotion to God is a step in the right direction. It was not the original intention to worship the picture or the image, but rather to concentrate the mind on That which it represented. When ways and means serve an uplifting purpose, according to the mentality and development of the worshiper, who can say that they are or were bad? In the same manner, it was not intended to take Mystic Texts literally as an objective Reality or Knowledge, but as a food for the higher mind and the soul.

The Prophets who fought Idolatry in Israel for centuries, were really against the licentious ways to which such means had been bent, until there was no Truth, no uplift, no devotion nor sincerity in any of its practices. It had deteriorated into nothing but hindrance toward the liberation of the soul, a worship of false idols of man's own desires and cravings, and the expressions of them.

When one sees the ruins of such huge temples or pyramids all over the world of ancient times, it seems as though the major energy of the nations was spent in erecting such monumental edifices. Their Deity was the central idea around which the glory and accomplishment of whole nations was built.

Their effort, with simple means, was certainly supreme in this respect. If individuals or any nation of today were to spend a fraction of such **sincere effort in conquering themselves** and would devote that amount of energy and time to **know themselves** and **find** their true place in the Universal Essence, that would leave a greater monument to posterity than all the others which can be seen with the physical eyes. It would have an uplifting and practical effect. External things eventually crumble, but internal values flourish throughout eternity.

When external forms and customs rule, the Truth is obscured by them, and It leaves behind only those forms which have no life nor devotion to sustain them. Where the Light of Truth leads the Way, there all forms take their proper place, as a natural sequence of Cause and Effect.

God geometrizes energy fields and substances into myriads of shapes and forms and functions, hut He is not caught or confined in any shape or form. Man imitates God and is caught in the trap of pride and possessions by his own ego and his personal glory of accomplishments. The hungry soul goes away empty, because the Mystic point and Essence which can link the soul back to the ONE WORD, the HIDDEN NECTAR OF LIFE, is lacking in the external forms and ceremonies. The entire purpose of human life is to have a mystic temple for the soul, wherein God can dwell in living communion with man in deed and in Truth. This is the impulse behind all the external efforts of temple building in all times. Memories in stone do not help the soul. God is a God of the living, not of the dead forms, for all live unto Him (Luke 20:38). A living devotion is needed by which all souls may aspire to God-Realization.

"Know ye not that ye are the temple of God, and that the Spirit of God dwelleth in you?"

(I COR. 3:16)

"If any man defile the temple of God, him shall God destroy; for the temple of God is holy, which temple ye are."

(I COR. 3:17)

CHAPTER XX
RECAPITULATION

We also find obscure verses in Genesis 6:2-4 Who were the sons of God? Were not all His creation His children?

It has been previously explained and shown clearly that the new creation of *'desire bodies'*, in the realm of Eden, was the creation called *'woman'* or the race of individual Eves. So the *'sons of God'* were the souls of pure energy essence, who had not as yet entertained a desire to incarnate into these lower bodies until

"the sons of God saw the daughters of men that they were fair; and they took them wives of all which they chose."
(GEN. 6:2)

The Nephilim or giants referred to in Gen. 6:4 as the mighty men of renown, were the offspring of these unions.

In the Bible and other Sacred Scriptures, incarnating souls are referred to as *'man'* or the race of Adams, before the physical universe was created. These souls had a latent desire to be free and create in the vast expanse of space. This is called the original desire or *'Adi Karma'* in the East. That is the *'original sin'*. So a free will was given them, to do this. This was a boon granted to souls by the Creator, for incarnation and experience, and it conditions everything that is done by and for man. In other words, man was given a free will in the beginning; but once acted upon, that very act and every thought, word and action thereafter, conditions him. This is called the *karma* of each individual.

Only when the soul desires to return to its Home can it find the Way. God is not dependent souls for praise, goodwill and service. He doesn't need a fraction of it from all the myriads of beings or particles of creation. But for the individual souls, it is the only way back to this Sublime Source, his real Security, his Haven of Rest, and the Eternal Home for the Soul. By riveting his attention and devotion on God Who is the only help and center of guidance, especially when incarnated as a Great Master or Savior, can he start the Homeward journey.

Praise and gratitude to the Giver of all, keeps the mind simple and humble. There is no occasion then for the '*Ahankar*' or ego of the mind to get puffed up and take glory unto itself for putting a few things together in a little different way and combination in matter than it was done before. All praise and glory goes to Him Who gives the understanding to the soul and also furnishes the materials with which it can work. We are all like children who feel that the parents just could not get along without us.

No matter which road or path the soul selects, it requires time and attention to do the traveling. The goal of selection is at the end of the Road or Way which the soul has chosen. Therefore, anyone can see how **important** it is to **set the right goal before the soul**, through the mind, the heart's desire and in the daily consciousness of life, even when at work. All roads lead to their goal, or blind endings in nowhere; in fact, worse than nowhere, for we may not only be off course, but even traveling perilously in the opposite direction at great speed, without being conscious of it. Only devotion and true discrimination can assure the soul of attracting to itself the right Path of Life. All real growth is slow and gentle, almost imperceptible, like in Nature. We don't see the grass grow, but we know that it needs cutting regularly.

The accomplishment of success or the gaining of powers is not the objective here; but rather the conditioning of the soul in the qualities of the Eternal Nature so it can blend ultimately with that One Source. The soul struggles and endures, that it may be cleaned of its own lower desire vehicles of self and selfishness, to prepare it for Eternal Blessings. However, the soul must never lose sight of its goal for one moment, nor fail in the practice of Humility.

All Saints who struggled upward in devotion, testify to this Truth. Saint Thomas A' Kempis wrote some beautiful lines on this way of life in his book, *The Imitation of Christ*. Many other devotees in the western world, who were later proclaimed saints, have written the same testimony in their books. Among them were St. Augustine, St. Theresa, St. John of the Cross, St. Francis of Assisi, etc.

Of course, there is a vast difference between the great Teachers called Gurus and Saints in the Eastern world, and the terminology in the West. In the **East it was and is** a Science of the Soul, and every title given was according to the realm which the soul had consciously entered on its Inner Mystic Way of Travel, called Transport. The title was not decreed by others, nor can it be given in that way. The extent of the inner wealth of the Essence of the Lord, the Lost Word, the Pearl of Great Price, determines the degree of Sainthood.

Great souls merely call themselves servants or slaves of the Lord and their followers, even when they are duly appointed Successors of Great Masters. Such is their simplicity and humble devotion to their Guru and the Supreme Father. They accept nothing for their service to mankind, but are content in earning their living by some simple toil or profession, as all other beings do. They go about their Spiritual duties, even while performing their family and civic duties. And when their following becomes so great that it requires all of the hours of the day and even way into the night to serve the congregation, then some provision is made even before this occurs, such as a pension earned by their years of labor either for the government or some private concern, or an inheritance which enables them to carry on the good work. Spiritual labor is also worth its hire; but it is not paid in material coin. The reward consists of Spiritual values of more Grace to make more effort, and inner Jewel of greater devotion and uplifting Love and Bliss. Jesus declared this principle very clearly when He said:

"Render therefore unto Caesar the things which are Caesar's; and unto God the things that are God's."

(MAT. 22:21)

CHAPTER XXI
METHODS OF DEVELOPMENT
IN THE OLD TESTAMENT

The burning bush which Moses saw (EXODUS 3:1-7) was the flame of the Yod or Yoti, also called Jot or Jyoti in eastern terminology, in the plane of Paradise or Akash. The inner perception, by God's grace, may go far ahead of the actual development of the entire being; as was the case with Moses.

Spiritual things always come through Kether the crown and the higher cerebral centers and faculties of the human being. But to **hold** the consciousness there is the problem which Joshua solved when he made the inner sun stand still upon Gibeon, and the moon stand still in the valley of his brain called Ajalon (JOSH. 10:12-14). That is a great day for the soul. There is none like it in its inner experience of conscious entrance to the Inner Sky and its realms. Moses could not do it, and, therefore, he could not take the children of Israel (the souls) into the Promised Land.

The progress of each initiate was measured by the actual inner psychic *chakras* which he had conquered. That means where he could **hold** his consciousness steady, without a ripple of thought or emotion. These methods of the conscious development of the lower chakras or centers in the body were used in all systems of teachings of the Sacrosanct Art and Science in India, Egypt and in the Middle East as well as in the Old Testament.

The New Testament teaches the same Truth by means of the path of Love and Devotion, without the need of the steps of inner conscious development in the centers of the body below the eyes. This was easier for the majority, and a number of the early Christian Saints have written accounts of their inner experience of spiritual progress consciously attained. Some of them are: St. Augustine, St. Francis of Assisi, St. Theresa, St. Thomas A' Kempis and many others. Their writings reveal similar inner experiences of spiritual enlightenment, and it is profitable to read them.

In the Orient, the conscious development of the five lower *chakras* was still taught at the time of Kabir Sahib in the fifteenth century. Kabir Sahib was a real Saint of a very high order.

Param Sant Sat Guru Swami Ji of Agra started and taught all development beginning with the center of consciousness between the eyes, upward, and covered all the regions in man's brain, clear to the top of man's latent Spiritual Potential. Several others who preceded Him also taught this Science of the Soul upward from the center between the eyes. Their names were: Guru Nanak, Dadu Sahib, Paltu Sahib, Jagjivan Sahib, Tulsi Sahib and a few others.

Swami Ji formed the Sant Mat system, also called the Radha Swami Faith or Science. 'Sant' means Saint; 'Mat' means system of teaching. 'Radha' means soul; and `Swami' means Lord. The teaching reveals how the human soul may attain God-Realization—be consciously united with the Lord God—while living on this earth. It teaches the union of the soul with God, its Source. It embraces the teaching of **the Lord of souls** in relation **to each soul** as a path or way of going Home by first being united within to the Holy Sound Current which Job called the Redeemer who liveth, and it was also called the Spirit of Jehovah in the Old Testament. In the New Testament it is called the Logos, the Word of God, the Holy Spirit, the Holy Ghost, the Comforter, etc.

Each age received its revelation and its inspiration through some Great Teacher, Saint, Savior or Prophet.

CHAPTER XXII
A DIET FOR MYSTICS AS POINTED
OUT IN THE BIBLE

"And God said, Behold, I have given you every herb bearing seed, which is upon the face of all the earth, and every tree, in which is the fruit of a tree yielding seed; to you it shall be for meat." (Gen. 1:29)

"For he shall be great in the sight of the Lord, and shall drink neither wine nor strong drink; and he shall be filled with the Holy Ghost, even from his mother's womb." (LUKE 1:15)

"Now therefore beware, I pray thee, and drink not wine nor strong drink and eat not any unclean thing." (JUDGES 13:4)

"She may not eat of any thing that cometh of the vine, neither let her drink wine or strong drink, nor eat any unclean thing: all that I commanded her let her observe." (JUDGES 13:114)

"But Daniel purposed in his heart that he would not defile himself with the portion of the king's meat, nor with the wine which he drank:" (DANIEL 1:8)

"Prove thy servants, I beseech thee, ten days; and let them give us pulse to eat, and water to drink." (DAN. 1:12)

"And at the end of ten days their countenances appeared fairer and fatter in flesh than all the children which did eat the portion of the king's meat." (DAN. 1:15)

"And be not drunk with wine, wherein is excess: but be filled with the Spirit;" (EPH. 5:18)

"For a bishop must be blameless, as the steward of God; not self-willed, not soon angry, not given to wine, no striker, not given to filthy lucre;" (TITUS 1:7)

"Do not drink wine nor strong drink, thou, nor thy sons with thee, when ye go into the tabernacle of the congregation, lest ye die: it shall be a statute for ever throughout your generations:" (LEVITICUS 10:9)

The above quotations clearly indicate the necessity for mystically inclined souls to adopt a vegetarian diet, free from alcoholic drinks.

It is a natural condition for the body of earth to live on the products of it in its earthy environment. In this way the body can get the products of the earth direct and the magnetism of the earth, if the foods are properly chosen and prepared according to the individual's needs.

The sap in all vegetation is the life thereof. This rises in the plants in daytime by the attraction of the sun energy which causes oxidation in all foliage. At night this energy in the sap retires to the root system for nourishment and absorption into the entire plant structure. In this manner all vegetation responds to the sun and moon energy in our universe. Heaven bestows warmth and air, and the earth and waters respond and bring forth substance and fruits, each after its kind.

All vegetation and life need these four essential elements to grow and maintain health: Warmth and sunshine, air, moisture, and the soil of the earth. Human beings too need these things in substance and essence, either from the sources direct or through the medium of food and liquid. In this simple way can the body of man, the microcosm, keep in rhythm and tuned to the natural vibrations of the macrocosm or the universe. This causes no suffering or hardship for animals. They also have a right to live and fulfill **their** *karma*. So here is a more considerate way of life for all other life, which interferes with none. It is a graceful way of living, worthy of mankind full of Love and thoughtfulness, and freedom for all.

The animal creation is a lower realm and keynote of life, as a whole, than the human form. The animal spines are usually horizontally placed in relation to the earth. Animal life is mostly a life of force and quick reactions, the element of fear predominating. With a few exceptions, life lives upon life everywhere, whether on land or in the sea. This animal nature is also within man, **as his lower** nature, which he must overcome and surrender completely before he can become a full-fledged human being of spiritual stature.

In the Old Testament the sacrifices of the animals were used to show man that he must give up these animal qualities **within himself**, one by one, as a sacrifice for each sin or animal tendency, until the humble and contrite heart **became a natural thing** with man. Then his Spiritual evolution could start in earnest and the human element and the fuller Love Nature of the soul could have a chance for expression in life, thoughts and deeds.

This is why Spiritual Masters usually require a non-flesh meat, non-egg and non-fish or fowl diet of their disciples. The avoidance of alcoholic drinks is also necessary as they stimulate the animal nature in man.

St. John the Baptist was a vegetarian. He is supposed to have lived on the locust pods, also called Karob or St. John's bread and wild honey. The apostles stripped wheat stalks and chewed the wheat when they were hungry. They also had their coarse bread as the mainstay of their diet. Jesus lived a very simple life and ate very little. His disciples often begged him to eat something. It was then that he told them that he had food to eat which they knew not of. He referred to the Spiritual Nectar, the Holy Sound Current within. This was his mainstay; not the food of the earth:

> "But whosoever drinketh of the water that I shall give him shall never thirst; but the water that I shall give him shall be **in him** a well of water springing up into everlasting life." (JOHN 4:14)

Jesus met the needs of his time and its purpose. Love was the keynote of his message, and that included and covered even thing. Love is God, God is Love!

> "For the kingdom of God is not meat and drink; but righteousness, and peace, and joy in the Holy Ghost." (ROM. 14:17)

> "It is good neither to eat flesh, nor to drink wine, or anything whereby thy brother stumbleth, or is offended, or is made weak." (ROM. 14:21)

CHAPTER XXIII
HARD SAYINGS OF JESUS

The object of this book is the clarification of biblical texts so they may be put to practical use which every good Christian can follow and become a better disciple of his beloved Master. No matter how difficult a saying in the Bible may be, there is always a real and practical meaning and a definite message of Spiritual value within that sealed parable or arcane speech. The disciples of Jesus also had this difficulty and would say many a time,

"this is an hard saying"   (JOHN 6:60)

Many of the disciples left him because of this (JOHN 6:66, 67). According to Luke 10:1, Jesus had 70 disciples at one time; and according to some teachings, he had twelve apostles and seventy-two disciples.

Sayings of Jesus, like:

"If any man come to me, and hate not his father, and mother, and wife, and children, and brethren, and sisters, yea, and his own life also, he cannot be my disciple."
(LUKE 14:26)

are hard for one who advocates that "ye love one another' and gives his life for the principle. Here again, the practical teachings of the Saints make this difficult advice very clear, understandable and useful for Spiritual growth. In the writings of the Param Sant Sat Guru, Swami Ji Maharaj, in the book called 'Sar Bachan', published by the Radhas Soami Satsang at Beas, Punjab, India, on page 114, this problem is clearly stated:

"Internally the soul is entangled in the net of passion, anger, greed, attachment and vanity; while externally it is attached to mother, father, son, wife, friends, wealth, honor and all the sensual pleasures of the world."

It is the external **attachment** to all external relations which Jesus refers to in the above quotation from Luke. How can the soul grow spiritually when it is bound hand

and foot by external and internal attachments which bind the life of the soul to sensual pleasures, possessions, etc., from which it cannot free itself?

These **bonds of attachment**, within and without are to be hated and overcome; within, as bad habits and undesirable qualities mentioned in the above quotation, and without, as the bondage of the soul by customs, forms, possessions, position, honor, etc.

Love never stands in the way of the soul's progress, because real Love is above possession and personal attachment. True Love sees God in all things and beings. Man owns and possesses nothing. Everything belongs to God.

"and ye are not your own" (I. COR. 6:19)

"The earth is the Lord's and the fulness thereof; the world, and they that dwell therein."

(Ps. 24:1) (*also* I. COR. 10:26)

All is God's gift to His children. Jesus stated plainly that this negative attachment and possessive attitude must be hated and forsaken before anyone could be his disciple. The same requirements are mentioned in many places in the Bible as well as in other Sacred Scriptures.

Real Love and respect toward parents, etc. are always highly recommended in the Bible and by all Great Teachers. This principle is even brought out clearly by Shakespeare. Romeo was chided by the friar for doting, not for loving.

True Love is the soul's own nature and essence. But attachment forms bondage and is the opposite to Love because it wants to hold onto everything for selfish reasons. Such attachment must be hated and forsaken in order to free the soul from all such bondage, internally and externally.

Such is the true principle of complete surrender to the Will of God. It is the Master's message of real Love and devotion to Him as the first requisite in soul growth and discipleship. True Love transcends all law and all bondages. It is the lack of Love and faith in God which forms the chains of attachment.

CHAPTER XXIV
THE SOUL'S TRAVEL

The preceding chapters will help to clarify and unify the principles and ideas in the Bible with other Sacred Scriptures. God is Light and gives it to all nations and peoples of the earth and in the heavens. He alone can decree who should and who should not be conscious of Him. His Light is everywhere, but we do not behold it because our interest and attention are far removed from that high key of Love and Devotion. Neither do we hear the blessed Sound of Shabd, His Word, in any realm because we do not ascend to it, but live mostly in the ego and in our personal interests and desires. We live in a world of our own creation. God's creation is but a vague ideal which we have not yet consciously entered.

The admonition throughout the Bible and every Sacred Text is the same. Many wonderful sayings in the Psalms and in Old Testament generally, concerning the Spirit of God or the Holy Spirit, will have a new and deeper meaning for us, with a practical explanation, if we but choose to use it and find the Way Within. The Highway to the King's Palace is open to all, but few there be who find it and walk thereon. The Path is only narrow at the gateway and is as broad as Light itself in Reality! It expands to Infinite Unity Within.

That blessed sight of *'His Vision'*, called *'Holy Darshan'*, is also a wonderful gift of the Beloved. It is bestowed on mortals through the true Mystic Masters, Gurus and Saviors who are the Custodians of God's Treasure House. If we would have such jewels, we must **find One Who has them** in deed and in Truth. That is the real *'Pearl of Great Price'* (MAT. 13:45). All other symbolism in the Bible cannot compare to the Song and Sounds of the Light of Love in the Beloved One. Where He is not, there are but sideways and byways, dead-ends and back-tracks. Only One Road is **the** Highway of the Holy Spirit, and that is the Holy Shabd. The Hidden Will and His Mystery, for which all creation was made, is within mankind. Man is like a precious jewel formed in the depths of the earth by heat and pressure from without.

The descent of the Children of Israel into Egypt symbolizes an involutionary necessity because of the great drought, spiritually and physically, which made it necessary for them to go into that realm of experience of servitude of the mind, the ego and the senses. The group of souls called the *'Children of Israel'* is described as a unit in relation to inner struggles and outer experiences. In reality, each individual soul goes through this same conditioning, only it is not recorded in this material world. God's Will, and cosmic energies as His servants, work in every realm and region in the heavens and on earth.

All *karma* is individual, no matter how it is grouped or classified in the description. Similar *karmas* have similar vicissitudes, and that is why it looks like national *karma*. But if even one righteous man, as in the case of Lot or Abraham, lives in that nation which is to be destroyed, he must be taken out of the area before disaster can strike. The same is true today as it was in ancient times.

Saints never interfere with the orders of any rulers, nor with the running of the universe by lesser powers and principalities. **Their mission and interest is purely Spiritual**. Goodness is above destruction everywhere, because it is of the Eternal Substance. So is Beauty, Love and Truth. Evil is but a cover over such Reality, like a shadow of darkness. Evil destroys itself, because it is void of the current of Love. Yet the Great Saints have such compassion on mankind that When man has piled up so much *karma* that he is about to be destroyed, the Saints Themselves pay this debt to the extent of saving mankind from complete destruction, and at the same time save Their devotees from physical destruction.

The Truth is the same in every land, creed and country. The universe is run by principles and laws which were established in the very beginning. This is the world of the pairs of opposites. Until we reach beyond the realm of good and evil, there will be joy and sorrow, sickness and health, life and death. The pattern of energy descends and crystallizes into definite geometric proportions, in the direction of energy travel which is as precise as the weaving of any design. **There can be no favoritism in the law of Cause and Effect**.

Even the law of Grace does not upset this mathematically balanced procedure; it merely transcends it by a higher vibratory keynote of finer energy. All polarity effects are from above, downward. Hence, the Higher always rules the lower. The Positive, above, has power over the Negative, below. The Cause rules the effect. The Life rules the form. Mind patterns and will, rule matter. Effort is the exertion of mental, emotional and physical energies in one direction.

Love is not an evasion, but is a **fulfillment of all law**. Mercy and Grace of the Lord, which come down through His Holy Shabd, constitute an influx of the highest energy and lift the soul out of negative effects. It is the Transcendent Energy which is greater than all else. To illustrate this point, let us say a pilot in a helicopter dropped a life line to a drowning man. Would he be violating any laws of the water or of navigation? Also, would that in any way prevent the drowning person from making an effort to save himself? Does it prevent him from exercising his free will to drown if he prefers, or to catch hold of the rope which will lift him to its Source and safety?

All that pertains to the involution and evolution of souls is necessary for equilibrium in life and motion. Understanding of them helps much to comprehend our position in daily life. This, in turn, helps to clarify Scriptural Texts which are based on the laws of the Universe, or on the Cause and the Effect of causes, termed 'karma', set in motion by our own free will, desire and action.

Even as a simple business cannot be run without payment of debts and earning of income, if it is to remain solvent; so are these obligations, called 'karma', to be cleared by the soul that wishes to be liberated. When we are off guard, or not on the beam, our scattered attention of mind and emotions sets many of these causes into action. Therefore, a better training and tuning of the mind and senses, through **concentrated attention**, should be very helpful toward avoiding irresponsible or idle thinking, and thoughtless or inconsiderate action. It is the only logical and real means of progress, and is available to every human soul, if he will but make the necessary effort to **reach** for this Life Line!

Education, as we have it today, is not the answer to the deeper, Spiritual problems in Life. Our training is geared mostly for intellectual and physical pursuits. The consciousness of the soul is beyond the reach of the mind. And that portion of the mind which is used and trained for advancement in the highest educational circles in this world, is still within the lower phase of the mind! The higher mind and soul need training and developing in order to be useful on their planes of consciousness, just as we need the training of the lower mind for functioning in this world.

However, soul progress, in order to be of a permanent nature, cannot be swift and without effort on our part, nor can it be forced. Soul progress should always be free, and should never be subject to anything but the individual's desire to be liberated. The True Masters Themselves never force nor lasso a soul against its own desire. But once the soul reaches for the Holy Shabd, and, having caught hold of It, **holds on**, the Master does the rest. This freedom is essential to all **true growth**, from within outward.

Compulsion and force are of the mind, and can be employed only in that sphere and in matter. Even there, it is subject to constant reactions and necessary re-adjustments. This constitutes the struggle in life. Soul struggle is similar, between upward and downward impulses of energy travel and use. However, this impact is much deeper and it takes a keener attention and devotional firmness to hold the balance.

Therefore, constant attention and concentrated inner awareness are necessary to guide the finer and deeper energies of the soul upon its course. And there must be a Goal or a fixed point of inner attraction to which to direct the devotional energy and attention. Wherever the attention or consciousness dwells, there it acts and expands itself. This is the law of life and growth, internally and externally. This is the very core and substance of our being, and the heart of the universe itself, as the Causeless Cause of all existence. If we aim high, top fruits will be reached.

Consciousness is like the sun, and attention forms its rays. Wherever these are directed, expansion and growth take place, as in Nature. The direction of energy rays may be aimed high or low, and that is where we dwell. To keep the conscious awareness high, above the eyes, in the higher centers and *chakras* in the brain, is the aim and object of the teachings of the Saints. Only thoughts of Love and Devotion to God and to the Guide Who is consciously One with Him, have that inward central whirl of attraction toward that Eternal Core. The Eternal Essence will attract its own substance and lift it up unto Itself, and man's consciousness along with it, if it is attached to it. Such is the law of Grace and Love.

The Holy Ghost, Holy Spirit, Holy Word, Holy Shabd or Holy Sound Current is such an Energy River of Reality which is the Essence in all and flows through the very Core of all there is — soul, mind, feeling, body — within us and in every being in creation. This is the True Science of the Soul, from the very beginning. It is also the middle as well as the end and object of all existence and being. It is Consciousness, it is Bliss and it is the Essence of all Knowledge; for only in the heart and center can anything be truly known. The effects are external, while the causes themselves are always inside. If we would know them, we must go deep within. Life itself is the deepest River of Energy. Awareness of its flow is conscious experience.

The soul's involution and evolution is the game in Life. As our chest rises and falls with each respiration, so do our energies expand and contract, and produce phenomenal results called health and happiness. The soul does not live by physical bread at all, but by the Word or the Eternal Sound Energy **which is** of **the same Essence as the soul. Only that Holly Essence, as living Water or Nectar of Life is food for the soul.** The One Word of God is truly the only food for the soul. It lives on nothing else. Even as the body lives on food of a material nature, like itself, so does the soul live on the One Essence which is its own true nature and its Home Substance.

Mind is fed by mind substance and thoughts. Emotions feed on feelings and sensations. **Each body** must have its own substance in Nature on which to feed, or it starves and dies. The soul feeds on Love and God's Grace, from the very center of the Sound Current. The Essence of the One Word which created all universes and realms and beings, is its only food and support. All other attempts to satisfy the soul end in misery and frustration.

Like feeds on like throughout Nature. Scientists have proved the immense power contained in a little speck of energy called the atom. How much more potent, **for good,** can be the energies of the soul if they are let loose to have their way, like the atom when it is released? And even greater is the energy of the Sound Current. It is **beyond** the scope of comprehension and description or imagination.

Can the soul be an exception to this law in Life? Man does not realize the great Truths of his own being, or he would not try so hard to evade them for material pleasures and thus find himself on highways and anyways of suffering and misery.

Even in mechanics, we know that every machine must have the proper lubrication and fuel to make it endure and serve efficiently. This is all studied and tabulated down to a fine art. As man is not a senseless machine, but subject to constant shifting of desires and mind impulses, no such rules could be applied. Each person is a rule or law unto himself. Only he can find what he needs for the next step, **according to his desire impulse** and mental makeup, if he will study himself. **We**, ourselves, **are the unsolved** problems to ourselves. Intelligent interest always finds a way. "Where there is a will, there is a way." But all this pertains only to the body, the mind and the emotions. What about the soul, our real self, beyond the mind and senses?

Our mind cannot transcend itself to prescribe for the soul in its position and its reach. That would be like the servant ruling the master; and the soul is in exactly that position as long as it allows the mind and the senses to dictate and lead the way. This is the theme of a whole set of beautiful symbolism in Free-masonry. When an apprentice in any trade or profession usurps the position of his master and benefactor, he is in for trouble even in this world.

When force **compels**, then **Life rebels**. Force is the law of suffering and unhappiness. However, the problem is not simple because the mind and the desires are not simplified. We ourselves cannot meet that constant flux and impact of desire without inner conflict. Then how much more so in the without? This is the obstacle toward obtaining happiness in this life. To still the mind and to **simplify desires** is the Way. How simple that sounds until we try it!

That can be accomplished only by contact with a Positive Energy Current from above. How to contact that Current? By seeking the guidance and protection of a living Master Who will instruct us **how to reach for and hold on** to the True Positive Energy Current called the Holy Shabd, which sustains and governs all. Under such able guidance and by genuine devotion to the Guide, the soul can direct its energy toward **that** Goal within itself. This concentration is not on any external point or object, nor does it consist of hypnotizing or locking the mind in any conditioning of belief, as that would only interfere with the soul's progress.

The True Mystic Guide teaches us how to direct the soul's own energy inward and upward to its center of consciousness, to discover itself as that One Essence in Eternal Love and Grace, like a drop of water merging with the ocean. To leave our own ego and its desires and creations, and enter the Land of Promise provided Within ourselves, is the keynote and promise throughout the entire Bible.

In the Old Testament the Spirit of Jehovah God works valiantly to lead the Children of Israel into this Promised Land flowing with Energy Rivers of Milk and Honey, as the Nectar and Wine of Life. This was promised to the seed of Abraham who had faith and devotion beyond themselves. Through this Righteousness was the promise extended as a Covenant with all followers having such faith and inner devotion.

In the New Testament, the simplicity of this faith and devotion is extolled without the external forms of symbolism used in the Old Testament. This was hard to comprehend and not easily acceptable to those who only externally followed the forms and customs of old. Love alone seems a stranger in this world. It is a bright light itself, for which each one is his own lamp.

When the real man himself becomes the object of his own search, then he is not led astray by external interests and discoveries or new theories. The full attention of his mind can then be drawn to a point of consciousness in the center of his forehead, preparatory to the inner travel, upward, known as Transport or elevation of the consciousness. The soul, as well as the mind, must reach beyond its present state for a fulcrum by which to lift itself up. Neither soul nor mind can do this at its level of consciousness. That is where the grace of Shabd Energy comes in and does it for them, through the Mercy and Grace of the Sat Guru, the Real, True Mystic.

Such is the simple way, according to the teachings of Sant Mat, also known as the Radha Swami Faith. This is the practical way of "doing by not doing", of selfless effort coupled with Grace, of rising above self in a transcendent Love, to the One Reality.

Following is quoted a poem composed by the Great Saint, Swami Ji Maharaj, in the latter part of the nineteenth century, and translated into English by Professor Jagmohan Lal of Beas. It beautifully illustrates how helpless mankind is, and how compassionate and merciful the Saints are in helping those who wish to be Liberated:

Request of the Soul to the Mind

1. A request of mine, oh mind, please grant!
   Thy humble servant have I been for numerous incarnations and thou hast been my lord.
2. Known as lord of the three worlds; E'en the three gods[2]. are thy servants.
3. Rishis, Munis, all thou dost rule.
   Within thy orbit are the ascetics and celibates.
4. Gods and men and yogis, all are under thy control.
   None dare thee disobey.
5. Whomsoever you wish, you may involve in the world. And whom you like, set free.
6. Thus have I heard your greatness praised;
   Hence, this humble request.
7. Why be content to live in this body
   Like a prisoner in a dark cell?
8. The Master once said to me:
   "Let the mind be your escort."
9. I therefore entreat, why delay?
   To `gagan`[3]; let's mount up soon.
10. Decide, even now.
    On sensual pleasures turn your back.
11. A peerless companion, thou;
    Thine am I e'en as thou art mine.
12. Grant this prayer of thy slave.
    And in 'gagan' take up abode.

---

2 'Gods' Brahma, Vishnu and Shiva.
3 'Gagan' The sky of Trikuti or Trikuti itself, the home of the mind.

13. Thus be as once you were.
    Why suffer so much here?

14. Sat Guru gave me this tip:
    "Take the mind with you and Homeward turn."

15. '*Surat*[4]' am I, but under thy control.
    Unaided by thee, I cannot catch the Shabd.

16. If to this request you don't accede,
    The round of eighty-four we'll both have to undergo.

17. Now please be kind, to my entreaty pay heed,
    And that pure '*Dhun*[5]' investigate.

18. Let us both go up
    And on 'Mount Sumeru[6]' encamp.

19. There you will live and rule
    And I to Radha Swami abode speed on.

Reply of the Mind to the Soul

1. Thus the mind to '*Surat*' made reply:
   Hard it is to give up pleasures

2. And follow this advice.
   Enslaved am I by the senses.

3. All courage and strength have I lost,
   Helpless before the senses I stand.

4. Sensual pleasures I wish to renounce.
   When face to face, I cannot control myself.

5. I resolve before and repent afterwards;
   But at the moment I am overcome.

6. How shall I rise to '*gagan*', dear?
   I am restless like a galloping horse.

7. (Soul): May I suggest a way out?
   Let's turn to the Sat Guru and pray for help.

8. (Mind accedes): Let's together in Sat Guru take refuge, And by His '*Satsang*[7]' grow strong.

---

4 '*Surat*' means 'soul'

5 '*Dhun*' means the melody or tune of Holy Shabd.

6 '*Mount Sumeru*'—one the three prominences in Trikuti.

7 '*Satsang*' means 'association'. The highest form of Satsang is to merge with Shabd, and the prescribed meditation practice generally; secondly, the association with and serving the Guru or Master and His Sangat, and listening

9. When the Sat Guru showers His Grace,
   He will check me every time.
10. It is impossible for me to go up of my own *'accord'*[8],
    Till I contact the Perfect Guru, the Liberator.
11. Hearing this, the *'surat'* was exceedingly happy:
    "Let us then hurry up and break the bonds."
12. Now both of them have taken refuge in the *'Satsang'*
    And drink freely of this Nectar.
13. Together to *'gagan'* they mount,
    Eagerly drinking the Nectar of Shabd.
14. Radha Swami showers His Grace on them;
    They gather the Spiritual Treasures.
15. And thus, through the wonderful Grace of Radha
    Swami, The pitiless Kal was overcome!

---

to His discourses; thirdly, reading about and speaking of the incidents in the life as well as the teachings of one's Guru and other Saints, as well as reading and discussing Radha Swami literature and other Spiritual Writings.

8 *'accord'*—It is impossible for even the mind to return to its home without the help of Sat Guru because the mind is the slave of the senses just as the soul is the slave of the mind. By following the master's instructions, the mind may return to its home in Trikuti and be truly happy, leaving the soul free to go to its true Home of Everlasting Bliss.

CHAPTER XXV
HOW SHALL I ATTAIN THE LORD, OH MASTER?

(A translation into English by PROF JANAK RAJ PURI
from 'Rag Gauri Purbi' by GURU ARJUN DEV,
from Granth Sahib.)

How shall I attain the Lord, Oh Master?

That can be only through a Saint Who has attained the
bliss of Sahaj[9], and will show me the path.

The Unseen is within, but remains invisible because of
the veil of ego.

Infatuated by Maya, the whole creation is asleep. How
can we ever wake up from this delusion?

Dwelling in the same house[10], living together, we know
not each other.

For lack of One Thing[11], the Five torment us. But That
Thing is not easily accessible.

The One Who made this house, has locked it and entrusted the key to the Guru.

Try however one may, he shall never obtain the Treasure unless he takes refuge in the Guru.

Those whose shackles are to be cut by the Guru, are
granted the love and company of the Holy[12]?

When, in Their (Saints') company, they will sing the
song of rejoicing (practice Shabd),

There will be no difference left between them and the
Lord, says Nanak[13].

It is thus that the Lord is attained,

---

9 "Sahaj" means easy and natural; it also refers to the spiritual stage of
having passes the transition from the stage of 'becoming' into that of "being"
One with Supreme Being.

10 by "house" is meant this physical body.

11 "One Thing" is the Treasure of Nam and Shabd.

12 by "the Holy" is meant the Saints and devotees.

13 Whatever has been written in the Adi Granth Sahib by the first five Gurus and the ninth Guru has been credited to Guru Nanak Sahib by each of
the succeeding Gurus; therefore, "says Nanak" is mentioned in every Shabd
in the Granth.

Sahaj is achieved, delusion has vanished, the flame[14] has merged in the Light!

Translation of a discourse by
Sardar Charan Singh ji Maharaj
"How shall I attain the Lord. Oh Master?"

This is an explanation of a Shabd by the fifth Guru, Shree Arjun Dev Ji:

Man seeks the Lord because He is his origin. Having separated from Him, the soul has been entangled by Maya in the snare of attachment, and it has taken to the company of the mind. Further, the mind itself is not independent, but has been enslaved by the senses and the worldly desires. It thus gets still more entangled, and the soul has to bear the consequences of whatever thoughts and acts emanate from the mind, whether good or evil; because the mind and the soul are tied together in a knot. The soul has to suffer the pain—sometimes of one birth, sometimes of another, and remains imprisoned in the jail of Chaurasi (the cycle of 8,400,000 births).

To whichever birth we go, we find pain and suffering. We can get deliverance from this cycle of birth and death only when our soul returns to its origin. The only outlet from this jail is through the human form. In other words, of all the forms, it is only in the human form that the soul has the privilege of uniting with the Lord. The Hindus call it the House of God, the Muslims refer to man as the Highest Form of Creation, and the Jews and the Christians hold the belief that God has created man after His own image. It is for this reason that, in the human form, man seeks the Lord according to his limited understanding. He employs various ways and means to find Him out, but all this proves in vain.

The seeker asks the Master to enlighten him as to how and where he can find the Lord. The Master says that if a seeker could meet a Saint Who had attained to the stage

---

14 The flame merging into the Light, has the same meaning as "The drop merging in the Ocean"

of Sahaj; and if the Saint would disclose the secret and the path of meeting the Lord, and if he would follow the path, only then could he unite with the Lord. What is meant is that whenever we succeed in being re-united with the Lord, it is brought about through the Saints. The stage of Sahaj can be attained only when we transcend the limitations of mind and Maya. The Saints say that the Lord Whom man seeks is not hidden in forests and mountains, nor does He dwell in temples and mosques, in Gurdwaras and churches, nor is He asleep somewhere in the skies. He dwells within Man himself. Whenever He will be found, He will be found within us; and whosoever has found Him, has found Him within. But when we close our eyes, we find nothing but darkness. Why can we not behold Him? This is because there is the veil of our own ego between Him and us.

What is the ego? It is "I", "me" and "mine". It is the self. It is what we day in and day out express by saying "This is my son, my family, my wealth, my property, my achievement, my high position, my religion, my country, my race, my nation," etc. All that exists belongs to the Lord, but we think ourselves to be separate from the Lord. We desire to possess and try to make them our own, but they never become ours nor have they ever become any-one else's. Having become attached to them, we exist only for them, and we continue to be born and to die here. It is not the family, relatives, wealth, etc., but **our own attitude of attachment and possessiveness** which is the obstacle.

The soul is within us and so is the Lord, and this has been so for thousands of *yugas*; yet, how strange it is that those who live together, dwelling in the same house, never meet each other. This is the cause of the veil of ego.

How can this veil be lifted when we are fast asleep? In this hypnotic trance of attachment, no one ever thinks of Him; taking the world to be real, they have become at-tached to it. They are wasting days and nights in the pur-suit of pleasures. So long as we do not have a longing for the Lord, we cannot come out of this delusion. In the first place, we do not show, devotion to the Lord. Even if we sometimes think of Him, it is for our own comfort and happiness. We pray for some high position or honor, or to be saved from sorrow and pain. So long as we do not seek the Lord for His Own sake, we cannot have love for him. True longing, true reverence, true devotion, are necessary preludes to True Love for the Lord.

Nam or Shabd is the link between man and God. Without that One Thing, we are being pursued by the five enemies, and we suffer various kinds of pains and sorrows at the hands of these enemies. Who are these enemies? They are lust, anger, greed, attachment, egotism. What is that One Thing? It is the practice of Nam. We are entrapped by these five thieves because there is no practice of Nam. To illustrate: When the owner of the house is asleep, the thieves may take away anything they like, but when the owner is awake, the thieves dare not come near. In the same way, when we practice Nam, we wake up from this hypnotic state of numerous births and deaths.

The Lord Who created us has placed the Treasure of Nam within us, and has entrusted the key and the secret to the Master. So long as He does not impart to us the method of the practice of Nam, we cannot obtain that Treasure. The Master will not prepare something and put it within you, but will enable you to unlock the hidden Treasure. The Treasure is yours and It is within you. The Master will show you the Path, traversing which, you can obtain It; just as the power of knowledge is within all of us, but is dormant, and when we go to schools and colleges, work diligently, burn the midnight oil, follow the instructions of the teachers, then the dormant faculty is awakened and we become graduates and scholars. Those who do not go to the teachers and do not work hard, remain uneducated. Thus, whatever devices or means we may use to get the Treasure of Nam, they will be of no avail unless we **unconditionally surrender ourselves to the Master** and travel the Path shown by Him.

Now the biggest question of all arises. What do the Saints mean by Nam? Where does that Nam reside? And by what means can that Treasure be obtained? We have called the Lord by thousands and thousands of Names. We have many countries, and in each country, there are many languages, and in each language we remember the Lord by various Names. Some call Him Wahi Guru, some call Him Allah, some call Him Jehovah, some call Him Radha Swami, and some call Him God. All these Names are Varnatmak; that is, they come within the scope of writing, reading and speaking. But the Name which is described and praised by the Saints is Dhunatmak; that is, it can neither be written, nor can it be read, nor can it be seen. Huzur Maharaj Ji used to describe It as "Unwritten Law, Unspoken Language".

All the Varnatmak Names have a history behind them and had their origin in Time. They may be hundreds of years old or thousands of years old. We have given many names to the Lord, and many have been forgotten; and many more names there will be by which we shall call Him. But the Nam of which Guru Nanak Sahib is singing praises here, has no time-limit. In the beginning was Nam, and everything else came through that Nam. According to the Granth Sahib, "All creation has come out of Nam." And the Bible refers to It as Word. "In the beginning was the Word, and the Word was with God" etc. All the planets and the stars and the entire universe were created by It. Again, in the Granth Sahib we find, "The earth has come out of Shabd, the sky has come out of Shabd, the entire creation has come out of Shabd." In various languages That Power has been described by different Names. The Sikhs have called it Gurbani, Sachi Bani, Nam and Hukm; the Hindus have called it Akash Bani and Anahad Shabd (Unstruck Sound); the Muslims have called it Kalma, Bang-i-Asmani (Sound that comes from the skies), Kalam-i-Illahi (Speech of God), and Isme-i-Aazam (the Greatest Name); Christ has described it as The Word. It is through the Varnatmak or the spoken and the written word that we have to retrace our attention inside and connect it with the Dhunatmak Nam. We should not make ourselves attached to these words and become tied with the strings of ceremonies of various religions nor get embroiled in religious feuds between various nations and creeds. The very nature of the mind is that it must attach itself to something. If we practice devotion to Dhunatmak Nam, we shall be freed from the bonds of nationality, race, creed, ceremonies, etc. We shall perform our duties to the best of our ability, but **without attachment** to anything but Nam; and so, automatically, we become better citizens, better husbands, better wives, etc. It is for such Nam that we go to Saints.

Now the second question arises: Where can we get that Nam? In the religious books and the holy scriptures, we find the praises of Name or Nam, and perhaps even a description of the method of Its practice. There is talk about the Holy Name or Nam in the temples, mosques, Gurdwaras, churches, tabernacles, in Satsangs, etc. When we go there, the desire to attain it is aroused. But that True and Great Treasure of Nam is within us. Whenever we shall get It, we shall get It from within ourselves.

There are prescriptions in the doctors' books, but the medicine itself lies on the shelves; the account books of the money lenders contain **accounts** of credits and debits, but the money itself lies in the vault; likewise, the Holy Scriptures contain only a description of Nam, but not Nam Itself. Just as a disease cannot be cured by the reading or reciting of prescriptions; just as money cannot be obtained from the money-lenders' account books; so also Nam cannot be obtained by merely reading or studying holy books. Huzur Maharaj Ji used to say, "If a person goes on repeating 'Laddoo' (an Indian sweet) all his life, he will not be able to taste it nor satisfy his appetite. However, if one prepares the Laddoos according to the instructions in the cook book, he will not only be able to satisfy his appetite, but will also be able to relish the taste."

By this I do not mean that we should give up the reading of sacred books. Rather, the reading with understanding is very beneficial. Reading of the sacred writings will generate a longing for union with the Lord. It also enlightens us as to the method by which we can find Him. But if you think you can **obtain Him**, by mere reading or studying, then you are mistaken. Reading is like cleaning a utensil. The cleansing of a utensil is useful only if you wish to put something in it. We have to cleanse the mind in order to fill it with the Nectar of Nam.

What are the sacred books? The Rishis and the Munis, the Gurus and the Saints, and the Holy Men worked hard and attained God-Realization. Whatever sights they experienced within, whatever obstacles they encountered on the way, they have set them down in writing for our benefit and guidance. Now, by mere reading of these books, neither can the obstacles be removed from the way nor can the sights be seen. This is a subject for **practice**.

The Treasure of Nam is within us as fire is in wood, but we cannot see it nor can it be of any use to us in its present state. If we rub one piece of wood with another, in the proper way, fire will be produced, and we can make use of it. In the same way, the Treasure of Nam is within us, but we can obtain it only when we give up the path of the mind and take to the Path of the Master. It is then that we shall be able to derive benefit from it.

Now this Treasure is no doubt within us, but where exactly shall we find It? There are two parts of the body — one below the eyes, and the other above the eyes. Below the eyes are only the nine apertures and the sensual pleasures. Our center of thinking is above the eyes. Whenever we think deeply, we usually place our hands or fingers up to the forehead. The more we can concentrate, the better we can think. Daily our attention descends from here to the nine apertures, and through them becomes scattered in the outside world. Saints tell us we have to stop our attention from going out, and that which has already spread out, has to be brought back behind the eyes. So long as our attention is not concentrated between the eyes, **from whence the Shabd takes it behind the eyes and up**, we cannot return Home. When our attention has been concentrated behind the eyes, we find the sweetest and most melodious Sound resounding, attracting and calling us towards Itself. There is no question there of nationality, race, creed, wealth, authority, possession, etc. It is the same which the Saints call Shabd and Nam. When our attention is fixed on It, we shall reach from whence It comes. That Shabd comes from Sach Khand, where the Lord resides.

Withdrawing our attention from the nine apertures and connecting it with the Shabd within constitutes reaching the door of Mukti (Liberation). For, when we have reached the first rung of the ladder, there is hope of reaching the top as well. The secret of the withdrawal of the attention from the nine apertures, and the technique of connecting it with the Shabd, is imparted to us only by the Saints.

Those souls whom the Saints wish to liberate from the ocean of this world and unite with the Lord, They first bring them into Their company and Satsang. When we attend Their Satsang, various doubts and difficulties disappear. We come to know our origin, our Home, and then a longing for union with the Lord is awakened in us. Satsang and good company are necessary preludes for devotion to the Lord. The mind is easily influenced by the company it keeps. If we keep bad company, we become wicked; and if we keep the company of Saints and devotees, we follow their example and, like them, we become devoted to the Lord. If, perchance, we are kept away from the Satsang of the Saints, then we should continue to read their writings so that the mind should keep detached from worldly objects and free from all **desire** to dominate anyone or to obtain power, position, wealth, etc., and we should continue with regular and daily practice of Nam. When we obtain the company of Saints, and practice Nam, we attain union with the Lord. Then there is no distance or difference left between us and the Lord.

This, then, is the method by which we can find the Lord. Having realized Him, we shall obtain the stage of Sahaj. We shall get deliverance from all our delusions, the drop will merge into the Ocean and will become the Ocean Itself. The Atma (soul) will merge with Parmatma (Highest Soul — God) and will become One with Him.

CHAPTER XXVI
SUMMARY A CONCISE DESCRIPTION OF MAN'S PURPOSE AND OPPORTUNITIES IN LIFE

by
THE LATE SARDAR BAHADUR JAGAT
SINGH MAHARAJ JI

"Man is the top of all creation, the perfect handiwork of Nature in all respects. He contains within himself the key to unlock the mystery of the Universe and contact the Creator. It is the greatest and the highest good fortune of any sentient being, to be born in the form of man.

"But his responsibilities are also correspondingly great. Having come up to the top of the evolutionary ladder, he should now step on to the ladder of NAM, and tread the spiritual path that would ultimately lead, him to the Divine Home whence he came.

"If he fails to do so he slides down and, according to his Karmas, his desires and inclinations, will have to sojourn in this world of change and go through the various forms of creation.

"In the human body the eye center is the spot which represents the end of the one course and the beginning of the other. He may go up or he may slide down.

"This is the message which all Saints and Masters have in their time given to the world."

The Bible refers to man's coming and going, the descending and ascending of souls on the *'Jacobs's ladder'*:

"and behold, a ladder set up on the earth, and the top of it reached to heaven: and behold the angels of God ascending and descending on it." (GENESIS 28:12)

An example of the people's search for TRUTH in the mountain of the Lord (the human body) is given in Isaiah 2:2 and 3.

The soul is a spark of the Eternal Essence of God. As such it cannot rest or find peace except in God's Essence.

The link between the soul and God is His Eternal Sound Current Energy called the Holy Shabd, the Word of God.

The Word is described in Holy Scriptures, but it takes a living Saint to link the soul in reality to that Current; one who is himself in touch with it, just as one candle lights another. Then by following the instructions of the Saint or Master, the soul can make daily effort and progress in raising the consciousness to that level set by the Teacher as the objective of inner attainment.

First the mind is detached from temporal things by devotional practice which raises the consciousness until it can tune into God's Music of the Holy Shabd, while living in the world but not of it, carrying on with our duties and earning our own living.

The mind must be stilled and devotion must take the place of the ego until all dross is cleared and the tuning is perfect. Then is the soul merged in complete Bliss of His Eternal Sound, His Word.

The soul if the real being, the eternal wanderer seeking its home. It appears in every shape and form for the sake of experience and sensory recordings. The soul is a particle of God Himself, exploring the outer limits of His form or space, away from the center of Light and Life. Through this outer experience the soul has gathered impressions which make it feel a separate being or ego, independent of all things. In this illusion the soul suffers much through the mind and sense impulses which are outward bound and which exhaust the soul's energy, the only treasure it has.

Each manifestation and experience is given a measure of energy. When that is used, a new cycle or experience is necessary for the soul. Being eternal its wanderings are many in time and space; but always consciously or unconsciously looking and longing for Home.

We are here because we desired to be here and gain through external knowledge, pleasures and experiences, which built up the ego and many other illusions. When the soul gets weary of its rounds of pleasures and pains, then it seeks an answer to this riddle of Life and its merry-go-round. And like the Prodigal Son of the Bible, it finally remembers the Father's House and the High calling as His son.

Realizing this, in all humility, it turns all its energy to the Homeward Journey instead of outer sensory pleasures and achievements. Then ways and means are opened to the soul by the Gracious Father, by which the soul can find its way to that distant Home, left long, long ago.

The soul's earnest longing is rewarded by the Father's helping hand of guidance and by His Love. He calls His children Home at the end of the Cosmic Journey and there is great rejoicing and Bliss in daily growth of consciousness until the soul becomes One with Him, as it was in the beginning. Only now it is richer in experience of humility and of Love in Him. Absence made the heart grow fonder through aeons of travel and individual suffering because of the illusion of the mind and senses which ruled the consciousness. When freed from these external accretions, the soul can rise again to the One Essence in the Father's House of Eternal Bliss and Unity.

The True Teacher and the Way will be found by a sincere seeker. The return process is slow and steady. Love guides the way when the soul sets its face toward Home and its faith in the Father. Inner progress will blend into outer changes until all is ONE IN HIS LOVE.